UNLOCKING
Literacy

UNLOCKING
Literacy

Effective
Decoding & Spelling
Instruction

by

Marcia K. Henry, Ph.D.

·P·A·U·L·H·
BROOKES
PUBLISHING CO.®

Baltimore • London • Sydney

Paul H. Brookes Publishing Co.
Post Office Box 10624
Baltimore, Maryland 21285-0624

www.brookespublishing.com

Typeset by Barton Matheson Willse & Worthington, Baltimore, Maryland.
Manufactured in the United States of America by
Victor Graphics, Inc., Baltimore, Maryland.

The vignettes in this book are based on the author's actual experiences. In all
instances, identifying details have been changed to protect confidentiality.

Library of Congress Cataloging-in-Publication Data
Henry, Marcia Kierland
  Unlocking literacy : effective decoding and spelling instruction / by Marcia K.
  Henry.
        p.   cm.
  Includes bibliographical references and index.
  ISBN 1-55766-664-4
  1. Reading—Phonetic method. 2. English language—Pronunciation—Study
  and teaching. 3. English language—Orthography and spelling—Study and
  teaching. I. Title.

  LB1050.34H46 2003
  372.46'5—dc21

                                                          2003045340

British Library Cataloguing in Publication data are available from the British Library.

Contents

About the Author

Marcia K. Henry, Ph.D., brings more than 40 years of experience working in the field of reading and dyslexia as a diagnostician, tutor, teacher, and professor. Dr. Henry received her doctorate in educational psychology from Stanford University. Prior to her retirement in 1995, she was a professor in the Division of Special Education at San Jose State University, where she taught and directed the Center for Educational Research on Dyslexia. Dr. Henry taught as a Fulbright Lecturer/Research Scholar at the University of Trondheim, Norway, in 1991.

Dr. Henry speaks frequently at regional, national, and international conferences on topics related to intervention strategies for dyslexic learners. She also writes for a variety of professional journals and serves on the editorial boards of *Dyslexia* and *Annals of Dyslexia*, the journals of The British Dyslexia Association and The International Dyslexia Association (IDA), respectively.

Since retirement Dr. Henry has taught at the University of New Mexico, the University of Pittsburgh, and the University of Minnesota–Duluth. She provides teacher training related to the teaching of reading and related language arts and consults with several school districts and states on informed reading instruction. Dr. Henry is the author of teaching materials for integrated decoding and spelling instruction. She is a past president (1992–1996) of The Orton Dyslexia Society (now known as IDA). She is a fellow of the Orton-Gillingham Academy and received the Margaret Byrd Rawson Lifetime Achievement Award from IDA in 2000.

Dr. Henry now lives on Madeline Island in Lake Superior, where she spends much of her time writing. She volunteers as a tutor at the island's two-room elementary school when needed. She compiled and co-edited *Dyslexia: Samuel T. Orton and His Legacy* for IDA's 50th anniversary in 1999.

Foreword

Unlocking Literacy: Effective Decoding and Spelling Instruction contributes several significant ideas to the field of early reading. Each of these important in its own right, the collection is valuable for its synergy, and the package is wrapped in accessible writing, accompanied by lists of web-based resources. Below is a sampler of those ideas that hold particular appeal for me.

Orthography is the foundation for decoding and spelling. This idea might seem obvious, but it isn't. The book persists in its emphasis on the historical and morphophonemic roots of English orthography, a principle for bringing clarity to chaos. As Venezky (1970) pointed out several decades ago, English is not a one-to-one system linking letters and sounds, but neither is it the cacophony described by advocates of a more holistic approach. The portrayal of English writing system as a historical-morphophonemic matrix (see Figure 3.1) is clearly a simplification. But we manage our daily lives by simplifications—those of us who drive to work every day operate on the "simplification" that other drivers are going to stay in their lanes! English continues to evolve in strange and mysterious ways, but readers and writers who understand the matrix possess the foundation for dealing with the many print worlds that they encounter, ranging from newspapers to the web. The matrix aims not to constrain ("everything has to fit into a cell"), but to offer a starting point for wrestling with the next message that may come downstream.

Of particular importance is the emphasis on the interplay between decoding and spelling, between reception and production. To be sure, the relation is not symmetrical. The correspondence between a graphemic sequence and the most likely phonemic sequence (print to sound) in English is generally quite predictable; you can usually say what you see. The "conventional" spelling of a phonemic sequence (sound to print) is much less regular. This problem becomes serious in second grade, when phonetic spellings begin to bother teachers and parents. Students can make lots of "mistakes" in spelling what they want to say. This volume does not present a satisfactory resolution to this conundrum, and perhaps that is the point. The goal of an orthography is to support a particular style of communication, one that relies on a simple technology based on orthographic symbols. When a child reads a message, we can infer how he or she is interpreting the symbols. When a child writes a message, a complementary interpretation is also available. In both instances, the primary issue centers around communication—to what degree is the intended message exchanged between the participants? Communication, to be sure, depends on audience, purpose, and style. You should be able to read the following message—"Ths buk wl halp U reed hppoptumus"—even though it might not be considered appropriate in some contexts. Under what conditions might it be acceptable for a second grader? And what does the message reveal about the writer's understanding of English orthography?

Teacher knowledge is the basis for effective instruction. This book will disappoint the reader who is looking for a set of ready-made prescriptions. From the outset it focuses on a fundamental question: What do qualified teachers need to know and do to adapt the decoding–spelling curriculum to individual differences? The answer is clear. Teachers need the concepts and technical language that illuminate the interplay between spoken and written language and, more importantly, between natural and academic language. This book offers a substantial amount of developmental psycholinguistics along the way.

The teacher of elementary students confronts an incredible array of challenges that demand the capacity to handle virtually every subject matter and then some. How reasonable is this expectation? In my judgment, it depends on integrating the "basic skills" approach typical of phonics instruction along with the opportunities for content-based projects. What might phonics have to do with literature, social studies, science, art, and so on? The answer to this question is implicit in this book, which treats decoding-spelling not only as a basic skill, but as a domain that emphasizes understanding as well as performance. Learning how to connect the letter *B* with the sound /b/ is joined with more substantive concepts about the print–sound relationship. Henry's book aims toward promoting exactly these linkages for the teacher who reads between the lines.

The CIAO model provides the elements for instantiating this conceptualization. CIAO is a framework from the professional development program called Project READ (Calfee & Henry, 1986; later renamed Project READ Plus to reduce confusion with Enfield and Greene's Project Read in Minnesota). CIAO brings together the key elements that undergird the monograph: curriculum, instruction, assessment, and organization. We created CIAO because in our meetings with teachers and administrators, we had been searching for a way to pull all of the pieces of the READ-Plus staff development model together, in much the same way that Opening–Middle–Closing–Follow-up seemed to make sense for lesson design.

For *curriculum* in the elementary grades, *Unlocking Literacy: Effective Decoding and Spelling Instruction* emphasizes establishing initial phonemic awareness and then rapidly moving to the consonant and vowel building blocks (Chapter 6). But the recommendation is that students also quickly explore the creation of "big words," first Anglo-Saxon compounds and then Latin and Greek patterns. The advantage of this approach is that the teacher has the foundation to take students quickly from the phonemic (sounds) to the semantic (meaning) in a seamless fashion.

Henry proposes *instruction* that is interactive and productive, rather than strict reliance on direct instruction and the interrogate-respond-evaluate

(IRE) pattern (Cazden, 2001) emphasized in most phonics programs. The Opening–Middle–Closing–Follow-up models in the lessons in this book provide teachers with an alternative that employs "discussion of sounds and corresponding letters" as an instructional strategy (p. 9). Equally important is the use of spelling in the construction of letter–sound patterns.

Assessment is closely intertwined with instruction. For example, Chapter 4 explains the use of letter cards to promote constructivist activities by students. As students move through these activities, the observant teacher can see the students' thinking. The book says less about the role of writing as a vehicle for representing spelling capacities, and what to do with spelling errors. But the teacher who understands the matrix will possess the foundation for dealing with this arena.

Organization—the developmental integration of decoding and spelling during the years between kindergarten and the upper elementary grades—is implicit in the text, and the knowledge base in this volume provides the foundation for bringing teachers together.

In earlier times, the ancient Greek elite were taught to read by slaves who employed cookies shaped like letters of the Greek alphabet (which had very regular letter–sound correspondences) as teaching devices. Data on the effectiveness of these procedures are of course lacking, but today's context is clearly quite different and far more demanding. On the other hand, some constancies warrant consideration. English is clearly a dynamic, multicultural polyglot, and today's writing system for English is equally complex. For the classroom teacher, a few principles provide a roadmap through this maze: 1) the importance of a clear conceptualization of the concepts underlying the orthography, 2) the creation of a pragmatic design for linking these principles to instructional practice, and 3) an efficient transition from acquisition of orthographic tools to purposeful applications of these tools. Henry's volume captures the essence of these constancies.

In conclusion, it is indeed a delight to celebrate another accomplishment by Marcia Henry, a longtime colleague and friend. This work reflects a career dedicated to helping teachers ensure that all students acquire competence in handling English orthography. Marcia and I first met when she entered Stanford's doctoral program in the early 1980s; she brought a remarkable background of experiences from her teaching career and her activities with The Orton Dyslexia Society (now known as The International Dyslexia Association). She joined the research group that constructed Project READ (Calfee & Henry, 1986), a "balanced" literacy program before the label had been imagined. This volume brings to mind what was a truly halcyon time and an extraordinary group of committed educators—to Marcia, thanks for the memories!

Robert Calfee, Ph.D.
Dean, School of Education
University of California

REFERENCES

Calfee, R.C., & Henry, M.K. (1986). Project READ: An inservice model for training classroom teachers in effective reading instruction. In J.V. Hoffman (Ed.), *Effective teaching of reading: Research into practice* (pp. 199–229). Newark, DE: International Reading Association.

Cazden, C.B. (2001). *Classroom discourse: The language of teaching learning* (2nd ed.). Portsmouth, NH: Heinemann.

Venezky, R.L. (1970). *The structure of English orthography*. The Hague, The Netherlands: Mouton.

Preface

The publication of this book coincides with what we know about effective reading instruction today. Much of the current research validates work that has intrigued me for most of my professional life. Thus, this book was written to share insights gained over 40 years of working in the field of reading and specific reading disability, which is often called dyslexia. My own education in this field began when I began tutoring students at the Rochester Reading Center in Rochester, Minnesota, in 1959. Encouraged by the center's directors, Paula Dozier Rome and Jean Smith Osman, I began to learn more about reading acquisition and instruction—an entirely new field for me at that time.

It was in Rochester that I learned the actual teaching techniques that are recommended today for all children learning to read. I learned the importance of giving children strategies that empower them to read and spell, including the use of phonology and understanding the role it plays in learning to read and the significance of morphology, and the importance of teaching morphemes (the meaningful units of language, e.g., prefixes, suffixes, and Latin roots and Greek combining forms) to older students. I found that although teaching the structure of the language is important with all children, it is essential with those who are dyslexic or need explicit instruction to acquire the alphabetic code.

I discovered that almost all children appear to benefit from a multisensory approach in which all modalities used in learning—visual, auditory, and kinesthetic-tactile—are linked and sound, letters, and letter formation all play important roles. I continued more formal education at Santa Clara University and Stanford, where I took more courses related to reading acquisition, psycholinguistics, and psychology. All of this experience prepared me for my work with children and with preservice and in-service educators and for the writing of this book.

Only one component of the reading/language arts curriculum, the decoding–spelling continuum, is featured in this book. Before students can comprehend text, they must be able to decode words fluently and accurately. Before they can compose stories, they must spell accurately. Learning sentence structure and construction, paragraph elements, and comprehension of narrative and expository text are also important components of any child's reading/writing instruction, but these topics are not covered in this book.

In Chapter 1, along with the rationale for the ideas expressed in this book, current research on decoding and spelling is summarized. The implications of this research are clear: Instruction cannot be piecemeal or scattershot. It must be cohesive, systematic, explicit, and direct. This instruction allows students to understand the structure of English orthography (the spelling system) and provides numerous strategies for decoding and spelling.

Chapter 2 presents a brief history of written English. Knowledge of the historical factors inherent in English words provides useful clues for accurate decoding and spelling. Written English took years to form and is still changing, as all artifacts do. Children enjoy learning about the history of words and especially about the English words they are learning to read and spell.

Chapter 3 describes the structure of English orthography based on both word structure and word origin. I discuss the structure of English words, focusing on the letter–sound correspondences, syllable patterns, and morpheme patterns of English words of Anglo-Saxon, Latin, and Greek origins.

In Chapter 4, reading fundamentals, including lesson concepts, lesson format, and lesson procedures, are discussed. Lessons take place as dynamic discussion sessions with the teacher acting as facilitator as well as instructor. The multisensory approach of these lessons encourages active learning through metacognitive strategies, introduction of useful patterns found in thousands of words, and numerous opportunities for practice. Lessons are connected to real reading and writing in context.

Chapter 5 discusses prerequisites for effective decoding and spelling, including preliteracy events, readiness skills, and phonological awareness tasks. Informal assessment as well as lessons and activities beneficial in preschool and kindergarten are presented.

The last three chapters of the book include sample lessons along with content and opportunities for practice. Chapter 6 introduces patterns and rules needed by primary grade students, including letter–sound correspondence patterns and related rules, compound words, syllable patterns, and common prefixes and suffixes. Examples of possible supplemental activities are provided.

Chapter 7 focuses on specific instructional lessons and activities useful for upper elementary and middle-school students. The Latin and Greek layers of language are introduced. Latin word roots and their corresponding affixes, along with the common Greek combining forms found frequently in science and math texts, are emphasized. In Chapter 8 additional, less common Latin roots and Greek combining forms are presented. Teachers will gain information related to activities useful in high school content area classes.

This book also contains substantial back matter. The appendices begin with surveys of language knowledge for teachers that were developed by Louisa Cook Moats (2003). In addition, there are appendices of common nonphonetic words, compound words, prefixes, suffixes, Latin roots, and Greek combining forms. Words often found in elementary and secondary content area textbooks are also presented. The glossary defines terms that are used in the book and that are beneficial for teachers and their students to learn.

This book will be useful to teachers in general or special education, to tutors and therapists working with small groups or individuals, and to parents wishing to know more about effective decoding and spelling instruction.

I hope that students will discover the joy of language as they acquire reading fluency and accuracy in decoding and spelling words.

REFERENCE

Moats, L.C. (2003). *Speech to print workbook: Language exercises for teachers.* Baltimore: Paul H. Brookes Publishing Co.

Acknowledgments

My profound thanks go to the wonderful team at Paul H. Brookes Publishing Co. Among them, special thanks to Elaine Niefeld, who encouraged the writing of this book, and Jessica Allan, who skillfully guided me through the initial drafts. Mika Sam Smith, who has as great an interest in the English language as I do, provided masterful queries and suggestions in the copyediting phase.

I am deeply grateful that Paula Dozier Rome and Jean Smith Osman of the Rochester Reading Center started me on this journey more than 40 years ago. Their support and love continue to guide me. Robert Calfee and several other Stanford professors provided opportunities for learning, teaching, and research in the fields of education and psychology. I am extremely appreciative of their confidence in me. I also consider the late Norman Geschwind, Isabelle Y. Liberman, and Margaret Byrd Rawson, with whom I served on the Orton Dyslexia Society's board of directors, among my best teachers.

I am indebted to Susan Brady and Keith Stanovich for supporting the writing of this book as they reviewed the original prospectus. To Martha Renner and Marjorie Smith, best friends who are also keen writers and thinkers, my heartfelt thanks for the many hours spent reviewing the draft chapters. They know how much I value their recommendations. Appreciation also goes to my colleagues at San Jose State University and at other universities where I taught and to members of The International Dyslexia Association (formerly The Orton Dyslexia Society), who continue to influence the field of reading disabilities with enthusiasm and professionalism.

I acknowledge with loving memory my parents, Bob and Margaret Kierland, who inspired me in many ways. I am grateful to my brother Pete, who first made me aware of the struggles of children who do not learn to read easily. To all my children who are "30- and 40-something," thanks for continuing to make life diverse and eventful. My hope is that my six grandchildren will enjoy the gifts that books provide. Finally, I thank my husband Burke for his steadfast support of all my endeavors and for his constant love. Without his encouragement this book would never have been written.

To my students of all ages, from whom I continue to learn,
and to the teachers who know how important reading
and spelling is for their students
and who persist in learning more about written language.
They make it all worthwhile!

SECTION I

Preparation

Decoding
and Spelling

Keys to Unlocking Literacy

Literacy ranges from the basic ability to read and write (or functional literacy), required in everyday life, to advanced literacy, reflecting knowledge of significant ideas, events, and values of a society. For many children, literacy comes easily, but others need help unlocking the complexities of reading and writing. Two significant factors in acquiring literacy are decoding (or word identification) and spelling.

Reading is probably the most important scholarly activity a person masters. Every subject in school requires at least grade-level reading ability. Just as important is the ability to read for pleasure. Much of what we learn about the past and present is found in books and magazines. Thus, reading adds to our knowledge of the world and our understanding of human relationships.

Reading has two major elements: decoding and comprehension. Decoding comprises the skills and knowledge by which a reader translates printed words into speech. More simply, decoding is the ability to pronounce a word subvocally in silent reading or vocally in oral reading. Comprehension, in contrast, is the ability to understand the words, sentences, and connected text that one reads. Perfetti asserted that "only a reader with skilled decoding processes can be expected to have skilled comprehension processes" (1984, p. 43). Gough and Tunmer (1986) urged educators to consider that decoding is a necessary part of reading because print cannot be understood (comprehended) if it cannot be translated into language (decoded). When children have access to words important to the gist of a story or to the meaning of text, the chil-

3

dren's understanding is enhanced. Butler and Silliman (2002) contended that to date, researchers are uncertain exactly how decoding affects comprehension, but they know that without decoding one cannot comprehend. We need to decode the words in order to assign meaning to words, sentences, and texts.

In this book, I deal with the integrated teaching of decoding and its linguistic counterpart, encoding, or spelling. Decoding is a receptive language process in which letters on the page are received by the reader. The alphabetic principle, the systematic correspondences between spoken and written forms of words, informs the reader. Spelling, on the other hand, is a productive language process; the speller hears the sounds and must translate them to alphabetic symbols by writing or by speaking letter names.

Decoding and spelling share a common orthography, or writing system, so it makes sense to teach the two in conjunction. The patterns useful in decoding are reinforced by spelling and vice versa. In addition, readers who have difficulty in reading usually have difficulty in spelling (Bruck & Waters, 1990; Ehri, 1987; Henry, 1988b, 1989; Moats, 1995; Templeton, 1995). Bruck and Waters observed that "although spellers of all ages and skill levels use sound–spelling information for spelling, accurate knowledge of these correspondences differentiates the more skilled from the less skilled speller" (pp. 165–166).

Decoding of unfamiliar words requires that children recognize the common symbols, or letters, of the language. These symbols have corresponding sounds. Instruction in the letter–sound correspondences is called *phonics*. In order to develop adequate decoding and spelling skills, children need explicit instruction in phonics that is systematic, structured, sequential, and multisensory (McIntyre & Pickering, 1995).

Two themes flow through this book: word origin and word structure. The first theme comes from an examination of the history of written English and the way this history has influenced the English orthography, or spelling system, over centuries (see Chapter 2). Word origin reflects the historical and geographic origin of a word. The second dimension of this book comes from three major structural components: 1) letter–sound correspondences, 2) syllable patterns, and 3) morpheme patterns (the units of meaning in words such as prefixes, suffixes, and roots; see Chapter 3). An understanding of the historical forces influencing written English, along with an understanding of the structure of the English spelling system, provides teachers and their students with a logical basis for the study of English. Yet, few teacher preparation programs include these knowledge bases in the curriculum (see Berninger, 2000, and Moats, 1994, 2000, 2003, for examples of texts that do cover these domains). Berninger concluded that reading problems are more related to the instructional program than to the child because teachers often do not use systematic, explicit instructional strategies. In addition, teachers may have an insufficient understanding of the structure of language at multiple levels (e.g., phonology, morphology, syntax) and may not understand the ways that phonology is represented in the orthography.

Appendix A provides an opportunity for teachers to check their language knowledge before proceeding through this book.

The framework for the decoding–spelling continuum in this book is based on word origin and word structure (Henry, 1988a, 1988b). This framework provides a structure to present and organize information, allowing teachers to avoid presenting skills in isolation. The three languages of origin most influential to English are Anglo-Saxon, Latin, and Greek. Students who recognize letter–sound correspondences, syllable patterns, and morpheme patterns in words of Anglo-Saxon, Latin, and Greek origin hold the strategies necessary to read and spell most unfamiliar words.

Figure 1.1 illustrates the framework undergirding the integrated decoding and spelling instruction. The cells in the blank 3 × 3 matrix shown in Figure 1.1 refer to the origin and structural categories of language. Both word origin and word structure guide what is to be taught. The great majority of English words come from Anglo-Saxon, Romance (primarily Latin), and Greek origins. Brown (1947) noted that 80% of English words borrowed from

	Letter–sound correspondences	Syllables	Morphemes
Anglo-Saxon			
Latin			
Greek			

Figure 1.1. Blank word origin and word structure matrix. (*Source:* Henry, 1988b.)

other languages come from Latin and Greek and make up 60% of words used in text. By receiving instruction in all of the components in this framework, students will learn the significant patterns found in English words. A completed matrix appears in Chapter 3 (see Figure 3.1) as the specific word origin patterns are presented. As the patterns are introduced, teachers and their students will become familiar with terms in the "Decoding–Spelling Instruction Register" (see Chapter 4) that are necessary in discussing decoding and spelling concepts.

THE CONTINUUM OF INTEGRATED DECODING AND SPELLING INSTRUCTION

The decoding–spelling continuum across the grades is supported by the work of several researchers in the field of reading and spelling who have theorized that learners move through developmental stages as they begin to read and spell (Bear, 1992; Chall, 1983; Ehri, 1985; Frith, 1980; E.H. Henderson, 1990; Perfetti, 1984, 1985). These stages generally move from prealphabetic, to partial alphabetic, to mature, and then to consolidated alphabetic phases for reading multisyllabic words. Chall (1983) proposed the following stages of reading development. In Stage 0 (prereading), children develop the prerequisites of visual, visual-motor, and auditory skills. This stage contains many of the skills we now know as phonological awareness ability, or understanding of the role that sounds play in the language. During Stage 1 (initial reading or decoding), first and second graders learn the alphabetic code and recognize sight words. In Stage 2 (confirmation, fluency, or ungluing from print), second and third graders gain fluency and pay less attention directly to spelling–sound relationships. In Stage 3 (reading for learning new information), fourth through eighth graders become more efficient readers as they relate print to ideas, although they read text that is limited in technical complexity. During high school, Stage 4 (multiple viewpoints) strategies include the ability to deal with layers of facts and concepts added to previous knowledge. Stage 5 (construction and reconstruction) is found at age 18 and beyond. Stage 5 readers depend on analysis, synthesis, and judgment as they construct abstract knowledge.

E.H. Henderson (1990) and Bear (1992) described similar developmental stages for spelling as 1) preliterate, 2) letter name, 3) within-word pattern, 4) syllable juncture, and 5) derivational principles. During the preliterate stage, 1- to 7-year-olds begin to scribble, identify pictures, and draw. They listen to stories and identify some symbols. These children may pretend to read, even holding a book upside-down. By the letter-name stage, between 5 and 9 years of age, children use "invented" spellings, know most common sight words, recognize initial and final sounds, and read orally but disfluently. The within-word pattern stage, from 6 to 12 years old, finds students recognizing short (lax) and long (tense) vowel markers. Readers are comfortable with silent reading. Oral reading becomes more fluent with appropriate expression. During the stage of syllable juncture, between 8 and 18, students understand the consonant doubling principle (e.g., *boat/boated* but *pat/patted*). Errors are common at the juncture where syllables come together and in schwa positions. (A schwa is a vowel in an unaccented syllable.) Students in the syllable juncture stage begin using prefixes and suffixes. Although students in this stage prefer silent reading, oral reading becomes even more fluent with good expression. The final stage, that of derivational principles, occurs from age 10 through adulthood. Students in this stage understand etymological principles and know roots and bases, predominantly from Latin and Greek. These students have "new control and correctness in regard to polysyllabic words" (E.H. Henderson, 1990, p. 74). Metalinguistic reasoning and classical vocabulary expand rapidly.

Even those students who learn phonics for decoding and spelling short, regular words often have difficulty at a more advanced level because they have only learned rudimentary sound–symbol association rules. The decoding–spelling continuum illustrated in Figure 1.2 begins with an introduction to phonological awareness and continues through Latin and Greek morphemes. The term *phonological awareness* is generally used to indicate awareness of and facility with all levels of the speech sound system, including word boundaries, stress patterns, syllable patterns, onset–rime units, and phonemes.

Phonemic awareness, the most advanced level of phonological awareness, requires the conscious awareness of individual phonemes in a given word, along with the ability to manipulate these sounds. Students with phonemic awareness understand that *sand* and *sick* begin with the same sound /s/ and that *told* and *laid* end with the same sound. These students are able to complete the more difficult task of removing one sound from a consonant blend, such as deleting /l/ from *plant* to get *pant* and removing /m/ from *blimp* to get *blip*.

After phonological awareness training, in which children learn to rhyme, segment, and blend orally (described in Chapter 5), children begin learning

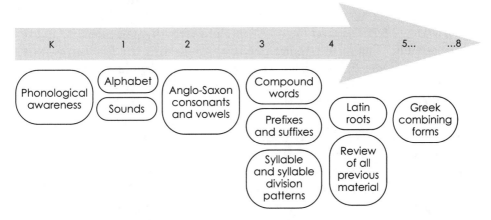

Figure 1.2. The decoding–spelling continuum. All of the topics listed should be taught by eighth grade. (*Source:* Henry, 1997.)

the upper- and lowercase alphabet letters and letter–sound correspondences while continuing to improve their phonological awareness skills. Students need to automatically name each letter and give the sound(s) each letter makes. Children learn a variety of patterns found within the domain of letter–sound correspondences (see Chapters 3 and 6). By second grade, children need exposure to common patterns of syllable division, compound words, and frequently used prefixes and suffixes (see Chapter 6). Third grade is a transition year in which more multisyllabic words are introduced. These longer words are not necessarily harder to read once children know the common prefixes and suffixes.

In the upper elementary grades, many words found in text are multisyllabic and often contain Latin roots and affixes and Greek combining forms. Thus, additional strategies must be taught to those students who have not acquired an automatic level of word recognition for longer words. By fourth grade, children begin learning common Latin roots, along with additional prefixes and suffixes. Greek word parts come next, early in fifth grade. By the end of sixth grade, most common Latin roots and Greek combining forms should have been taught (see Chapter 7). For students in middle school or high school, review of all patterns should continue. Less common roots and combining forms and other linguistic concepts must be acquired in middle school and high school (see Chapter 8).

APPROACHES TO DECODING AND SPELLING INSTRUCTION

Decoding

The teaching of decoding and spelling has undergone numerous changes over the years. A pendulum appears to swing between the phonics side and the sight-word side of instruction. Chall and Squire (1991) summarized the history of readers and textbook publishing. They found that the first widely used reader was *The New England Primer*, with alphabetic rhymes, pictures, and religious content. The most popular reader through the early 1800s was Noah Webster's *American Spelling Book*, emphasizing the "sounding" out of words and "standard" American pronunciation and spelling. McGuffey's readers, with a focus on the alphabetic/phonetic method, were popular between 1836 and 1920. By the 1930s the *Dick and Jane* series by William S. Gray introduced the whole-word method, controlled vocabulary, word recognition, and stress on comprehension. In this whole-word (or sight-word) approach, students memorized words by seeing them over and over again. For example, students saw the word *Jane* over and over again. Students did not learn that *J* sounds like /j/, that *n* sounds like /n/, and that *a* represents a long vowel sound because of the final silent *e*. This approach was the basis for the later whole language instruction.

Whole language instruction assumes that through exposure to good literature and opportunities to read and write, children will pick up the alphabetic code and make their own phonics generalizations. In the whole language approach, any phonics instruction is embedded in "real," predictable text. Unfamiliar words are to be guessed from the context, not sounded out. Stanovich and his colleagues (Stanovich, West, & Feeman, 1981; West & Stanovich, 1978) found that reading was not a "psycholinguistic guessing game" as proposed by Goodman (1967, 1976), but rather that only poor readers guess words from context, whereas good readers do not. Stanovich and his colleagues inferred that skilled readers did not need to rely on context information because their word recognition processing was so rapid and automatic.

Adams concluded, after careful examination of many studies and her own research, "The single immutable and nonoptional fact about skillful reading is that it involves relatively complete processing of the individual letters of print" (1990, p. 105). She noted that skillful readers of English process individual letters with comparative ease and speed as they recognize, at an automatic level, many of the ordered sequences of letter patterns. She provided this conclusion as one of the reasons that phonics instruction is so important.

Chall (1967) encouraged a move back to phonics for beginning reading instruction. During phonics instruction, students learn to connect letters with sounds. Instruction in phonics in the 1970s and early 1980s centered on a drill-and-practice format, often with worksheets guiding the practice. In this type of instruction, students rarely heard the sounds they were to practice; rather, they might look at a picture of a boy and write the letter related to the first sound of the word *boy*. In contrast, the type of phonics advocated in this book is based on frequent discussion of sounds and corresponding letters providing practice in actual reading and spelling from dictation. Beginning phonics instruction usually is accompanied by reading decodable text or text based primarily on patterns that have been or are being taught.

In the late 1980s and early 1990s, opposing camps advocated either phonics or the whole language approach. Stahl and Miller (1989) suggested that whole language is not very effective in developing decoding skills and found nothing to favor the use of whole language beyond kindergarten. Many teachers, reading researchers, and teacher educators support an informed and balanced approach to teaching reading based on research outcomes (Brady & Moats, 1997; Pressley, 1998). Pressley concluded that upon finding an unfamiliar word, "sounding out a word is the preferred strategy of good readers" (p. 23). Many teachers find that teaching explicit phonics is useful but also know the value of having students read good literature, work on comprehension, and receive composition instruction.

More school districts throughout the United States are reemphasizing the teaching of specific skills such as phonics, especially in the primary grades. The goal stated by Presidents Bill Clinton and George W. Bush is that by third grade, all students will read at grade level. Although this goal is laudable, it assumes that all of the necessary skills can be taught by third grade. Yet, many of the content area words required in fourth grade and above contain elements that would not be taught in a lower elementary grade reading/ spelling curriculum. Children need to read few words beyond two syllables in the early grades. Children study few prefixes, suffixes, and roots important for upper-grade success in reading. Without recognizing the value of syllabic and morphological patterns, however, students are constrained from using clues available to identify long, unfamiliar words found in upper-grade text. Unfortunately, most decoding instruction largely neglects syllable and morpheme patterns, perhaps because these techniques are only useful for the longer words found in literature and subject matter text beyond second and third grade, at which point decoding instruction becomes virtually nonexistent in most schools.

Spelling

Spelling instruction has changed little since the 1950s in most classrooms. A typical procedure is that children receive a list of 20–25 words on Monday. They go over the words with the teacher and are expected to memorize the sequence of the letters in each word. Children practice during the week, often having a pretest on Wednesday or Thursday. The real test comes on Friday. Most children, even those with reading and language problems, do well on the Friday test but often cannot write the word correctly in context 2 or 3 weeks later.

During the height of the whole language movement, children were encouraged to use "invented" spelling that was based on what they thought was correct. Although this practice makes sense developmentally for kindergartners and first graders, children soon need to spell correctly. They benefit from explicit and direct instruction in the alphabetic code. Carney (1994) emphasized that spelling errors detract the reader from the message. Poor spellers are often thought to be careless or unintelligent. Carney contrasted errors of competence with performance errors. Errors of competence are fairly consistent misspellings, whereas performance errors tend to be temporary. Children with reading and spelling problems are consistent in their misspellings. Teachers need to analyze carefully the error patterns displayed by their students. Carney also urged teachers to be aware of the part that dialects play in spelling. For example, a child who pronounces *saw* as "sore" and *law* as "lore" may tend to spell the words as they sound to him or her. The closer a person's dialect is to standard English pronunciation, the easier spelling is for the person.

Ehri (1989) encouraged teachers to provide beginning readers with a full knowledge of the spelling system, including its orthographic and phonological connections. She urged teachers to perfect the way they teach children to read and spell.

Templeton and Morris (2002) pointed out that although memory plays an important role in learning to spell, it is not the only role. Students must also learn to understand how words work. Knowing word structure and how this structure signals both sound and meaning is important. Templeton and Morris concluded that the instructional emphasis should be placed on exploration of patterns as opposed to memorization of the 5,000 most frequently occurring English words.

CURRENT RESEARCH AND IMPLICATIONS FOR INSTRUCTION

Elementary Grade Instruction

Research sponsored by various educational institutions has focused on prerequisites for reading acquisition and the specific literacy tasks that influence future reading ability. Historically, educators have looked at the maturity and readiness of future readers. Children's use of oral language, fine and gross motor skills, general intelligence, concepts of print, and basic perceptual-motor skills all play a part in reading readiness.

In the mid- and late 1990s, Scarborough (1998) studied the prerequisites for reading acquisition. Four factors stood out as the strongest predictors of reading: expressive vocabulary, general language ability, sentence/story recall, and phonological awareness. Scarborough noted that

> Not surprisingly, measures of skills that are directly related to reading and writing—including knowledge about letter identities, about letter–sound relationships, and about the mechanics and functions of book reading—have yielded the highest simple correlations with subsequent reading scores. (p. 91)

Somewhat weaker effects were obtained for all measures of general ability and various narrower facets of language skill. Even weaker average correlations were obtained for the other kindergarten abilities examined, including speech production and perception, visual and verbal short-term memory, and other nonverbal abilities.

Research initiated by Liberman and her colleagues (Liberman, 1973; Liberman & Liberman, 1990; Liberman & Shankweiler, 1991; Liberman, Shankweiler, Fischer, & Carter, 1974) found that children's phonological awareness is extremely important in learning to read. Results from many studies suggest that the common trait running through the reading ability of children and adults with reading disorders appears to be impairment in phonological, and primarily phonemic, awareness. Even in the 1920s, Samuel T. Orton (1937) remarked on the fact that many of the children under his care lacked an understanding of the role that sounds play in words and noted the difficulty the children had with understanding letter–sound relationships.

Since the early 1990s, the U.S. Department of Education and the National Institute of Child Health and Human Development (NICHD) of the National Institutes of Health have conducted numerous studies on reading acquisition. The 24 research network center sites and the 22 noncenter re-search sites funded by the NICHD have focused on prerequisites for learning to read and factors necessary in early reading instruction. More than 1,000 teachers have been trained, and more than 10,000 children are involved in prevention and intervention programs at almost 300 schools in 1,285 class-rooms (Lyon, 1999; Lyon, Fletcher, & Barnes, 2003). Scientific advances from these studies are described in more than 2,600 peer-reviewed publications for the following areas of investigation:

- Behavioral/linguistic predictors of reading disorders in children ages 5–6 years

- Early identification of reading disorders in children ages 5–6 years

- Prevention and early intervention programs for reading disorders

- Remedial treatment of reading disorders

- Developmental course of reading disorders

- Cognitive profiles/subtypes of reading disorders

- Causal mechanisms in reading disorders: genetics and neurobiology

- Definitional model of dyslexia

- Epidemiology of reading disorders

- Disproving of the developmental lag hypothesis that some children have delayed maturity for typical reading acquisition

- Gender differences in reading disorders

- Genetic and environmental contributions, including development of pedi-atric structural and functional neuroimaging methods

- Development of neural circuitry for children and adult readers without impairments and for children and adults with reading disorders

The NICHD research has concluded that approximately 20% of children in the United States have substantial difficulties learning to read (Lyon, 1995). Research in numerous studies converges on the importance of phonological awareness in learning to read (see Chapter 5). Although phonological aware-ness may be a necessary condition for learning to read, it is not sufficient. Ehri found that orthographic knowledge has a profound influence on phonological awareness (Ehri, 1998; Ehri & Soffer, 1999). Ehri proposed that *graphophonemic* awareness is a necessary condition of learning to read. As children learn graphemes (the written symbols that represent speech sounds) such as *ch* and *tch*, children must reconcile the sounds with the appropriate spellings. Ehri suggested that graphophonemic analysis is central for retaining sight words in memory and contributes mainly to early reading and spelling acquisition: "The big chore is grappling with the correct spelling of individual words and figuring out how the graphemes and phonemes come together in a systematic way" (1998, p. 108). This task is so critical to learning to read that, as Lyon stated,

> Unless identified early on and taught by expert teachers using detailed and intensive approaches emphasizing teaching both in phonological awareness and phonics instruction, children who learn poorly in the third grade can be expected to learn poorly throughout middle- and high-school grades. (1996, p. 71)

Seidenburg and McClelland (1989) noted that children must come to understand at least two basic characteristics of written English as they acquire word recognition skills. First, children must understand the alphabetic principle. Second, they must learn about the distribution of letter patterns in the lexicon. That is, children must learn that only some combinations of letters are possible in English and that the combinations differ in frequency. Of all of the possible combinations of 26 letters, only a small percentage yield letter strings that are permissible in English. In addition, Seidenburg and McClelland noted that skillful word reading depends on the coordinated and interactive processing of the appearance or orthography of the words, their meaning, and their pronunciation.

Stanovich noted that children with little phonological awareness have trouble acquiring alphabetic coding skill and thus have difficulty recognizing words: "When word recognition processes demand too much cognitive capacity, few cognitive resources are left to allocate to higher level processes of text integration and comprehension" (1996, p. 281).

Adams (1990) reminded us that students with specific reading disability, or dyslexia, do not easily discover the alphabetic code and therefore exhibit considerable difficulty in learning to decode and spell (see also Ehri, 1991; Perfetti, 1985; and Stanovich, 1986). Students must be able to apply this knowledge when reading and spelling. Knowledge of the alphabetic code is useful not only in attacking new words but also in storing words in memory as students build a sight vocabulary, read words by analogy, and make informed predictions about words in text. This working knowledge grows and changes as beginning readers become more fluent.

Several prevention and intervention studies support the need for explicit teaching of patterns and rules for successful decoding and spelling (Berninger, 2000; Berninger et al., in press; Felton, 1993; Foorman, Francis, Beeler, Winikates, & Fletcher, 1997; Scanlon & Vellutino, 1996; Torgesen, 2000; Torgesen, Wagner, & Rashotte, 1997). Barbara Foorman and her team in Houston concluded that second and third graders "who received an Orton-Gillingham, synthetic phonics approach [Alphabetic Phonics] outperformed children receiving a combined synthetic/analytic phonics approach or a sight-word approach in the development of literacy related skills" (1997, p. 63).

Other studies concluded that the ability to read and comprehend also depends upon rapid and automatic recognition and decoding of single words. Fluency and automaticity should not be confused as identical constructs.

Rather, fluency is seen as the speed of decoding that is gained as one masters the alphabetic code (Stanovich, 1980). The National Reading Panel (2000) suggested that practice and exposure to print are essential to fluency. Automaticity, in contrast, is the immediate recognition of words. Improvements in fluency and automaticity appear to be harder to obtain than improvements in decoding and word reading accuracy (Wolf & Katzer-Cohen, 2001). Interventions for both fluency and automaticity are discussed in Chapter 6.

Rapid automatized naming (RAN) has also been investigated since the mid-1970s as a correlate to reading acquisition. The rapid naming of colors, numbers, and objects appears to have a significant effect on later reading ability (Bowers, Sunseth, & Golden, 1999; Denckla & Rudel, 1976; Wolf, 1991). The most difficult task for young poor readers is naming common objects, colors, and symbols. By second grade, problems with letter and number naming are more reliable markers of poor reading ability. In fact, Adams (1990) noted that one of the best predictors of first-grade reading ability is the fast and accurate skill of naming and recognizing shapes of letters. Naming speed is thought to provide a marker for processes sensitive to precise and rapid timing requirements.

Children who have problems with both phonological awareness and RAN are said to have a "double deficit" and will have more trouble learning to read and spell (Badian, 1997; Bowers & Wolf, 1993). Dyslexic children with phonemic awareness weaknesses and few problems with RAN show relative orthographic strength. Those with RAN impairments have poor orthographic skill and poor text reading speed.

Hammill, Mather, Allen, and Roberts (2002) noted that it is not yet possible to say specifically which predictors (e.g., semantics, grammar, phonology, RAN) are most meaningful to accurately identify children who will have trouble learning to read and spell. Hammill et al. encouraged more research and more explanations to predict who will and will not be good at word identification.

Numerous researchers now conclude that decoding and spelling should be taught explicitly, at least through eighth grade (Snow, Burns, & Griffin, 1998). This instruction is important for all children but is essential for the children who do not readily acquire reading and spelling skills. These children may be identified as having learning disabilities, and 80% of these children have specific reading disability or dyslexia. Others who do not learn to read and spell easily may include children whose first language is not English and children without any special category label who need explicit instruction in learning the alphabetic code. Students who do not master the alphabetic code prior to secondary school may need direct instruction in reading and writing throughout and perhaps even beyond their formal schooling.

Upper-Grade Instruction

Studies of older students find that many who are identified as having learning disabilities read and spell at a second- or third-grade level (Henry, 1988b).

Even those students who learn rudimentary sound–symbol association rules for decoding and spelling short regular words often have difficulty at a more advanced level. In the upper elementary grades, many words in text are multisyllabic and often contain Latin and Greek word parts. Thus, additional strategies must be taught to those students who have not acquired an automatic level of word recognition for longer words.

Just as awareness of the sounds of language provides clues for accurate decoding and spelling, knowledge of morphemes (the smallest units of meaning in language) provides additional information (Berninger et al., in press; Carlisle, 1987, 1995; E.H. Henderson, 1990; L. Henderson, 1982, 1985; Henry, 1988a, 1989), such as knowing that the addition of -*s* to nouns makes them plural (e.g., *cat*, *cats*). Prefixes and suffixes provide additional meaning. Prefixes tend to hold specific meaning (e.g., *re-* means *back* or *again*), whereas suffixes provide grammatical distinctions (e.g., *-ous* signifies an adjective ending). Roots, the base elements of words, provide consistent patterns used in thousands of words.

Studies suggest that proficient readers and spellers use morphological knowledge as they read and spell, whereas poor readers and spellers "lack awareness of the presence of base forms within derived counterparts, and they lack specific knowledge about how to spell suffixes and how to attach suffixes to base words correctly" (Carlisle, 1987, pp. 106–107). Henry (1988b) found that even good readers lacked morphemic awareness and often could not use knowledge of prefixes, roots, and suffixes while reading and spelling.

Singson, Mahony, and Mann (2000) investigated upper elementary graders' knowledge of derivational suffixes. Derivational suffixes are morphemes that are added to roots or base words and that usually change the grammatical category of a word (e.g., the suffixes *-ion* and *-ive* can be added to the verb *instruct* to make the noun *instruction* and the adjective *instructive*, respectively). Singson et al. concluded that the upper elementary grades are an important time for the development of derivational morphology in both written and oral language and that this understanding of morphology contributes to decoding and spelling ability.

Scandinavians Elbro and Arnbak (1996; Arnbak & Elbro, 2000) found that morphological awareness training significantly increased comprehension and spelling of morphologically complex words in fourth- and fifth-grade dyslexic children. In one study with secondary students, Elbro and Arnbak indicated that "dyslexic adolescents use recognition of root morphemes as a compensatory strategy in reading both single words and coherent texts" (1996, p. 209).

Abbott and Berninger (1999) concluded that older underachieving readers benefited from learning structural analysis, including study of syllable structure and morpheme patterns. One experimental group focused on structural analysis based on the *WORDS* curriculum (Henry, 1990) as they learned a core group of Greek combining forms. The researchers noted that had all students mastered beginning word recognition skills, including phonological awareness, orthographic knowledge, and application of the alphabetic princi-ple to phonological decoding, prior to the study, training might have provided stronger effects.

In 1997 the director of the NICHD, in consultation with the U.S. Sec-retary of Education, convened the National Reading Panel, a team of leading educators, reading researchers, teachers, educational administrators and par-ents to assess the status of research-based knowledge, including the effective-ness of various approaches to teaching children to read. Major findings from the National Reading Panel (2000) included the importance of teaching phonemic awareness skills; teaching systematic, synthetic phonics skills; as-sisting students in gaining fluency, accuracy, speed, and expression in reading; and applying reading comprehension strategies to enhance understanding and enjoyment of reading material. The panel also concluded that teachers need to understand how children learn to read, why some children have difficulty learning to read, and how to identify and implement the most effective in-structional approaches. The panel also noted that although silent reading is an accepted practice, the research demonstrated that it was not as effective as guided oral reading in helping children become fluent readers. In addition, the panel encouraged rigorous research in order to understand the potential of computers in reading instruction.

Use of Technology

What role should technology play in reading instruction? Clearly, many re-cent advances suggest that technology can be a powerful tool in reading in-struction, especially for children with reading problems. Improved software and devices for speech production and recognition make possible the reading of text on the computer screen or the conversion of speech into electronic text (Wise, 1998). A computer can be used as a compensatory tool to improve writ-ing or as a remediation tool to improve reading and spelling. Wise, Olson, and Ring (1997) found that children benefited from reading stories with accurate computer speech feedback for difficult words. Wise et al. acknowledged that the gains were enhanced with intensive training in phonological awareness without the computer.

Elkind (1998) reported on specific programs (the Kurzweil 3000 and the WYNN [Arkenstone]) that offered increased accuracy of character recogni-tion and fidelity of speech. Children using this technology increased reading rate and also enhanced comprehension on timed and untimed tasks. The chil-dren also increased endurance for the reading task. These machines can show an electronic image of an actual page with pictures, graphics, page layout, and text formatting faithfully reproduced in color. West (1998) discussed how technology moves verbal literacy to visual literacy, or a "world of images," which is important in the lives of children.

There are, however, some caveats. Catts and Kamhi (1999) concluded that children need language skills, world knowledge, and metacognitive and self-regulatory strategies to perform computer tasks. Catts and Kamhi noted that some children are poorly prepared in these prerequisite areas.

In the primary grades, computer programs developed for reinforcement and drill and practice appear to be motivational. In addition, they require no special keyboarding skills. Once computers are used for writing assignments, however, upper elementary and secondary students need to learn effective keyboarding skills.

Raskind (1998) reminded us that research on computers in instruction remains scarce. More studies need to be designed for different settings, not only the lab but also pull-out situations and the classroom. One meta-analysis of 42 studies involving computer-assisted instruction concluded that these programs generally have a positive, though small, effect on beginning readers (Blok, Oostdam, Otter, & Overmaat, 2002). The National Reading Panel (2000) report noted that few systematic studies of computers and other technologies related to reading instruction exist. The panel did find that the talking computer (i.e., the addition of speech to print) may be a promising instructional alternative. The panel concluded that a great deal of additional exploration must be undertaken.

Students often rely on spell checkers to correct spelling errors. Yet, consider this explanation from an anonymous dyslexic professor:

> The computer spell check is a wonderful invention. However, there are a number of ways the process can go awry. The spell checker leaves me with many spelling errors. Computers are considerable help in catching such errors as *worgn* for *wrong*, *apirently* for *apparently*, *wemon* for *women*, *alian* for *alien* and such garbles as *inderrent* for *indifferent*. A common problem comes when I type a correctly spelled word but with a meaning not intended and often humorously alien in my sentence—for example, *impalement* for *impairment*. The spelling program gives me a pass on spelling the word and I am not aware that an error remains. Often what I type are nonwords. Sometimes the word is so far off the mark that the spelling program can think of no possible words to suggest. I sit there frustrated.

The professor gives more examples of his errors with the incorrect word choices (each of which is *spelled* correctly and would not be caught by a spell checker) in italicized type and the intended words in brackets:

> I remember being in a small *rome* [room].
> . . . a place where ships at *see* [sea] were located.
> My typing teacher *latterly* [literally] took me by the hand.
> In *collage* [college] my reading difficulty . . .
> *Finely* [finally] I found . . .
> . . . and *low* [lo!] I missed every word on the spelling test.

Male (2000) suggested that computers can function as a tool to help a child perform. But, human "communication partners," in the form of peers or teachers, are essential to the process of developing spoken and written language skills. Nothing gives children the feel of success like independently reading a book and writing a story. For that, instruction is usually necessary.

SUMMARY

By teaching the concepts inherent in the word origin and word structure model across a decoding–spelling continuum from the early grades through at least eighth grade and using technology when it serves to reinforce the concepts to be taught, teachers ensure that students have strategies to decode and spell most words in the English language. This framework and continuum readily organize a large body of information for teachers and their students. Not only do students gain a better understanding of English word structure, but they also become better readers and spellers (Henry, 1988b, 1989).

A Brief History of Written English

Language is one thing that differentiates mankind from any other species of animal. Linguists continue to try to discern the beginnings of vocal language and look for a universal, ancestral tongue. The vocal system for oral language was present with first man. Today approximately 6,800 languages are spoken throughout the world. Linguists predict that 90% of these languages are at risk, as only 600 are currently being taught to children (Sampat, 2001). Over time the major languages have surpassed many regional tongues.

English is one of approximately 130 languages composing the Indo-European linguistic family. Although English is the first language of more than 320 million people and is spoken as a second language by approximately 350 million people, Mandarin Chinese is the most common tongue, spoken by nearly 900 million people (Sampat, 2001). King (2000) estimated that perhaps as many as 1 billion people are learning English as a foreign language. Students throughout the world study English as it is becoming the common world language for global communication in business, primarily via the web.

The term *language* refers to both spoken and written language and to the use of words. Human language, both oral and written, must be learned; it is not just acquired. The language learner must be born into a linguistic community where the relationship between sound and meaning is prescribed by local customs. By listening to the world around them, young children learn the meanings of words already understood by the adult speaker (Barnett, 1964).

Portions of this chapter are from Henry, M.K. (1999). A short history of the English language. In J.R. Birsh (Ed.), *Multisensory teaching of basic language skills* (pp. 119–140). Baltimore: Paul H. Brookes Publishing Co.; adapted by permission.

In those cultures with written languages, children begin formal written language instruction between 5 and 7 years old.

English is a dynamic, constantly changing language, with numerous historical forces shaping its development. The historical perspective is of primary importance to the study of word formation in English and explains some of the consistencies and inconsistencies in English words. By giving students an understanding of how words entered the language, we can dispel some of the difficulties surrounding the exceptional spellings of some common English words. English orthography, when understood from this perspective, begins to make sense.

It is difficult to say when early writing systems were first established, but early cave paintings at Lascaux, France, were made approximately 30,000 years ago. Other findings (Henshilwood et al., 2002) suggest that modern, human written communication developed in Africa even as early as 77,000 years ago. The Blombas Cave, east of Cape Town in South Africa, holds etchings on numerous ochre stones that contain intricate geometric patterns and chiseled lines. Henshilwood and his colleagues assumed that these symbols were drawn to be interpreted by other cave dwellers or nomadic peoples. Such early drawings were not considered languages but usually represented agricultural or religious symbols important to the culture.

The advent of written language marked the beginning of civilization and the start of history. The first written languages began with visual symbols impressed in clay or inscribed on papyrus scrolls 5,000 years ago by people in Sumerian and Egyptian cultures. These cuneiforms or pictographs were a form of logographic writing in which each symbol stood for whole words or syllables. These forms were often difficult to interpret, took considerable space and time to create, and required some artistic talent. Other pictographs include the Scandinavian Stone Age and Bronze Age carvings found frequently in Norwegian fields and the drawings found on teepees of the 19th-century American Indians. As life became less nomadic and as people began to own property, written accounts became necessary. Language as a medium of drama or narrative came somewhat later.

Around 3200 B.C.E. (Before the Common Era) or earlier, hieroglyphics developed in ancient Egypt. These pictograms connected symbols and sounds and represented associated ideas, abstractions, or metaphors. Even in ancient societies, writing was taught systematically through educational systems and transmitted to successive generations.

Today the Chinese language uses a form of logographic writing. Literate Chinese writing requires 6,000 characters representing 40,000 words. Even larger numbers of characters must be learned by those in the professions. Thus, well-educated Chinese people must learn a significant number of characters. Contrast the thousands of Chinese characters necessary to become literate with the 26 letters of the Roman alphabet used in English writing.

Phonetic writing is the final major type of writing, in which written language corresponds to spoken language and signs represent sounds. Both syllabaries and alphabets correspond to spoken language and use signs to represent sounds. Japanese Kana is a syllabary in which symbols stand for the sounds made when words are separated into syllables. Alphabet writing is easier to master as it uses fewer elementary symbols. The very first alphabets contained only consonants. Although the vowels were sounded in speech, they were considered unnecessary in writing. Arabic and Hebrew alphabets made up entirely of consonants still exist.

Early writing went from right to left on a page. In the sixth century B.C.E., the Greeks changed to the boustrophedon order, which alternates right-to-left and left-to-right directions (as an ox plows a field). The Greeks created the first true alphabet by reassigning some early Semitic and Phoenician consonant symbols to symbols that represent vowel sounds. The Greeks also modified letters to signify other sounds they needed. The Etruscan alphabet evolved from the Greek and contained 23 letters.

The Roman alphabet, which is the basis for the English alphabet, developed between 1700 and 1500 B.C.E., as the Romans adapted Etruscan script and wrote left-to-right. By the first century B.C.E., letter formations were refined and mastered. Capital letters were used exclusively; uncial letters (precursors of modern lowercase letters) appeared in the fourth century C.E. The English alphabet reached 26 letters after medieval scribes added *w* and Renaissance printers separated *i* and *j* as well as *u* and *v*.

The alphabet has been crucial to mankind since its invention. Indeed, Logan (1986) noted that

> Of all mankind's inventions, with the possible exception of language itself, nothing has proved more useful or led to more innovations than the alphabet. . . . The alphabet is one of the first things that children learn once they are able to speak. It is the first thing that is taught in school because it is the gateway to learning and knowledge. (pp. 17–18)

HISTORICAL MILESTONES

Among the important languages of the world, English is one of the youngest. The original inhabitants of the English Isles, the Celts, spoke a different language in the Indo-European family. They were conquered by Julius Caesar, a Roman, in 54 C.E. (Common Era). The Britons continued to speak Celtic, while the Romans spoke Latin. The Romans departed and returned almost a century later and stayed for nearly 400 years. During this second stay, Celtic and Latin were spoken side by side. Many place names, especially city names ending in *-chester* and *-caster*, such as *Manchester*, *Winchester*, and *Lancaster*, still exist based on the Latin root *castr*, meaning *camp*.

Table 2.1 depicts a time line (based on E.H. Henderson, 1990, and Henry, 1999) highlighting important events contributing to the changes in written English over the years.

Table 2.1.   Events related to periods of the English language

Period	Year(s)	Event
Pre-English	54 B.C.E.	The ancient Britons (or Celts) defend their land from Julius Caesar and are defeated.
	50 C.E.	Roman Emperor Claudius I colonizes Britain; Celtic and Latin languages co-exist.
	450 C.E.	Romans leave Britain; the Teutonic tribes (the Jutes, Angles, and Saxons) invade.
	600	England divides into seven kingdoms; Northumbria emerges as the dominant Christian kingdom affiliated with the Roman Catholic Church.
Old English	800	The Danes (or Norsemen or Vikings) invade England and are defeated by King Alfred in 878.
	900	Old English reaches its literary peak under the West Saxon kings.
	1000	The Danes successfully invade Britain, yet the Anglo-Saxon language continues its dominant role.
	1066	William the Conqueror, Duke of Normandy, invades Britain; Norman French becomes the official language of state while English remains the language of the people.
Middle English	1350	Edward III takes control; English again becomes the official language of state.
	1400	Geoffrey Chaucer dies, leaving his classic *The Canterbury Tales*.
	1420	Henry V becomes the first English king to write in Middle English.
	1475	The Renaissance reaches England. English borrows from Latin and Greek languages. William Caxton begins printing in English.
Modern English	1600	Queen Elizabeth I and William Shakespeare write in Modern English.
	1755	Samuel Johnson compiles the first comprehensive dictionary of English.
	1828	Noah Webster compiles a dictionary of American English.
	1857–1928	The *Oxford English Dictionary* is developed and published in parts; it is published in full in 1928.

From Henderson, Edmund, *Teaching Spelling*, Second Edition. Copyright © 1990 by Houghton Mifflin. Adapted with permission.

Period of Old English: 450–1150 C.E.

During the fifth century C.E.,[1] Germanic groups—the Angles, the Saxons, and the Jutes—began to settle in different parts of England after terrorizing the inhabitants of the land during the Teutonic invasions. They did not adopt the Celtic language and did not practice the religion of the Celtic people (Balmuth, 1992). Rather, Anglo-Saxon became the dominant language, and the vocabulary stressed the people, objects, and events of daily life. The Roman alphabet, which the Romans had adapted from Greek via Etruscan, was reintroduced to the British Isles by Christian missionaries at this time.

---

[1]Dates of the periods of the development of English vary by author. The dates used in this chapter are those of Nist (1966). See Table 2.1 for a chronological listing of language-related events.

Five major segments of evolution shaped the English language during this period of Old English. First, the language was influenced by Teutonic invasion and settlement. Next, Northumbria, in what is now Northern England, emerged as the dominant Christian kingdom affiliated with the Roman Catholic Church around 600 C.E. Third, with poetry such as *Beowulf*, a national English culture began to emerge. Later, Scandinavians primarily from Norway and Denmark invaded and brought political adjustment and racial assimilation but were defeated by King Alfred in 878. The Norman Conquest, led by William the Conqueror, Duke of Normandy, brought the decline and subjugation of Old English (Nist, 1966). During the Old English period, Germanic, Celtic, Latin, Greek, Anglo-Saxon, Norse, and French words entered the language. Words in the Old English period were phonetically very regular as they almost always followed letter–sound correspondence. For example, *why* was spelled *hwy*, and *where* was spelled *hwær*. Sounds and symbols had even more of a one-to-one correspondence than they do in English today. Only the Christian priests, monks, and nuns were able to write the Roman alphabet, which was the language of the Roman Catholic Church.

King (2000) estimated that about 4,500 words from Old English survive in some form today, including *freond (friend)*, *cild (child)*, and *hus (house)*. Note that prefixes and suffixes, known together as affixes, entered the language even during the period of Old English. For example, the Old English suffix *-scipe* has been passed down as *-ship*. Thus, *freondscipe* translates as *friendship*. Some Old English suffixes remain in use today, such as *-ness*, *-less*, and *-ful*.

The Norman Conquest in 1066 was the transition point to Middle English. According to Nist, at the end of the Old English period, "that language was no longer the basically Teutonic and highly inflected Old English but the hybrid-becoming, Romance-importing, and inflection-dropping Middle English" (1966, p. 107). Coulmas (1996) deduced that the Normans brought the *ou* vowel spelling to English and inserted *g* in front of *h* as in *night*, which had been spelled *niht*. They replaced *u* with *o* before *m*, *n*, and *v* as in *come*, *son*, and *love* because a series of arcs were difficult to read. The Normans also introduced *qu-* to replace *cw-* as in *queen*, which had been spelled *cween*.

Period of Middle English: 1150–1500

The period of Middle English brought great changes in the native tongue of Britain. In the beginning stages, Early Middle English (1150–1307) sounded much like present-day German and was the language of commoners and the uneducated. This period also brought words spelled with less phonetic regularity, such as *rough*, *cough*, *although*, and *through*, which use one spelling (*-ough*) to represent different sounds.

Claiborne estimated that after the Norman Conquest "more than ten thousand French words passed into the English vocabulary, of which 75 percent are still in use" (1983, p. 112). Anglo-French compounds and affixed words (e.g., *gentlewomen*, *gentleman*; *faithful*, *faithfulness*) appeared during this period. Words borrowed from French became increasingly important, especially words related to government, law, and the arts such as *parliament, justice,* and *prologue.* As a result of the Norman Conquest, England was actually a bilingual country, as the upper classes spoke French and the rest of the country spoke English at home and in the community. By 1300 nearly everyone in England spoke English rather than French due to antagonism by native-born English and strong nationalism by landowners (Claiborne, 1983). In addition, by the mid-1300s, the mayor and aldermen of London ordered that all court proceedings there be held in English.

A renewed Latin influence penetrated the language during the period of Mature Middle English (1307–1422) in the 14th and 15th centuries. Chaucer, regarded by many as the first great master of the English tongue, wrote his Canterbury Tales in the late 1300s. This was the time of the Renaissance, which brought a wave of cultural advancement. Hanna, Hodges, and Hanna observed that

> The Latin vocabulary was felt to be more stable and polished and more capable of conveying both abstract and humanistic ideas than was a fledgling language like English. Further, Latin was something of a lingua franca that leaped across geographical and political boundaries. (1971, p. 47)

Many of the words used in English today are borrowed from the Romance languages of the Mature Middle English period. The use of the term *Romance* implies Latin-based terms coming primarily from France, Italy, Portugal, Romania, and Spain.

At this time, too, Latin affixes entered the language in great numbers. The affixation of roots greatly expanded the number of words formed by any one Latin root (e.g., *rupt: rupture, ruptured, disrupt, disruptive, abrupt, erupt, eruption, interrupt, interruption*). Prefixes and suffixes were added to roots to form words such as *adjacent, inferior, lunatic, moderate, necessary, prosecute, rational, solitary,* and *testimony.* Thus, through affixation, English words grew in length and English vocabulary grew at an astounding rate (Claiborne, 1983). During this time, prefixes such as *counter-, dis-, re-, trans-, sub-, super-, pre-, pro-,* and *de-,* along with suffixes such as *-able, -ible, -ent, -al, -ous,* and *-ive* entered the language.

Late Middle English (1422–1500) is known for the growing importance of the written word. English became the language of private and public and informal and formal correspondence. Gutenberg first developed the printing press in 1452 and printed 200 copies of his 42-line Bible (in Latin) in 1456. Soon other printers advanced his work by using illustrations and printing stories and poems. The English pressman William Caxton introduced the printing press to England using the English spoken in London by the well-to-do. Caxton's translation and printing of *Recuyell of the Historyes of Troye* in 1475 was the first book printed in English. The advent of printing in English encouraged new spelling conventions to be set in place at this time. For example, the spelling of *gost* became *ghost* when Dutch and Belgian printers inserted *h.* By the year 1500, more than 1,000 printers throughout Europe had printed millions of books (Krensky, 1996).

Modern English: 1500 to Present

Modern English is typically described in three periods: Early Modern English (1500–1650), Authoritarian English (1650–1800), and Mature Modern English from 1800–1920). Even more of English orthography was locked into convention during the period of Early Modern English. During this period, the sound patterns of the language were changing, especially among vowel sounds. This shift in vowel sounds was so marked that it is often referred to as the "Great Vowel Shift" (Jespersen, 1971, as cited in Nist, 1966, p. 221). In Chaucer's time, the vowel sound in *house* was pronounced as /ōō/ as in "hoos"; by Shakespeare's time in the early 1600s it shifted to /ō/ as in "hose"; and by the Mature Modern English of T.S. Eliot's time in the 20th century, the vowel sound had become /ou/. Pronunciation of consonant and vowel spellings often changed. For example, in the word *sweord* in Old English, both the sounds of *s* and *w* were pronounced. The Modern English spelling, *sword*, keeps *w*, although it is no longer pronounced. In Old English, all five letters in *cniht* were pronounced. The Modern English spelling, *knight*, includes the silent letters *k*, *g*, and *h*.

During the periods of Authoritarian and Mature Modern English, vocabulary continued to expand, especially with the use of Greek and Latin morphemes in scientific terms. In fact, many Latin roots came directly from Greek. Changes continued through the Mature Modern English period to reach the pronunciation of today.

English, then, is a polyglot, with Anglo-Saxon, Latin, and Greek all playing a role in establishing the words read and written today (Balmuth, 1992; Hanna et al., 1971; Nist, 1966). Indeed, Claiborne, in *Our Marvelous Native Tongue*, noted,

> The truth is that if borrowing foreign words could destroy a language, English would be dead (borrowed from Old Norse), deceased (from French), defunct (from Latin) and kaput (from German). When it comes to borrowing, English excels (from Latin), surpasses (from French) and eclipses (from Greek) any other tongue, past or present. (1983, p. 4)

Figure 2.1 summarizes the three major language origins influencing English and provides a brief description of the types of words and several examples from each layer; however, other cultures also added to the English language, especially to American English. American English differs primarily from British English in its vowel sounds and orthography (e.g., *organizing* versus *organising*; *color* versus *colour*; *traveled* versus *travelled*); the vocabularies in both are almost identical and syntax remains virtually the same. Claiborne (1983) emphasized that most early British immigrants to America were barely literate. He noted, "Their language, therefore, was not, as has sometimes been said, the tongue of Shakespeare, but the plain, homely English of the King James Bible, at its best capable of eloquence but seldom marked by elegance" (p. 200).

Few books were available during Colonial times, but new terms were needed, especially to describe the natural wildlife, such as its plants, trees, crops, and animals. From the Native Americans, British immigrants took

Figure 2.1   Layers of the English language. From Calfee, R.C., et al. (1981–1984). *The book: Components of reading instruction.* Unpublished manuscript, Stanford University, California; adapted by permission.

names for the land such as *Penobscot, Merrimac, Passaic, Susquehanna,* and *Savannah,* along with words for animals such as *chipmunk, moccasin, skunk,* and *moose.* Dutch settlers provided names such as *Breukelyn (Brooklyn)* and *Haarlem* (Harlem) and words such as *brandy, golf, duck, wagon,* and *uproar.* Words from African slaves in the 1600s included *gam, chigger,* and *goober* (peanut). English colonists used words that were already in their language but assigned them new meanings such as with the words *underbrush, clearing, log cabin,* and *corn crib.*

American English became partly standardized through the diligence of Noah Webster. From 1783 to 1785 he published a speech book, a grammar, and a reader. The publication in 1828 of his *American Dictionary of the English Language* reflected American and British English usage in vocabulary and definitions. Webster tried to simplify spellings somewhat. If two spellings were current in England, he picked the simpler of the two. Thus, *musick* became *music* and *risque* became *risk.* It was Webster who dropped the *u* in such English words as *honour, favour, colour,* and *labour.* He also changed the spellings of words ending in *-re* to end in *-er* such as with *theater* for *theatre* and *center* for *centre.*

Many new words also formed during the westward movement. Words like *cantankerous, rambunctious,* and *caboodle* became part of the daily vocabulary of settlers in the American West. Words from other cultures also entered the American English lexicon during the 19th and 20th centuries. Consider all of the foods from various countries that are now familiar to most Americans, such as Mexican *burritos* and *tacos*, French *bouillabaisse* and *Brie*, and Chinese *chow mein* and *won ton* soup.

American English continues to expand with new immigrants and innovations. Think of the terms that radio, television, computers, and space exploration have added to English! Many of these new words, such as *bandwidth*, *videocassette*, *microbits*, *astronaut*, and *television*, are made up of existing word parts that are used to mean something different.

The 1980s and 1990s brought numerous new words and phrases to the language. Lederer (1991) acknowledged terms such as *baby boomer, couch potato, awesome, hunk, channeling, airhead, microwave, Jazzercise*, and *proactive*. Soukhanov (1995) discussed the word *pharming*, a genetic engineering technique that the *San Francisco Chronicle* described as "a marriage of high-tech biology and low-tech agriculture" (as cited in Soukhanov, p. 97). This word was voted the most interesting new word in 1992 by the Canadian press but has not become a part of everyday usage. Ayto (1999) described new terms such as *cybercafe, decluttering, intermercials* (advertisements on the Internet), and *technoplegia* (paralysis brought on by fear of using technical equipment). The 1990s also brought us *infomercial, heli-hiking, mudwalking*, and *gephyrophobia* (a fear of crossing bridges). Computer standardization, too, has led to interesting changes, especially in foreign words. For example, some writers may omit the diacritical markings in words, such as an umlaut in German or a tilde in Spanish, as many computer programs cannot show them or do not have characters to represent them.

Westbrook (2002) described the contributions of the language of hip-hop culture, which he called "slanguage." He noted that this language is based not only on the jive talk of the 1920s but also on the earlier coded language used by slaves, who were forbidden to read and write. Through hip-hop culture and MTV and other media, terms such as *cronies* (friends), *cool* (acceptable), *blower* (telephone), *'hood* (neighborhood), and *marinate* (consider) are filtering into the traditional American language.

STUDENT ACTIVITIES ON THE HISTORY OF ENGLISH

Students benefit from a variety of activities related to the historical perspective of the English language. The following exercises for students can supplement instruction on word origins and history:

- Make some cave drawings of events and objects of importance.
- Draw a time line of language events.

- Find out more about various early writing systems such as Sumerian cuneiform; Egyptian hieroglyphics; and the Greek, Etruscan, and Latin alphabets. Write your name in various alphabets.

- Find words from different language origins that are related to everyday activities and topics.

- Compare dictionaries to see if new words you use are listed in the dictionaries.

- Check for possible variations in a word's meaning among dictionaries.

- Make a chart of new words you hear and read. Research the language of origin or when the word was first used.

BOOKS ON THE HISTORY OF ENGLISH

Resources for Students

Brook, D., & Zallinger, J.D. (Illus.). (1998). *The journey of English*. New York: Clarion Books.

Klausner, J.C. (1990). *Talk about English: How words travel and change*. New York: Thomas Y. Crowell.

Krensky, S. (1996). *Breaking into print: Before and after the invention of the printing press*. Toronto: Little, Brown.

Samoyault, T. (1996). *Alphabetical order: How the alphabet began*. New York: Penguin.

Resources for Teachers

Ayto, J. (1999). *Twentieth century words*. New York: Oxford University Press.

Balmuth, M. (1992). *The roots of phonics*. Timonium, MD: York Press.

Barnett, L. (1964). *The treasure of our tongue*. New York: Alfred A. Knopf.

Bryson, B. (1990). *The mother tongue: English and how it got that way*. New York: William Morrow.

Claiborne, R. (1983). *Our marvelous native tongue: The life and times of the English language*. New York: Times Books.

Lederer, R. (1991). *The miracle of language*. New York: Pocket Books.

Logan, R.K. (1986). *The alphabet effect*. New York: St. Martin's Press.

Manguel, A. (1996). *A history of reading*. New York: Viking.

Martin, H.-J. (1994). *The history and power of writing*. Chicago: University of Chicago Press.

McCrum, R., Cran, S., & MacNeil, R. (1986). *The story of English*. New York: Viking.

Nist, J. (1966). *A structural history of English*. New York: St. Martin's Press.

Pei, M. (1965, 1949). *The story of language*. Philadelphia: Lippincott Williams & Wilkins.

Pinker, S. (1994). *The language instinct*. New York: William Morrow.

Soukhanov, A.H. (1995). *Word watch: The story behind the words of our lives*. New York: Henry Holt & Co.

Structure of the English Language

Teachers who comprehend the origins of the English language along with the primary structural patterns within words can improve their assessment skills, enhance their understanding of reading and spelling curricula, communicate clearly about specific features of language, and effectively teach useful strategies to their students. Influences on English orthography (the spelling system) stem from the introduction of letters and words from diverse origins, primarily from Anglo-Saxon, Latin, and Greek. When teachers and their students understand the historical basis and structure of written English, they can better understand the regularities as well as the few irregularities in English words.

A blank 3 × 3 matrix representing the word origin/structure framework for instruction was introduced in Chapter 1 (see Figure 1.1). Figure 3.1 illustrates the contents of the matrix. Each of the nine cells is discussed in this chapter.

Most students enjoy learning about the structure and origins of English words. Young students use these strategies to decode and spell short, regular words involving letter–sound correspondences, or phonics. These students also learn the common syllable patterns, the Anglo-Saxon compound words, and common prefixes (word beginnings) and suffixes (word endings). Upper-grade students and adult learners receiving instruction in more advanced language structure focus on Latin and Greek morphemes. These prefixes, suffixes, roots, and combining forms provide meaning. With an understanding of morphology, students learning English as a second language find that English, after all, is quite regular and is not a language of exceptions. Children with or

	Letter–sound correspondences	Syllables	Morphemes
Anglo-Saxon	Consonants *bid, step, that* Vowels *mad/made, barn, boat*	Closed: *bat* Open: *baby* VCE: *made* Vowel digraph: *boat* Consonant-*le*: *tumble* *r*-controlled: *barn*	Compounds *hardware shipyard* Affixes *read, reread, rereading* *bid, forbid, forbidden*
Latin	Same as Anglo-Saxon but few vowel digraphs Use of schwa /ə/: *direction spatial excellent*	Closed: *spect* VCE: *scribe* *r*-controlled: *port, form*	Affixes *construction erupting conductor*
Greek	*ph* for /f/ *phonograph* *ch* for /k/ *chorus* *y* for /ĭ/ *sympathy*	Closed: *graph* Open: *photo* Unstable digraph: *create*	Compounds *microscope chloroplast physiology*

Figure 3.1.   Word origin and word structure matrix. (*Source:* Henry, 1988b.)

without specific language learning disabilities benefit as they learn effective and efficient strategies to read and spell numerous words (Chall & Popp, 1996; Ehri, 1998; Henry, 1988a, 1988b, 1989).

The reader needs to recognize the sound patterns of speech in the symbols printed on a page. Print, however, does not represent the auditory pattern of heard speech in an exact way (speech is heard as a more or less continuous stream with pauses that do not necessarily correspond to the word or letter boundaries in print). For example, a child is apt to say "Whadjoosay" (What did you say?) as a single stream. One friend might ask another, "Jeetjet?" instead of saying the words separately as "Did you eat yet?" Teachers rarely point out the mismatch between spoken and written language. The problem for the learner is to decode the print to represent for him- or herself a coherent set of sound representations.

English contains approximately 40 phonemes (or discrete sounds). Fromkin and Rodman (1998) estimated that there are 25 consonant sounds and 15 vowel sounds. Some linguists count additional vowel sounds due to dialectical differences. English has many more graphemes (the letters and letter combinations forming patterns found in words) than phonemes. Paulesu et al. (2001) compared shallow orthography, having a more complete one-to-one sound–

letter relationship (as in Finnish, Italian, or Spanish), with the deep, less phonetic, and therefore more complex orthography (as in English and French). Paulesu et al. concluded that the orthography of language is especially important in learning to read, particularly for those children with specific reading disability (dyslexia). Unfortunately, because the media has emphasized the researchers' suggestion that there are 1,120 ways to represent 40 phonemes, using different letter combinations, readers might infer that English is an extremely nonphonetic language. Such a conclusion is often made by citing an uncommon spelling that is found in only one or two words in the English lexicon (e.g., *augh* as in *laugh* or *eo* as in *leopard*). Many teachers, unfamiliar with the structure of English, may conclude that English is an impossible language to teach. However, English has a relatively regular structure, and teachers and their students can readily learn many of the decoding and spelling patterns and rules in English.

Paul Hanna and his colleagues (1971) at Stanford found that in the 17,000 words most commonly used by adult speakers and writers, complete one-to-one letter–symbol correspondence was not uncommon. They estimated that 170 graphemes (letters or letter combinations) spelled their limited set of 42 phonemes that included consonants, vowels, diphthongs, and semivowels. Hanna and his group concluded that several almost perfect letter–sound correspondences exist in English. Moats (1995), in summarizing the Hanna et al. study, wrote that at least 20 phonemes have grapheme spellings that were more than 90% predictable and that 10 others are predictable more than 80% of the time.

The goal for teachers is to teach the very common letter–sound patterns and to teach the regularities of English orthography. Barnett (1964) explained that English is an extremely flexible system because we transfer meaning with minimal phonetic effort. Thus, with only three sounds, such as /ă/, /k/, and /t/, we can create several words with discrete meanings (*act*, *cat*, and *tack*).

ANGLO-SAXON LAYER OF LANGUAGE

Words of Anglo-Saxon origin are characterized as the common, everyday, down-to-earth words used frequently in ordinary situations. Nist provided a clever inventory of some of the Anglo-Saxon words in English today:

> English remains preeminently Anglo-Saxon at its core: in the suprasegmentals of its stress, pitch and juncture patterns and in its vocabulary. No matter whether a man is American, British, Canadian, Australian, New Zealander or South African, he still *loves his mother, father, brother, sister, wife, son and daughter; lifts his hand to his head, his cup to his mouth, his eye to heaven and his heart to God; hates his foes, likes his friends, kisses his kin and buries his dead; draws his breath, eats his bread, drinks his water, stands his watch, wipes his sweat, feels his sorrow, weeps his tears and sheds his blood; and all these things he thinks about and calls both good and bad.* (1966, p. 9)

Table 3.1.   English consonant spelling–sound correspondences with pronunciation examples

Consonant graphemes	Examples	Phoneme
b	bib	/b/
d	deed	/d/
f, ph; -gh (rare)	fife, phone, laugh	/f/
g	gag	/g/
h	hat	/h/
j, -dge, g	jam, ginger, fudge	/j/
k, -ck, c, ch, -que	kick, cat, chorus, unique	/k/
l, -le	lit, needle	/l/
m	mom	/m/
n	no, sudden	/n/
p	pop	/p/
r	roar	/r/
s, c, sc	sauce, science	/s/
t	tot	/t/
v	valve	/v/
w	with	/w/
y	yes	/y/
z, -s	zebra, dogs	/z/
ch, -tch	church, pitch	/ch/
sh	ship	/sh/
th	thin	/th/
th	that	/<u>th</u>/
wh	when	/hw/
si, su, -ge	vision, treasure, garage	/zh/

From Henry, M.K. (1999). A short history of the English language. In J.R. Birsh (Ed.), *Multisensory teaching of basic language skills* (pp. 125–126). Baltimore: Paul H. Brookes Publishing Co.; adapted by permission.

As the Nist passage shows, most words of Anglo-Saxon origin consist of one syllable and represent typical, everyday activities and events. Although consonant letters are fairly regular (i.e., each letter corresponds to one sound), vowel spellings are more problematic. Words that are learned early in school are often irregular and may cause difficulty for students with specific reading disabilities. Students must memorize these "outlaw," "red flag," or "weirdo" words, such as *rough, does, only, eye, laugh, blood,* and *said,* because the vowels do not carry the normal short (lax) or long (tense) sounds associated with these spellings.

Letter–Sound Correspondences

Letter–sound correspondences are the relationships between letters and sounds. Consonant letters of the alphabet represent the speech sounds produced by a

Table 3.2. English vowel spelling–sound correspondences with pronunciation examples

Vowel graphemes[a]	Examples	Phoneme
a	pat	/ă/
a, a-e, ai, ay, ei, eigh, ey	baby, made, pail, pay, veil, eight, they	/ā/
e	pet	/ĕ/
e, e-e, ee, ea, ie, y, ey, ei	me, scheme, greet, seat, thief, lady, alley, ceiling	/ē/
i	bit	/ĭ/
i, i-e, igh, ie, y, y-e	hi, kite, fight, pie, sky, type	/ī/
o	hot	/ŏ/
o, o-e, oa, ow, oe	go, vote, boat, grow, toe	/ō/
u	cut	/ŭ/
a	father	irregular /ŏ/
(schwa)	alone, item, credible, gallop, circus	/ə/
au, aw	fault, claw	/ô/
oo	book	/o͝o/
ew, oo, ue, u	chew, room, blue, lute	/o͞o/
oi, oy	coin, toy	/oi/
ou, ow	cloud, clown	/ou/
ar	car	/ar/
are	care	/ār/
er, ir, ur, or, ear	fern, bird, burn, corn, heard	/ûr/
er	butter	/ər/
ier, eer	pier, deer	/ēr/

From Henry, M.K. (1999). A short history of the English language. In J.R. Birsh (Ed.), *Multisensory teaching of basic language skills* (p. 126). Baltimore: Paul H. Brookes Publishing Co.; adapted by permission.

[a]A vowel letter followed by -e represents the vowel-consonant-e spelling pattern.

partial or complete obstruction of the air stream (e.g., *b, c, d, f, m, p, t*). Consonant letters include all those except the vowels (*a, e, i, o,* and *u* and sometimes *y* and *w*). Vowel sounds are created by the relatively free passage of breath through the larynx and oral cavity.

In learning phonics, students must link the phonemes and graphemes (the letter configurations corresponding to each of the phonemes) of English. Teachers generally use dictionary markings (phonic symbols) as guides to pronunciation, whereas linguists and specialists in speech and language disorders tend to use symbols from the International Phonetic Alphabet (IPA). Tables 3.1 and 3.2 show the common grapheme–phoneme correspondences using phonic symbols to represent the phonemes and provide examples of words that have these spelling and sound patterns.

Teachers and their students need to be able to link the phonemes with their corresponding graphemes. Graphemes are organized into either consonant or vowel patterns. Within these patterns, most of the graphemes will fit

Consonants		
Single	**Blends**	**Digraphs**
b c d f g h k j l m n p q r s t v w x y z	Initial: *bl-, cl-, fl-, gl-, pl-, sl-;* *br-, cr-, dr-, fr-, gr-, pr-, tr-;* *sc-, sl-, sm-, sn-, sp-, st-; tw-;* *scr-, str-; spl-; spr-…* Final: *-lf, -lk, -lp, -mp, -nd, -st…*	Initial: *wh-, gn-, kn-, wr-…* Initial or final: *ch, sh, th (thin), th (that)…* Final: *-ck, -tch…*

Vowels		
Short/long	**r- and l-controlled**	**Digraphs**
a mad/made e pet/Pete i pin/pine o rob/robe u cut/cute y my/baby	*ar* *or* *er, ir, ur* *al, all…*	One sound: *ai, ay, ee, oa, aw, au, ou, ue, ew, igh, eigh…* Two sounds: *ea, ie, ei, oo, ow, ey…*

Figure 3.2. Anglo-Saxon letter–sound correspondence matrix. (From Calfee, R.C., et al. [1981–1984]. *The book: Components of reading instruction.* Unpublished manuscript, Stanford University, California; adapted by permission.)

into one of three categories as illustrated in Figure 3.2. This 2 × 3 matrix showing Anglo-Saxon letter–sound patterns corresponds to the top left-hand cell in the 3 × 3 matrix shown in Figures 1.1 and 3.1. Anglo-Saxon letter–sound correspondences are the first symbol–sound relationships taught to children who are learning to read and write.

Single-letter consonant spellings seldom vary; for 17 of the 21 consonant letters, each letter stands for a specific sound. Thus, the letter *b* is almost always pronounced /b/, *m* pronounced /m/, and *p* pronounced /p/. The consonant graphemes *c* and *g* each have two sounds, but specific spelling patterns guide the reader. For example, *c* almost always has the sound /k/ before *a, o,* and *u* (as in *cat, cope,* and *cub*) but has the sound /s/ before *e, y,* and *i* (as in *cell, city,* and *cycle*). Informally, these are called the hard and soft sounds of *c*, respectively. Likewise, *g* before *a, o,* and *u* (as in *gate, go,* or *gun*) is considered hard, whereas *g* before *e, i,* and *y* (as in *gem, ginger,* and *gypsy*) is soft. The letter *s* usually says /s/ (as in *snake*), but often carries the /z/ sound in the final consonant position (as in *rose*) or as a plural (as in *dogs*). The letter *y* usually is a consonant at the beginning of words and syllables (as in *yard*) but is a vowel in the middle or end of syllables (as in *gymnasium, by,* and *baby*). Note that *x* is omitted from Table 3.1 because it represents two sounds: /k/ and /s/. Final *x* makes the sound of /ks/ (as in *box*) but makes the sound of /z/ at the beginning of some words (as in *Xerox* and *xylophone*).

Consonant blends (sometimes called *consonant clusters*) are made up of two or three adjacent consonant sounds in a syllable; they retain their individual sounds and are common (e.g., *bl* and *mp* in *blimp; spl* and *nt* in *splint*).

Interestingly, few English words begin with *kl* or *kr*. Instead, English words begin with the blends *cl* and *cr* unless they are proper names or unless Germanic terms are needed (e.g., *Kleenex, Klamath, Paul Klee, Otto Klemperer, Klondike, Kris Kringle*).

Consonant digraphs, in contrast, also have two consonant letters adjacent in a syllable but form only one speech sound. Digraphs often consist of a consonant letter followed by *h* and usually represent a new sound that is unlike the sound of either of the consonants in the digraph (e.g., *sh* as in *ship, ch* as in *chump, th* as in *this* or *thin, wh* as in *which*). Many students have difficulty discriminating between the voiced sound /w/ (as in *wail*) and the unvoiced /hw/ (as in *whale*), and not all English speakers use the unvoiced /hw/ sound. The letter combinations *kn-, gn-, wr-, -ck,* and *-ng* are considered digraphs in some systems (*-tch* and *-dge* are trigraphs, or three letters that represent one speech sound).

Vowel sounds tend to be more difficult to learn than consonant sounds, but even they have some consistency. Vowel sounds represented by single letters are generally either short or long. The short /ă/ is spelled with *a* (as in *hat, man,* and *staff*) nearly 100% of the time, and short /ŏ/ is spelled with *o* (as in *hot, mob,* and *lock*) more than 95% of the time (Smelt, 1976). Perfetti (1986) observed that alphabets fail to provide a unique letter symbol for each vowel sound; thus, we look at certain markers within the spelling of a word. These markers serve as clues to indicate whether the short or long sound should be used. A vowel with a syllable-final consonant after it in the same syllable carries the short sound (e.g., *a* as in *cat, e* as in *let, i* as in *fit, o* as in *fox,* and *u* as in *fun*). In contrast, a vowel at the end of a syllable has the long sound, or "says its own name" (as in *go, baby,* and *pilot*). The silent *e* at the end of a word after a consonant (as in *shape* and *vote*) also signals that the vowel within the word has a long vowel sound. The doubled consonant in *pinning* and *cutter* are there to mark the sound of the vowel before the doubled consonant as short. The doubled consonant cancels the long vowel signal that would otherwise be given by the *i* in *-ing* and the *e* in *-er*. The letter *y* serves as a vowel following a consonant at the end of a word or syllable (as in *my* and *baby*), or following another vowel (as in *day* or *toy*). The letter *w*, when it follows a vowel, also serves as a vowel (as in *few* and *claw*). In this case the vowel plus *w* or *y* is considered a vowel digraph.

Students will also read words with a vowel plus *r* or *l*. In syllables containing *r,* vowel sounds often change because of *r.* These patterns are best presented as combinations such as *ar* (as in *star*), *or* (as in *corn*), *er* (as in *fern*), *ir* (as in *bird*), *ur* (as in *church*), and *al* (as in *falter*).

Vowel digraphs are two adjacent vowels (e.g., *oa, ee, oi, ou, au*) occurring primarily in words of Anglo-Saxon origin. These digraphs usually occur in the middle of words. Vowel digraphs can be divided into two sets—those that are fairly consistently linked to a single sound (e.g., *ee, oa, oi, oy*) and those that may have two pronunciations (e.g., *ea* as in *bead* or *bread, ow* as in *show* or *cow*). Balmuth provided the historical origins of vowel digraphs and diphthongs and noted that during Middle English times the diphthongs were "especially varied in spelling because of the confusions that resulted from the separation of the written *i* and *y* and the introduction of the *w* and other French spelling conventions" (1992, p. 102).[1] Vowel digraphs are often difficult for students to acquire in Anglo-Saxon words because of their variability, interference from previously learned associations, and occasional irregularity.

By the end of second grade, children should have mastered all of the common letter–sound correspondences and spelling rules relating to these patterns. For example, at the end of a one-syllable word, the consonants *f, l,* and *s* are usually doubled when they come directly after a short vowel sound (e.g., *staff, chill, grass*). Students should recognize that in English words with a short vowel sound immediately followed by a final /k/ sound, *-ck* represents the final sound (as in *sick, stack, deck, clock, stuck*); only *k* is used after two vowel letters (as in *peak*) and directly after consonants (as in *milk*). The same is true for /ch/ spelled as *tch* and /j/ spelled as *dge* at the end of one-syllable words following a short vowel sound (as in *pitch* and *bridge*). Chapter 6 presents the spelling rules affecting words of Anglo-Saxon origin.

In addition to learning the common letter–sound correspondences, students must also know how to read and spell the 100–200 common irregular words found in primers and primary-grade text. Knowledge of letter–sound correspondences is not much help in either reading or spelling these nonphonetic words, such as *said, blood, love,* and *cough*. (See Appendix B for lists of the most common nonphonetic words.)

Melvyn Ramsden (2000) discussed the importance of knowing the meaning of a word before it is spelled. Although reading the words *mist* and *missed* is not so difficult, one must know the meanings of these homophones in order to know which one to use in a given context. Students must understand meaning to know which of the following to write in a certain situation: *meet* or *meat, here* or *hear, pail* or *pale, maid* or *made,* and numerous other homophones. As noted in Chapter 1, a computer spell checker cannot help correct spelling if the writer does not know the correct meaning of the words that he or she wants to use.

---

[1]Linguists differentiate between the terms *vowel digraph* and *diphthong*. Both contain two adjacent vowels in the same syllable. A diphthong glides from one sound to another. Diphthongs include *oi, oy; au, aw; ou, ow;* and *ue, ew*. Some linguists disagree about the number of diphthongs in English; Venezky (1999) suggested that this disagreement reflects dialect differences. (In this book, all vowel pairs are called digraphs.)

Syllable Patterns

Syllables are units of spoken language consisting of an uninterrupted sound formed by a vowel sound alone or a vowel sound with one or more consonants. Words with an Anglo-Saxon origin have a variety of syllable patterns. Students first learn that each syllable must have a vowel. Children generally have less difficulty hearing syllables in words than in recognizing written syllables (Balmuth, 1992; Groff, 1971). Therefore, teachers often begin by having children say their own names and counting the number of syllables. Later, students listen for accent or stress in words of more than one syllable. Anglo-Saxon base words, such as *sleep*, *like*, and *time*, tend to retain the accent when affixes are added (e.g., *asleep*, *likely*, *timeless*).

Groff (1971) emphasized that syllables are not units of writing, grammar, or structure, but rather units of speech. He noted that it is the boundaries of syllables rather than the number of syllables in a word that cause difficulty in their analysis. He made the distinction between how linguists may divide words based on morphemic boundaries and how dictionaries divide syllables based on sounds. For example, some linguists prefer to divide the word *disruptive* as *dis/rupt/ive* (prefix, root, and suffix), whereas the dictionary usually divides the word as *dis/rup/tive*. Groff questioned whether teaching syllable division is an important part of teaching reading. Although this argument continues, knowing the alternatives for dividing words into syllables provides students with another strategy for word analysis.

Teachers who know the following six major syllable types and the predominant patterns for syllable division can help children read multisyllabic words; teachers and students will also find syllable division useful in writing hyphenated words. The major types of syllables are 1) closed, 2) open, 3) vowel-consonant-*e*, 4) vowel digraph, 5) consonant-*le*, and 6) *r*-controlled (Moats, 1995, 2000; Steere, Peck, & Kahn, 1971).

Teachers introduce closed syllables first. In these syllables, the single vowel has a consonant after it, making the vowel sound short (e.g., *map*, *sit*, *cub*, *stop*, *bed*). An open syllable contains a vowel at the end of the syllable, and the vowel usually says its long sound (e.g., *go*, *me*, *Hi*, *ho/bo*). Stanback (1992) found that closed syllables alone make up 43% of syllables in English words. Open syllables and closed syllables together account for almost 75% of English syllables. The final *e* in a vowel-consonant-*e* (VCE) syllable makes the vowel long or "say its own name" (e.g., *made*, *time*, *cute*, *vote*, *Pete*). A vowel digraph (or vowel team or vowel pair) syllable contains two adjacent vowels (as in *rain*, *green*, *coil*, and *pause*). Children learn the long, short, or diphthong sound of each pattern. A consonant-*le* syllable usually starts with a consonant that is part of that syllable. For example, *bugle* has a long *u* because *gle* stays together, making the first syllable in the word an open syllable, *bu*. In contrast, *tumble* contains *tum* and *ble*, with *tum* being a closed syllable. *Little* requires two *t*s to keep the *i* in *lit* short. As discussed previously, vowel sounds in *r*-controlled syllables often lose their identity as long or short and are co-articulated with /r/ (as in *star, corn, fern, church,* and *firm*).

Students also need to learn some common rules for syllable division in order to make multisyllabic words easier to read and spell. By understanding and practicing identification of the various syllable types in monosyllables first, readers will recognize these common syllable types as they learn to divide words into syllables. Understanding how to spell the vowel sounds in syllables gives readers an advantage and a more productive understanding of the syllable division rules. Readers may recognize syllable division patterns such as VC/CV (as in *nap/kin*), V/CV (as in *ho/bo*), VC/V (as in *plan/et*), VC/CCV (as in *hun/dred*), and CV/VC (as in *cre/ate*) patterns. These are useful separations to know when one analyzes unfamiliar words.

Morpheme Patterns

A morpheme is the smallest meaningful linguistic unit. Compound words, prefixes, suffixes, and roots are the morphemes helpful for students learning to read and write because they are used in hundreds of thousands of words (Brown, 1947). By knowing the common morphemes, students enhance not only their decoding and spelling skills but also their vocabulary skills.

Linguists use several terms to reflect the main part in a word. The term *base word* or *base element* refers to the morphological base of a word stripped of its affixes, such as *jump* or *read*. The term *base word* can also refer to a complete English word, such as *transmit*, that in turn contains a root (*mit*). The term *root* refers to a word part from an origin language such as Latin or Greek; roots are usually bound in English. Although linguists sometimes use the term *stem*, it is not used in this book as it has a variety of meanings.

Anglo-Saxon morphemes are found in both compound and affixed words. Decoding and spelling these words tends to be simple because they contain regular orthographic features. A compound word is generally composed of two short words joined together to form a new, meaning-based word. That is, a compound word has a meaning that is based on the meanings of its constituent words. Children enjoy generating compound words such as *cowboy, blackboard, baseball,* and *campground*. Computer technology has been the impetus for many new compound words such as *software, firmware,* and *hardware* (with its computer-related, not tool-related, meaning).

Anglo-Saxon base words are generally free morphemes. That is, each can stand alone as a word in English (e.g., *spell, hope*). Anglo-Saxon base words may be combined as compounds (e.g., *football, blackboard*) and may also become affixed with the addition of prefixes and suffixes (e.g., *spell, misspell, misspelled; hope, hopeless, hopelessness*).

Morpheme affixes have two forms. Inflectional morphemes indicate grammatical features such as number, person, tense, or comparative forms (e.g., *dog, dogs; wait, waits; walk, walked; small, smaller*). Derivational morphemes, in contrast, are added to existing words to create new words that are often different parts of speech than the base words (e.g., *hope* is a noun and a verb, *hopeless* is an adjective, *hopelessly* is an adverb).

Students in first and second grades begin by adding suffixes to words requiring no change in the base form (e.g., *help, helpless; time, untimely*). By the middle of second grade and in third grade, students must learn suffix addition rules affecting some base words, such as when to double a final consonant (as in *big, bigger*), drop final *e* (as in *blame, blaming*), or change *y* to *i* (as in *copy, copied*).

The term *morphophonemics* refers to the condition whereby certain morphemes keep their written spelling even though their phonemic forms change (Venezky, 1999). This concept provides students with a logical reason for many English spellings. For example, in *knowledge*, the morpheme *know* is pronounced differently from the base word *know*. The meaning of *knowledge* is based on the base word *know*, however. Balmuth noted that

> It can be helpful to readers when the same spelling is kept for the same morpheme, despite variations in pronunciation. Such spellings supply clues to the meanings of words, clues that would be lost if the words were spelled phonemically, as, for example, if *know* and *knowledge* were spelled *noe* and *nollij* in a hypothetical phonemic system. (1992, p. 207)

LATIN LAYER OF LANGUAGE

The Latin layer of language consists of words used in more formal settings. Latin is the basis for the Romance languages. Romance languages include French, Italian, Portuguese, Romanian, and Spanish. Latin-based words are often found in literature or social studies texts in the upper elementary and later grades. Because Latin-based words are longer, many students expect them to be more complex. Yet, in most cases the words follow simple letter–sound correspondences.

Letter–Sound Correspondences

Most Latin roots contain short vowels, as in *rupt, script, cred, vent, tens, pend,* and *vis.* The syllable-final consonant combination *-ct* is a signpost for words of Latin origin, as in *dict, duct, tract, struct,* and *ject.* Words such as *disruptive, reconstructed,* and *extracting* provide examples of multisyllabic Latin-based words that cause little problem for children to read and spell once they learn the constituent patterns.

Vowel digraphs appear only rarely in Latin-based words. As mentioned previously, Anglo-Saxon vowel digraphs are often difficult for students to acquire. Similarly, in words of Latin origin, spellings for vowel digraphs are also difficult for students to acquire. These digraphs generally appear in suffixes such as *-ion, -ian, -ient,* and *-ial,* which are taught as units. Students, however, can learn some spelling patterns for these digraphs: The suffix *-ion* is usually preceded by *t* or *s* (as in *tion* and *sion*); the suffix *-ian* usually comes after *c* (i.e., *cian*); and the suffixes *-ient* and *-ial* usually come after *t* (i.e., *tient* and *tial*).

In addition, students may have trouble acquiring Latin-based words with vowel digraphs because the consonant before the digraph suffixes is typically variable. When a vowel digraph comes after the letters *c*, *s*, and *t*, it combines with those letters to create the /sh/ sound, as in *nation*, *partial*, *social*, and *admission*. (The suffix *-sion* is sometimes pronounced as /zhən/, as in *erosion* and *invasion*.)

Syllable Patterns

The main syllable types found in Latin roots include closed (e.g., *spect*, *rupt*, *script*), VCE (e.g., *scribe*, *-voke*), and *r*-controlled (e.g., *port*, *form*). Patterns of syllable division are similar to those found in words of Anglo-Saxon origin. For example, *disruption* has two VC/CV separations: *dis/rup/tion*. The V/CV syllable division pattern can be found in the words *re/port* and *pro/trac/tor*.

The stress patterns in Latin-based words are fairly complex. The schwa, or unstressed vowel sound, is often found in words of Latin origin (e.g., *excellent*, *direction*). When one pronounces *excellent*, for example, stress occurs on the first syllable, so the initial *e* receives the regular short sound. The following two *es*, appearing in unstressed syllables, have the schwa sound (/ə/). Listening for the unstressed vowels in open and closed syllables is an advanced skill that students with reading difficulties need to learn. Students who can discover the base word (e.g., *excel*) often are able to spell the longer word. The schwa is often found in unaccented prefixes and/or suffixes. Any vowel may be pronounced as schwa when it appears in an unstressed syllable. The schwa is discussed more fully in later chapters.

Morpheme Patterns

Although Anglo-Saxon base words can make up compound words (e.g., *sleepwalk*) and can have affixes added to them (e.g., *nightly*), Latin root words may only be affixed. Nist (1966) provided another key example: "So great, in fact, was the penetra*tion* of Latin *af*fixing during the Renais*sance* that it quite *un*did the Anglo-Saxon habit of *com*pounding as the leading means of word form*ation* in English" (p. 11). Words of Latin origin become affixed by the addition of a prefix or a suffix to the root, which rarely stands alone (e.g., *rupt*, *interrupted*; *mit*, *transmitting*; *vent*, *prevention*). Latin-based roots are nearly always considered *bound morphemes* because the root does not stand alone; a prefix and/or a suffix will be added. For example, the prefix *in-* can be added to the bound morpheme *spect* to get *inspect* and the suffix *-ion* can be added to get *inspection*.

The final consonant of a Latin prefix often changes based on the beginning letter of the root. For example, the prefix *in-*, meaning *in* or *not*, changes to *il-* before roots beginning with *l* (e.g., *illegal*), to *ir-* before roots beginning with *r* (e.g., *irregular*), and to *im-* before roots beginning with *m*, *b*, and *p* (e.g., *immobile*, *imbalance*, *important*). These changes are due to *euphony* (from Greek: *eu* meaning *well* and *phon* meaning *sound*). Thus, the words with the changed prefixes sound better and are easier to say than, for instance, *inlegal* or *conmunicate*. These "chameleon" prefixes have several forms and are explained in Chapter 7.

Numerous suffixes can be added to Latin roots. Students need to learn the rule for doubling final consonants in polysyllabic base words. If a word ends in one consonant, preceded by a short vowel, and if the accent is on the final syllable of the base word, double the final consonant when the suffix begins with a vowel. For example, *transmit + -ed* becomes *transmitted* because the accent of the base word is on the final syllable, *mit*.

Special note must also be made about the suffix *-ion* (*-tion*, *-sion*, *-cian*). Some sources, such as Barnhart (1988); Gillingham and Stillman (1956, 1997); and *Webster's New Universal Unabridged Dictionary, Second Edition* (1983), explain *-tion* and *-cian* as noun suffixes. Others teach *-ion* and *-ian* as suffixes added to roots, such as *invent, invention* and *music, musician*. A solution for students is to teach them that *-ion* and *-ian* are suffixes but that pronunciation dictates that the syllable be *-tion*, *-sion*, or *-cian*. The same is true for *-al* suffixes preceded by *ti* and *ci* (as in *substantial* and *judicial*): *-al* is the suffix and the syllables are *-tial* and *-cial*.

Latin word roots form the basis of hundreds of thousands of words (Brown, 1947; Henry, 1993). Longer words of Latin or Greek origin (the majority of words in the English language) are often easier to spell than short words because the longer words contain recognizable word parts that are used in thousands of words. Students can readily observe the prefixes, roots, and suffixes in words such as *prediction*, *incredible*, *extracting*, and *reconstructionist* and see that these common word parts assist in decoding, spelling, and enlarging vocabulary. Learning word roots is useful for all students, including those with reading disabilities, those studying for the SATs, and those who are English language learners (Henry, Calfee, & Avelar-LaSalle, 1989). In fact, the Latin word roots in English words are often the very same roots that prevail in Spanish words, such as *descripción (description)*, *prosperidad (prosperity)*, and *habitante (inhabitant)*. Note that the affixes, not the roots, are usually what differ between the Spanish and English spellings.

Understanding morphophonemic relations is especially important for learning Latin roots. When prefixes and suffixes are added, the stress often changes and therefore the entire word pronunciation changes. Think about words such as *excel, excellent; ridicule, ridiculous; prepare, preparation;* and *solid, solidify*. Vowel sounds can be heard in the accented syllables but not in the unaccented syllables. Not being able to hear the vowel sounds in the unaccented syllables makes spelling difficult, and students must try to find the base word before spelling the affixed word.

The Latin word roots are probably among the most productive elements for students to learn in the sense that the roots are important for enhancing vocabulary, for decoding, and for spelling. A relatively small number of Latin roots and affixes and Greek combining forms appear in hundreds of thousands of words.

GREEK LAYER OF LANGUAGE

During the Renaissance, Greek words entered English by the thousands to meet the needs of scholars and scientists. Bodmer noted that "the terminology of modern science, especially in *aeronautics, biochemistry, chemotherapy,* and *genetics*" (1944, p. 246) is formed from Greek. Greek word parts tend to be compounded and appear largely in scientific texts (e.g., *microscope, hemisphere, physiology*). The roots are often termed *combining forms* in modern dictionaries, although many teachers use the terms *Greek combining forms* and *Greek roots* interchangeably.

The following passage from a middle-school science text shows not only how short words of Anglo-Saxon origin mix with longer Romance words but also how the scientific terminology is couched in words of Greek origin (italicized):

> Suppose you could examine a green part of a plant under the *microscope*. What would you see? Here are some cells from the green part of a plant. The cells have small green bodies shaped like footballs. They give the plant its green color. They are call *chloroplasts*. A single green plant cell looks like this. *Chloroplasts* are very important to a plant. As you know, plants make their own food. This food-making process is called *photosynthesis*. It is in these *chloroplasts* that *photosynthesis* takes place. (Cooper, Blackwood, Boeschen, Giddings, & Carin, 1985, p. 20, emphasis added)

Letter–Sound Correspondences

Letter–sound correspondences in words of Greek origin are similar to those found in words of Anglo-Saxon origin, but words of Greek origin also often incorporate new letter–sound correspondences. Thus, in the word *chlorophyll*, students need to know that *ch, ph,* and *y* correspond to the sounds of /k/, /f/, and /ī/, respectively. These peculiar consonant combinations were introduced by Latin scribes and make words of Greek origin easily recognizable (Bodmer, 1944). Less common Greek letter–sound correspondences, found in only a handful of words, include *mn* as in *mnemonic, rh* as in *rhododendron, pt* as in *pterodactyl, pn* as in *pneumonia,* and the more well-known *ps* as in *psychology* and *psychiatry*.

Syllable Patterns

As words of Greek origin are often made up of two Greek combining forms, students need to know that syllables in each combining form usually retain their stress (e.g., *pho'/no/graph'* and *mi'/cro/scope'*). This occurs even in words containing three combining forms such as *pho'/to/he'/li/o/graph'*.

Syllable types most prevalent in Greek-based words are closed (CVC, as in *graph*) and open (CV, as in each syllable of *pho/to*). In addition, a unique syllable pattern, that of adjacent vowels in separate syllables, as in *the/a/ter, cre/ate, cha/os,* and *the/o/ry,* can be found. Note that although *ea* is often a vowel digraph (as in *read* and *teach*), in *theatre* and *create* the vowels represented by the letters *ea* are in separate syllables. In addition, *ao* and *eo* are never vowel digraphs. These "unstable" digraphs appear in distinct syllables and therefore have distinct sounds.

Syllable division in words of Greek origin generally follows the rules given for Anglo-Saxon words, especially for open syllables (e.g., *phono, photo, meter, polis*). The letter *y* sounds as short /ĭ/ in closed syllables (e.g., *sym/pho/ny, gym/na/si/um*), and these syllables divide after the consonant. The letter *y* sounds as long /ī/ in open syllables (e.g., *cy/clone, gy/ro/scope, hy/per/bo/le*), and these syllables divide directly after *y*. In words containing unstable digraphs, syllable division occurs between the vowels as in *zo/ol/o/gy* and *char/i/ot*.

Combining forms such as *semi* (VC/V), *hemi* (VC/V), and *micro* (V/CCV) do not follow V/CV or VC/CV division. Students rarely need to depend on strategies for syllable division in Greek-based words because they learn the orthographic patterns as wholes.

Morpheme Patterns

Greek combining forms can make up compound words just as Anglo-Saxon roots do. Students can learn to read and spell many thousands of words by recognizing relatively few Greek combining forms. While learning the common Greek combining forms that hold specific meaning, such as *micro, scope, bio, graph, helio, meter, phono, photo, auto,* and *tele,* students begin to read, spell, and understand the meaning of many words, such as *microscope, telescope, phonoreception, telephoto, telescopic, photoheliograph, heliometer, biography,* and *autobiography.* Many Greek combining forms are often called prefixes because they appear at the beginning of words (e.g., *auto* in *autograph, hyper* in *hyperbole, hemi* in *hemisphere*). Numeral prefixes such as *mono-* (1), *di-* (2), *tri-* (3), *tetra-* (4), *penta-* (5), *hexa-* (6), *hepta-* (7), *octo-* (8), *nona-* (9), *deca-* (10), and *kilo-* (1,000) become useful in the study of mathematics and geometry. (See Appendix D for Latin and Greek number prefixes.)

CONCLUSION

Treiman (1993) concluded that although children may pick up spelling patterns on their own, most children might learn the patterns more rapidly if regularities are spelled out for them. For example, teachers can point out that *-ck* and -*tch* never appear at the beginning of words and that consonant blends containing *r*, such as *cr*, *pr*, and *tr*, do not come at the end of words.

By learning the origin and structural framework of words, students gain strategies for decoding and spelling unfamiliar words. Students learn that words are made up of letters that have sounds and that words are also made up of syllables and morphemes and so can be broken down in several ways. Thus, children need to learn the following:

- A number of letter–sound correspondences within categories such as consonants, vowels, consonant blends, consonant digraphs, and vowel digraphs
- High-frequency, nonphonetic words
- The most common ways to divide words into syllables
- Common morpheme patterns—compound words, prefixes, suffixes, and roots
- The productive rules of the written form of the language
- An understanding of the history of written English

SECTION II

Instruction

Lesson
Fundamentals

The lesson format and procedures presented in this chapter and used throughout later chapters feature elements related to metacognition, multisensory instruction, and presentations in a discussion format. Teachers act as facilitators during these lessons.

METACOGNITIVE ASPECTS OF READING AND SPELLING

Although decoding has long been considered a cognitive activity, the related areas of metacognition, metalinguistic awareness, and metalanguage are also important. All three deal with knowing about knowing. Metacognition is the ability to reflect upon and monitor cognitive activity (Flavell, 1985). Metalinguistic awareness is the ability to think about and reflect upon the nature and function of language (Pratt & Grieve, 1984). Metalanguage is the language used to describe language—terms such as *phoneme*, *word*, and *phrase* (Tunmer & Herriman, 1984). The Decoding Instruction Register, a set of terms necessary for discussing and thinking about decoding and spelling concepts, is described in the metalanguage section. The ability to monitor whether what has been decoded is correct or incorrect and the capacity to reflect on alternative strategies for decoding unfamiliar words fit into the domain of metaknowledge.

Metacognition

Forrest-Pressley and Waller (1984) suggested that metacognition in decoding is knowledge about decoding and the ability to control decoding activities through monitoring, predicting accuracy, and changing decoding strategies deliberately. Strategies of interest to Forrest-Pressley and Waller were 1) recognizing whole words, 2) sounding out a word, 3) "guessing" from context, and 4) asking the teacher for the pronunciation of the word. They noted that in order for the teacher to assess the child's knowledge of cognitive processes, it is necessary for the child to have a conscious awareness of the processes and to be able to talk about these processes. Forrest-Pressley and Waller measured metacognitive aspects of decoding by assessing the child's use of decoding strategies and assessing the ability to verbalize the different strategies and predict their efficiency. They concluded that many readers, especially poor readers, have learned to cope instead of learning "why or how a particular strategy is useful" (p. 30).

Metacognition in decoding means simply that the reader is able to monitor reading in order to identify errors in decoding individual words and is able to select alternative strategies for word identification. Yet, unless the student actually knows that he or she has read the word incorrectly and knows how to correct it, the word will remain incorrect.

Metalinguistic Awareness

Metacognition involves reflecting on and monitoring any cognitive activity, whereas metalinguistic awareness and metalanguage focus on knowing about language function and structure. The earliest studies in metalinguistic awareness emphasized children's concepts of *reading* and *word* (Reid, 1966). More recent investigations have described the use of language to analyze and discuss language.

Most researchers dealing with metalinguistic awareness—or *linguistic awareness* as it is often called (Liberman, 1973)—refer primarily to spoken language. Holdaway (1986) viewed metalinguistic awareness as the ability to reflect upon the linguistic processes, not simply to use them. To understand phonics, for example, is to be explicitly aware of a very sophisticated stratagem. Liberman and Mann reviewed findings from a number of studies and concluded that the difficulty for most "children who have problems in learning to read is basically linguistic in nature—not visual, or auditory, or motor, or whatever—but rather in the ineffective use of phonologic strategies" (1981, p. 151). Liberman and Mann found that the ability to segment words by phonemes or by syllables was highly correlated with the ease of reading acquisition and concluded that "linguistic awareness may be necessary for the acquisition of reading" (p. 154).

Templeton broadened the scope of metalinguistic awareness by referring to it as "the ability to reflect upon and analyze the structures of both spoken and written language" (1986, p. 295). Thus, it provides the student with ways to talk about language.

The introduction to formal schooling and the act of learning to read brings about an increase in metalinguistic awareness. This awareness can be explicitly taught as teachers guide students to reflect on the patterns they are using and become more analytical.

Metalanguage

Closely related to metalinguistic awareness is metalanguage, the language used to talk about both spoken and written language concepts. Reid (1966) discussed the role of language as a mediating process in learning and concept formation. He described the "technical vocabulary" of 5-year-olds as they referred to *pictures, letters, writing,* and *names.*

Several researchers noted that the learner needs to develop concepts for thinking about reading (Adams, 1990; DeStefano, 1972; Downing, 1979; Yaden & Templeton, 1986) and that a specialized language is useful. The terms we use provide labels for the concepts we discuss. Few beginning readers (and even their teachers) have adequate vocabularies to discuss reading concepts. Teachers can explicitly teach terms related to language learning to enhance reading and writing instruction.

DeStefano (1972) coined the phrase Language Instruction Register for the technical terms used in discussing reading and writing. The terms useful for establishing an instruction register for discussing decoding are shown in Table 4.1. Sharing this common vocabulary facilitates discussion between teachers and students. When teachers in all grades in a school use the same terms, continuity develops throughout the grades for talking about decoding and spelling concepts.

Table 4.1. Decoding–Spelling Instruction Register

Linguistic terms	Letter–sound correspondences	Morphemes
grapheme	consonant	compound word
phoneme	vowel	prefix
morpheme	short vowel	root
word	long vowel	suffix
syllable	blend	combining form
phonics	consonant digraph	
schwa	vowel digraph	
segmentation	blending	

Source: Henry, 1988b.

MULTISENSORY INSTRUCTION

Multisensory instruction is the linkage of visual, auditory, and kinesthetic-tactile modalities. Students simultaneously link the visual symbol (what they see) with its corresponding sound (what they hear) and kinesthetic-tactile input (what they feel) as they write the pattern accurately and in when they say the corresponding sound(s). Teachers are encouraged to use a multisensory approach in these lessons.

Children do not learn only by phonics or by memorizing words by sight. In fact, the visual, auditory, and kinesthetic-tactile modalities are all linked as new spelling patterns and rules are presented. This approach to learning is not new—it was applied to reading in the 1930s by Anna Gillingham and her colleague, Bessie Stillman. Gillingham and Stillman were influenced by the theories of Samuel T. Orton, a physician who also studied reading and reading disorders. Orton proposed a multisensory approach for teaching children with reading problems. For the kinesthetic-tactile modality, he relied on the ideas conveyed by Grace Fernald and Helen Keller in 1921, when they wrote about several cases they had studied:

> Lip and hand kinaesthetic elements seem to be the essential link between the visual cue and the various associations which give it word meaning. In other words, it seems to be necessary for the child to develop a certain kinaesthetic background before he can apperceive the visual sensations for which the printed words form the stimulus. Even the associations between the spoken and the printed word seem not to be fixed without the kinaesthetic links. (p. 376)

This instruction is known today as the Orton-Gillingham approach (J.L. Orton, 1966). Gillingham and Stillman insisted that children with specific reading difficulties could not learn to read by sight word methods, even when these are later reinforced by functional, incidental, intrinsic, or analytical phonics. Gillingham and Stillman noted that their technique "is based upon the constant use of associations of all of the following, how a letter or word looks, how it sounds and how the speech organs or the hand in writing feels when producing it" (1956, p. 17).

In their manuals, Gillingham and Stillman (1956, 1997) directed the teacher to assist the children in making numerous linkages. For example, as a child sees a letter, he or she may trace it and say the letter name and/or sound. Or, the sound is made by the teacher and the name is given by the pupil.

Correct letter formation is emphasized while children are learning the letters and their corresponding sounds. Because children with dyslexia often persist in reversing letters or transposing letters within words, knowing how to form the letters helps in correcting the reversals. To assist children in correcting reversals, teachers point out the different order of strokes for letter formation. For example, to form *b*, the vertical line is drawn first, followed by

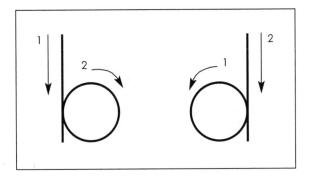

Figure 4.1. Print letter formation for b and d.

the circle. In contrast, *d* is formed with the circle (or a partial circle in the shape of *c*) first, followed by the vertical line (see Figure 4.1).

Slingerland (1996) guided students by having them talk through the process for both manuscript and cursive writing. For example, as students form *b*, the teacher guides their thinking by saying, "We start at the top and make the tall stem go all the way down. Now go up over the same line without lifting your arm, but stop and think which way the arm is going to go before making the round part" (p. 62). In contrast, as they write *d*, students learn to say "Round like an *a*, tall stem, straight down to the line" (p. 63). Slightly different directions are given to left-handers.

Margaret Rawson's thoughtful description of multisensory instruction is useful to consider:

> Dyslexic students need a different approach to learning language from that employed in most classrooms. They need to be taught, slowly and thoroughly, the basic elements of their language—the sounds and the letters which represent them—and how to put these together and take them apart. They have to have their writing hands, eyes, ears, and voices working together in conscious organization and retention of their learning (as cited in Henry, 1998, p. 1)

This form of instruction is beneficial for all children and is a real necessity for children with specific reading disabilities.

LESSON PROCEDURES IN A DISCUSSION FORMAT

Project READ (Calfee & Henry, 1986; Calfee, Henry, & Funderburg, 1988), was developed by a Stanford University research team in collaboration with several elementary schools in the San Francisco Bay Area. It provides a discussion-based format for instruction. (Project READ has since been renamed Project READ Plus to avoid confusion with Enfield and Greene's Project Read in Minnesota.) Lessons focus on specific spelling patterns within the historical and structural categories of the language (e.g., consonant blends, spellings of Latin

Opening

Middle

Conduct visual, auditory, and blending drills as needed.

Review taught pattern(s) and/or rule(s).

Teach new pattern(s) and/or rule(s).

   Students generate words, if appropriate.

   Discuss new pattern(s) and or rules(s) and related
      concepts.

   Students read numerous words

   Students spell numerous words from dictation.

Closing

Summarize and reflect on material covered.

Have final discussion.

Follow-up

Have students practice in groups or alone.

Give after-school assignments.

Figure 4.2. Project READ lesson format. (*Sources:* Calfee & Henry, 1986; Calfee, Henry, & Funderburg, 1988.)

affixes and Greek combining forms) and are designed to be presented sequentially in 30- to 50-minute sessions. Each lesson consists of a discussion related to language and reading/spelling concepts. Metalearning comes about not from isolated study but from social exchange. Students and teachers actively think about new patterns and rules. Teachers follow a procedure containing opening, middle, and closing activities (see Figure 4.2). In the opening, the teacher describes the purpose and content of the lesson and explains the lesson procedures. Following the opening, the teacher provides several middle activities. Patterns presented in previous lessons may be reviewed, and new patterns may be introduced. Students generate words fitting the targeted pattern or patterns. Students have the opportunity to read, spell, and discuss the patterns and concepts presented. Students also practice reading and writing the common irregular words (e.g., *the, said, love*), often in the context of phrases or sentences. Lessons can be adapted for individual tutorial instruction.

Although this discussion-based procedure may seem scripted, it is not, nor is it based on specific commercial materials. Teachers can bring their own teaching styles and choice of materials to enhance each lesson. For example, teachers may choose to use graphic organizers as they discuss word relationships or use magnetic letters or flip charts in a variety of activities to reinforce concepts.

A necessary part of these discussion-based lessons is having students fully discuss new patterns and concepts in a small-group format. The teacher facilitates the discussion, carefully introducing new terminology and concepts. Teachers may begin with visual and auditory drills to practice automaticity for letter–sound and sound–letter relationships. Students practice using strategies for decoding and spelling unknown words as they read and spell single words, phrases, and sentences. Older students practice analyzing long, unfamiliar words. While reading multisyllabic words, students follow the sequence that most fluent readers use when they try to decode a word. Students first check for recognizable morphemes (affixes and roots) and, if necessary, divide words into syllables. Only if these two strategies fail do students sound out individual letters (using letter–sound correspondences). In spelling, students are taught to repeat the word, to listen and count the number of syllables, and to identify common affixes and roots. As with decoding, students use letter–sound correspondences to spell only after attempting to use the morpheme and syllable strategies. Students learn productive spelling rules (e.g., rules for adding suffixes) to assist in spelling words from dictation.

Numerous opportunities for practice in both reading and spelling are provided for each pattern presented. Students read words, phrases, and sentences containing targeted patterns. Students also spell words, phrases, and sentences from dictation. Teachers should be aware that frequent review is necessary for many students and beneficial for all. (Sample lessons are provided at the end of this chapter and in the final four chapters of this book.)

At the end of each session, teachers and students review and summarize the concepts and patterns learned that day. This closing is an important facet of any lesson. During the closing, students and teacher summarize and reflect on the lesson content, structural patterns, and procedures. Teachers assign follow-up activities for many of the lessons in order to reinforce new concepts and strategies. Some of these take place directly after the lesson, and others are to be completed as homework. For example, students might be asked to underline vowel digraphs in a passage or find words containing Latin word roots in a newspaper article. Students might look for as many Greek words as possible in a chapter of their science text. Or, students may write a paragraph using specified patterns (e.g., consonant blends, prefixes, suffixes).

As each pattern and its corresponding sound are taught, the teacher should use the following sequence: Show a card with the new pattern printed on it. Give the sound and a key word (a common noun beginning with the new sound). Have the students repeat the sound and then write the target letter or letters. Models of the pattern should be provided on paper for each student. He or she traces the letter(s) several times while giving the sound. The student then copies the pattern and finally writes it from memory, always saying the corresponding sound.

Letter formation is of utmost importance. Teachers need to monitor letter formation as students begin to write new patterns. This kinesthetic-tactile reinforcement is necessary to promote learning of the pattern. Careful attention should be paid to pencil grasp, writing posture, and actual letter formation. Teachers should schedule writing practice for students having difficulty with either manuscript or cursive letter formation. Handwriting drills may in-

Consonants		
Single	Blends	Digraphs

Vowels		
Short/long	r- and l-controlled	Digraphs

Figure 4.3. Blank 2 × 3 letter-sound correspondence matrix. (From Calfee, R.C., & Associates. [1981–1984]. *The book: Components of reading instruction.* Unpublished manuscript, Stanford University, California; adapted by permission.)

clude tracing and copying a model, working at the chalkboard, writing in rice or in sand, or drawing large letters on newsprint. Connections between cursive letters need to be specifically taught. Difficult connections include cursive *br, be, on, own, ou, os, wh, wr, ve, vo, vy, exi, oxy,* and *of*.

As new consonant and vowel spelling patterns are presented, students can place the pattern in the appropriate cell in the blank 2 × 3 matrix (see Figure 4.3). Once students have mastered several consonant and vowel sounds, visual and auditory drills, along with blending drills, should be incorporated into each lesson. The following drills, modeled after Gillingham-Stillman (1956, 1997) drills, foster automaticity and fluency.

Visual Drills

The teacher should make or purchase 4 × 6 cards for each common grapheme (listed in Tables 3.1 and 3.2). For visual drills, the teacher shows students the patterns already taught, one pattern at a time. Students can respond individually or as a group with the appropriate sound(s). If the sound given is incorrect, students should trace the letter on paper or on their desk with the index finger of their writing hand. This kinesthetic-tactile reinforcement may provide a stimulus for the correct response. If not, the teacher should give the sound and have students write the pattern and simultaneously say the correct sound.

Auditory Drills

During auditory drills, the teacher says the sound and students can respond individually or as a group with the letter name(s). Students should repeat the sound for kinesthetic and auditory reinforcement. Students should not guess the sound. When the students do not know the correct response, they should be shown the appropriate card; they then write the letter(s) while saying the sound aloud.

Blending Drills

Blending sounds together is an extremely important linguistic task as students begin to read words. Card blending drills help students identify changes in syllable patterns as the teacher changes the letters that are displayed. Initial consonant graphemes, including blends and digraphs, are laid face up on the table, followed by medial vowels, and then by final consonants to make one-syllable words or nonwords. For groups, the teacher can set the cards on the ledge of the chalkboard or use a flip chart with three columns. The teacher exchanges one or more of the displayed cards with new cards to make new words, real or nonsense, and the students sound out each grapheme before saying the complete syllable. Cards should be placed in a logical order following correct orthographic sequence. For example, *x* would not come in an initial position and *-ck* would not follow a vowel digraph. The letters *l*, *f*, or *s* would not be placed singly at the end of the word because each is usually doubled following a short vowel sound. Beginning readers need a great deal of exposure to the card drills. Teachers are reminded to change the cards infrequently at first, giving students the opportunity to practice each new letter and sound. Figure 4.4 illustrates a drill for students with several learned consonant and vowel patterns.

In the setup shown in Figure 4.4, the teacher first lays cards on the table to spell the word *mad*. Students sound out and blend the word /măd/. Then the teacher takes away the *d* card and replaces it with *p*. Students then read /măp/. Then the teacher changes the vowel to *o*, and students read /mŏp/. They then read /sŏp/ when the teacher changes the initial consonant to *s*. When the teacher replaces the *o* card with the vowel digraph *oa*, students read /sōp/, and so forth as the teacher exchanges the cards. The teacher decides which graphemes to use based on the patterns that the students need to practice the most.

While blending the sounds on the cards, students should connect the vowel sound to the initial consonant sound (e.g., /mă/, /măd/; /mă/, /măp/; /mŏ/, /mŏp/) to prevent choppy blending. (Choppy blending produces a schwa after an initial consonant that does not actually exist in the syllable.) The teacher should be sure that students say each word as a whole after saying its separate sounds. Once students blend easily and fluently, the blending drills may be given less often, and word lists can be substituted to enhance automaticity and fluency. Students read the words in the lists, blending when necessary. Word lists are more effective for

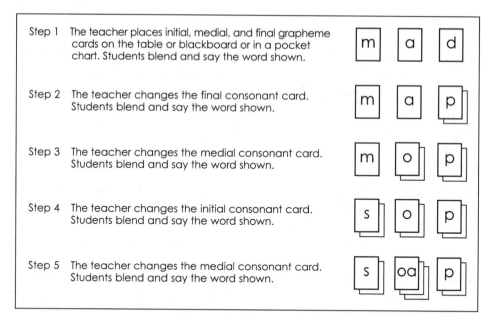

Figure 4.4. Card blending drills.

the learning of words and nonwords with four, five, and six sound units and for the learning of multisyllabic words (e.g., *stick*, *blimp*, *splint*, *basket*).

Following the card blending drills, teachers generally review a formerly taught pattern or rule with students, introduce a new pattern or rule, and provide numerous opportunities for practice. Students read words, phrases, and sentences containing the target patterns and spell words from dictation.

SAMPLE LESSONS

Two sample lessons, one for primary grade students and one for upper elementary or middle school students, may be useful to review. Although the format for discussion-based instruction is similar for lower- and upper-level lessons, the content differs between the levels, as shown in the second lesson, which focuses on Greek combining forms. Teachers are urged to overplan for discussion-based lessons. Teachers should try never to run out of things to teach. In addition, teachers should have a new nonphonetic word or a new spelling pattern ready to teach, a couple of sentences to dictate, or some phonemic awareness activities for review in case the lesson moves faster than planned.

In all of the lesson plans in this book, answers are presented as [*bracketed, italicized text*].

LESSON: CONSONANT BLENDS

Grade 1 or 2   Prerequisites: Knowledge of consonant and short vowel sounds

Opening

"Today we will continue to study consonant blends. You may remember that when two or three consonants are adjacent in the same syllable and keep their individual sounds they are called *consonant blends.* We will read and spell numerous words that contain consonant blends."

Middle

"Who can name some common blends?" Write the examples given by the students on the board. If students name a consonant digraph, remind students that in a consonant blend each sound has to be heard and then blended together.

Write the following words on the board one column at a time, or have them on a flip chart:

spot	frill	bulk
clap	left	help
blot	silk	blend
flat	best	drift
slot	rust	twist
plant	risk	blimp
crib	bend	swift
drab	melt	spend
stab	lump	plump
swim	next	stamp
twin	hint	crust
split	sift	print

"Let's read the first list aloud. Where are the blends?" [*at the beginnings of the words*] Circle the blends as students name them.

"Let's read the second list. Where are the blends?" [*at the ends of the words*] Circle the blends as before.

"Let's read the third list. Where are the blends?" [*at the beginnings and ends of the words*] Circle the blends as before.

Ask students to spell 10–20 words containing blends. Dictate each word twice before moving on to the next word. Alone or in groups, students should repeat each word, isolate the blend(s), then write the word while sounding it aloud.

Closing

"What kind of patterns did we work on today? Who can define a consonant blend? Where do they come in words? What did we do with consonant blends?"

Follow-up

Have students look for consonant blends in their literature book or in a content-area textbook.

After reviewing the concept of blends, present some patterns individually. Begin with *s* blends (i.e., *st, sl, sm, sn, sp, sk, sc, sw*) and go on to blends ending in *r* or *l*. Then add other initial and final blends. Have students trace, copy, write, and say sounds. Place new patterns in the consonant blends cell on the 2 × 3 matrix (see Figure 4.3). See if students can generate words beginning with each new blend before reading and spelling numerous words, phrases, and sentences.

From Henry, M.K. (1990). *WORDS: Integrated decoding and spelling instruction based on word origin and word structure* (p. 4). Austin, TX: PRO-ED; adapted by permission.

LESSON: INTRODUCING GREEK COMBINING FORMS

Grade 5   Prerequisites: Knowledge of most letter–sound correspondences

Opening

"You'll remember that many of the Latin word roots studied previously were actually borrowed from the Greeks. The Greek word parts are often called *combining forms* because the two roots are of equal stress and importance and compound to form a word, as in many Anglo-Saxon compound words. Some of the forms appear only at the beginning of a word (and so may be considered prefixes), others come at the end (and are sometimes thought of as suffixes), and some forms can be used in either position.

"Here are some words of Greek origin. Do any of you know what is "Greek" about the letter–sound correspondences in these words?" Show students that although Greek-based words contain many of the same letter–sound correspondences found in Anglo-Saxon and Latin-based words, Greek-based words also have unique letter–sound relationships (e.g., *ph* says /f/ as in *photograph*; *ch* says /k/ as in *chemist*; *y* is either a short or long /i/ sound as in *physician* and *typhoon*, respectively). Write words such as *photograph, phonology, physician, orchestra, chemical, chlorophyll,* and *hydrometer* on the board.

Middle

"Today we will be introduced to six new combining forms and their English meanings." Introduce the new combining forms, and have students carefully write each form, along with its meaning on their paper.

phon, phono (sound)

tele (distant)

photo (light)

ology (study), from *logos, logue*

graph, gram (written/drawn)

 (speech, word)

auto (self)

"Can you generate words containing the combining forms? You may add other suffixes or combining forms to make words." The teacher writes the students' words on the board or on a transparency. Students then read other words prepared by the teacher that contain some of the new forms, such as

phone	phonics	phonogram	phonology
phonological	phoneme	phonemic	photosynthesis
phonograph	graphite	graphics	autograph
photograph	photography	photographer	photocopy
photoflash	photogram	telecast	telegram
telephone	telephoto	telethon	automation
automatic	automobile	photology	telephotography
monologue	prologue	dialogue	epilogue

"Which school subjects might use these Greek-based words?" [*science, literature, social studies, often also math*]

Have students spell words containing the six target combining forms from dictation.

Have students read and spell sentences containing Latin- and Greek-based word parts, such as the following:

He *collected* several *autographs* from the *conductors.*
The *photographer* used her new *telephoto* lens on the *spectators.*
Phonics instruction is useful in *developing* reading and writing skills.

Closing

"What kind of words were we reading and spelling?" [*Greek-based words*]
"What is the meaning of *auto, tele, phon/phono*?" [*self, distant, sound*]
"How does knowing the meaning of the combining forms enhance your vocabulary?"

Follow-up

Have students look for Greek-based words in science and mathematics textbooks.

Continue adding additional combining forms in subsequent lessons, including these combining forms: *micro, meter, therm, bio, scope, hydro, helio, biblio, crat/cracy, geo, metro, polis, dem, derm, hypo, chron, cycl, hyper,* and *chrom.*

From Henry, M.K. (1990). *WORDS: Integrated decoding and spelling instruction based on word origin and word structure* (pp. 26–27). Austin, TX: PRO-ED; and Henry, M.K., & Redding, N.C. (1996). *Patterns for success in reading and spelling* (pp. 281–284). Austin, TX: PRO-ED; adapted by permission.

SUMMARY

Students need ample opportunities to read and spell many words containing the patterns targeted in discussion-based instruction. Words should be read and spelled as single words, in phrases, and in sentences. Teachers should follow up with reading of connected text as in textbooks, magazines, or newspapers. More examples of discussion-based lessons are found in the following chapters. In addition, interesting word facts and information for teachers appear in Word Wisdom highlights throughout the following chapters. Some of this material can be shared with students. Subsequent chapters also include numerous sample activities for reinforcement.

First Steps

Early Instruction for Effective Decoding and Spelling

As children gain more facility with oral language, their interests in "grown-up" activities may grow. They may see their parents reading books and magazines and writing grocery lists or letters either on paper or on the computer. Children become aware of print tasks. Parents often wonder how they can capitalize on these interests in a way that may improve their child's future academic performance.

Scientists have found that literacy development begins long before formal instruction. In 1985, the Center for Reading published *Becoming a Nation of Readers* (Anderson, Hiebert, Scott, & Wilkinson, 1985). The authors recommended that to promote reading and writing, parents provide books, letters, magazines, and other print matter in the home. Anderson et al. promoted literacy experiences in the home and community. These literacy activities might include frequently reading to the child, taking the child to libraries, subscribing to magazines, and linking familiar signs (e.g., McDonald's) with the words on the signs. Children do explore print on their own with active engagement from adults. Exposure to print plays an extremely important role as a predictor of many verbal skills, including reading acquisition (Stanovich, 1996).

Manguel wrote that as early as 1485, the Italian scholar Leon Battista Alberti noted that children should be taught the alphabet at the earliest possible age: "Children learned to read phonetically by repeating letters pointed out by their nurse or mother in a hornbook or alphabet sheet" (1996, p. 72). Manguel remembered, "I myself was taught this way, by my nurse reading out to me the bold-type letters from an old English picture-book; I was made to repeat the sounds again and again" (p. 72).

Hart and Risley (1995) discussed the quality interactions they saw in everyday parenting. They noted that both the vocabulary that parents use with their children and the sentences they speak transmit cultural values and expectations. Hart and Risley concluded that experiencing frequent though brief and encouraging interactions in the first 2–3 years of life contribute to

> Breadth of knowledge, analytic and symbolic competencies, self-confidence, and problem solving, which are among the interlocking attitudes, skills, and knowledge required for entry and success in an increasingly technological world of work (p. 192)

PRESCHOOL

The preschool years should be a time of exploration and discovery. Cicci stated that "children need the preschool years as a time of exploration and discovery—for general cognitive, language, emotional, and social development that form the undergirdings for the rest of their lives" (1995, p. 1). Parents and caregivers can foster later reading development through informal, everyday activities involving language in meaningful ways. Children benefit from pretend play as they give tea parties or as they "cook" a meal using plastic bowls, utensils, and measuring cups. Children need to learn to categorize and classify objects by following such instructions as "Put all the yellow objects here" or "Find all of the round objects on the table." Children can begin to match like objects as they find "the four red apples." The richer the oral language base, the better for reading acquisition. Parents can also encourage writing by having finger paints, chalk, felt-tip markers, and other tools available. Parents can play with their child as he or she explores this new domain. Oral and written language relationships between parent and child continue to be important throughout the first years of formal schooling.

Many children attend preschool or child care centers during their early years. Fielding-Barnsley recommended that preschool teachers prepare children for later reading instruction:

> To me, this means that the child arrives at school with five critical building blocks for literacy in place: (1) *letter identification*, the ability to recognize and label some letters of the alphabet; (2) *phonological awareness*, an appreciation that spoken words are made up of, and can be broken into, small speech elements; (3) *vocabulary knowledge*, an age-appropriate ability to produce and understand a wide range of terms; (4) *print concepts*, an understanding of the characteristics of books, the purposes for reading and writing, and so forth; and (5) *motivation*, a positive attitude toward books and reading and a desire to learn more. (1999, p. 6)

A comprehensive book on the importance of rich literacy environments during the preschool years for later literacy acquisition is that edited by Dickinson and Tabors (2001). The book includes three sections supporting language and literacy development in the home, the preschool classroom, and homes and classrooms together. This accumulation of research findings and implications for future instruction is invaluable for teachers and parents alike. Dickinson concluded that preschool teachers who use varied vocabulary, challenge students to think, and stimulate their curiosity and imagination support literacy development in kindergarten (2001).

The 5- to 6-year-old child typically speaks in complete sentences, has a vocabulary of about 2,500 words, asks questions using complex verb forms, and answers questions more specifically than a 4-year-old does. The American Speech-Language-Hearing Association says that the typical 4- to 5-year-old child

- Pays attention to a short story and answers simple questions about it
- Hears and understands most of what is said at home and in school
- [Makes] voice sounds [that are] clear like other [age-matched peers]
- Uses sentences that give lots of details (e.g., "I like to read my books")
- Tells stories that stick to topic
- Communicates easily with other children and adults
- Says most sounds correctly except a few like *l, s, r, v, z, j, ch, sh,* and *th*
- Uses the same grammar as the rest of the family (2002, http://www .asha.org/speech/development/dev_milestones.cfm)

Some educators believe that reading and writing develop simultaneously in natural contexts, and some children do appear to "pick up" the system with little difficulty. Indeed, preschoolers invent their own spelling system long before they are able to read (Read, 1971). This system persists well into first grade and may seem implausible to parents and teachers. Although students know a system of phonetic relationships that have not been formally taught, they do not know a set of lexical representations and the system of phonetic rules that account for much of standard spelling. Typical invented spellings include *da* (day), *kam* (came), *tabil* (table), *lade* (lady), *fel* (feel), *lik* (like), and *tigr* (tiger).

Clearly, many children require some formal instruction in order to learn to read, spell, and write. Children need to learn specific conventions of print such as writing from left to right, top to bottom, and front to back. When these conventions are taught, the following problem does not exist. Josh's preschool teacher told Josh's mother that her son was probably "dyslexic" because he copied three sentences from the board going from right to left and reversed or transposed many letters. Yet, Josh was only 4 years old, and no one had taught him the conventions of print, the letters, or even how to hold a crayon for writing.

KINDERGARTEN

Kindergarten marks that magical transition year when the child expands the more private, informal language of the home or child care to the more public, formal language of the school. Historically, kindergarten has been a time for oral language development in the form of listening and speaking activities and a time for developing physical and motor control. Today, however, the kindergarten curricula moves directly into reading and writing as formal instruction in literacy begins. Still, teachers and parents can encourage listening and speaking activities through poetry and rhyme, songs, and sociodramatic play. Listening activities such as listening for sounds and following directions need to be fostered. More formal speaking is encouraged through show-and-tell times as children bring their toys or pets to share or as they retell stories.

Prior to learning letter–sound correspondences, children benefit from training in phonological awareness tasks, such as rhyming, segmentation, and blending. When lacking the awareness of the role that sounds play in words, children rarely learn to read easily. Fortunately, the benefits of training in this area are often successful in teaching children to isolate individual sounds, to segment words into the sounds and syllables necessary for spelling in later years, and to blend sounds and syllables to make words (Ball, 1993; Tangel & Blachman, 1995).

The National Reading Panel reported that "teaching two PA [phonological awareness] skills to children has greater long-term benefits for reading than teaching only one PA skill or teaching a global array of skills" (2000, p. 2-21). The panel also noted that the two skills of blending and segmenting also produced a larger effect on spelling performance than did the multiple-skill treatment.

Phonological awareness is a key factor in reading acquisition. Parents and teachers can assess this ability through informal word play and games. Children can be asked to rhyme words and manipulate sounds. For example, the teacher can say the word *sat* and ask for as many rhyming words as possible. The teacher can say the word *meat* and ask the child to say the word without the /m/ sound or can say the word *plant* and have the child say the word without /t/. In order to assess blending ability, the teacher can say three sounds such as /t/ /ĭ/ /n/ and see if the child can pull the sounds together to say a word (*tin*). Segmentation requires the ability to break words and syllables into their constituent sounds. For example, the teacher can say *butterfly* and find out whether the child can segment the syllables as /bŭt/ /tər/ /flī/. Or, the teacher can say the word *map* and see whether the child responds with /m/ /ă/ /p/. These activities can be presented one-to-one, in small groups, or in large groups.

Note that these activities do not require knowledge of alphabet letters. Emphasis is on the sounds, at either the phoneme or the syllable level within words. The teacher must articulate all syllables and sounds very clearly and precisely. The teacher can give children visual cues by asking students to observe his or her lips. Remember that students can also receive direct training in phoneme segmentation, blending, and sound manipulation.

PHONOLOGICAL AWARENESS ACTIVITIES

Activities to develop phonological awareness skills include the following:

- *Rhyming:* The teacher says two or three words that rhyme and asks for additional rhyming words. For example, "Here are some rhyming words: *pat, sat, hat.* Can you tell me some other words that rhyme with these three words?" [*fat, mat, cat, flat, slat,* and so forth]

- *Syllable awareness:* The teacher says several multisyllabic words that are familiar to students and asks the students to count the syllables. For example, "How many word parts do you hear in *Carlos, Martha, city, rereading, population?*" [2, 2, 2, 3, 4] Or, "Clap the word chunks (or syllables) in these words: *Emily, Trevor, Allison, alphabet.*" [3, 2, 3, 3]

- *Sound awareness:* The teacher articulates clearly one-syllable words that have two to six sounds. For example, "How many sounds do you hear in *cow, sheep, stamp?*" [2, 3, 5]

- *Syllable deletion:* The teacher says compound words or other multisyllabic words and asks students to delete the initial or final syllable. "Say *railroad* without *road.*" [*rail*] "Say *sailboat* without *sail.*" [*boat*]

- *Sound deletion:* The teacher says a one-syllable word and asks students to delete the initial or final consonant sound or to delete a sound within a consonant blend. For example, "Say *pink* without /p/." [*ink*] "Say *belt* without /t/." [*bel*] "Say *blimp* without /m/." [*blip*] "Say *plan* without /l/." [*pan*]

 The deletion of blends, especially in the last two sound deletion examples, is considerably more difficult than the deletion of single consonants. Teachers should be sure to choose target words carefully. For example, do not say, "Say *wing* without /n/," because *n* in the *-ing* pattern does not say /n/.

- *Syllable blending:* The teacher says two syllables and asks children to put the syllables together to form a word. For example, "Blend these word parts and make a word: *Car/los, va/ca/tion.*" [*Carlos, vacation*]

- *Syllable segmentation:* The teacher says a multisyllabic word and asks students to separate the word into its parts. For example, "Break each word into its parts: *Lisa, cucumber.*" [*Li/sa; cu/cum/ber*]

- *Sound blending:* The teacher says three to six sounds and asks students to put the sounds together to make a real word. For example, "Blend these sounds to make a real word: /m/ /ă/ /p/, /m/ /ĭ/ /s/ /t/." [*map, mist*]

- *Sound segmentation:* The teacher says a one-syllable word and asks students to separate the word into its parts. For example, "Break each word into its parts: *pan, plan, grasp.*" [/p/ /ă/ /n/, /p/ /l/ /ă/ /n/, /g/ /r/ /ă/ /s/ /p/]

Blending and segmenting words into syllables are easier tasks than blending and segmenting syllables into sounds. Many 6-year-olds are unable to accurately blend and segment. Also, blending and segmenting words containing consonant blends are especially difficult for many children. (See the end of this chapter for several resources for teaching phonological awareness.)

BEGINNING TO READ AND WRITE

As mentioned previously, once children enter kindergarten, more formal literacy instruction begins. Most children are eager and willing to learn to read and look forward to learning to read and write. Even those with little exposure to print expect to begin to read in kindergarten. Children begin to become acquainted with symbols and what they represent. Informal activities to promote future literacy will be useful. While reading a story to children, parents or teachers can ask questions and ask children to predict what comes next. Children may begin to identify specific letters. As they do this, they can look for letters on billboards and street signs while in the car with their parents. Parents can play language games with their child and embed literacy experiences naturally into routine events.

Letter naming is an important factor in learning to read. Teachers need to know which letter names their students know. Children learn letter names at varying rates. Students who are at risk for reading disability need significantly more time learning letter names than those who are not at risk of having trouble learning to read and spell.

Teachers must also find out if their students know the relationship of upper- and lowercase letters. Many children do not automatically make these connections. The understanding of this relationship can be assessed by having children play a card game such as Go Fish or having children try to match upper- and lowercase letters placed in a bowl.

While beginning to learn letter names, children need to know how to form the corresponding symbols. As students learn to form letters, the importance of appropriate pencil grasp and correct writing posture cannot be stressed too much. Teachers need to provide a model of the target letter for children to trace, copy, and name several times before students write the letter from memory. Teachers should monitor pencil grasp, posture, and letter formation carefully.

In some kindergartens, students begin to learn the speech sounds that correspond with the letters. A suggested order of presentation can be found in Chapter 6.

Lessons can follow the format and procedures discussed in Chapter 4. The following lesson provides a possible script for a lesson on rhyming.

LESSON: RHYMING

Opening

"Today we'll talk about words that rhyme. Who knows what a rhyme is?" [*Students may respond by saying rhyming words, by noting they sound alike at the end, or by actually reciting a poem.*] "Listen to several common rhymes and hear words that rhyme. We'll practice listening for rhyming words together."

Middle

"A rhyme happens when words end in the same sounds. Listen to *at, cat, fat, sat.* How do they end?" [/ăt/] "Can you think of other words that end in /ăt/? [*mat, hat, rat, pat, that, chat, vat,* and so forth]

"Here's a favorite poem. I'll read it and you tell me why it's a poem." [*It has rhyming words, and poems often have words that rhyme.*]

Little Boy Blue, come blow your horn.
The sheep's in the meadow, the cow's in the corn.
Where's the boy that looks after the sheep?
He's under the haystack, fast asleep.

"Which words rhyme?" [*horn, corn; sheep, asleep*]

"Let's see if we can make some other rhyming words. Who can say a word that rhymes with *pin* and *thin*?" Write the words on the board, and show that the letter patterns at the end of rhyming words may be similar.

Closing

"What did we learn about today?" [*Rhyming words; they sound alike at the end of the word; words that rhyme may also look alike at the end.*]

Follow-up

"Get a partner and make up a poem together." You can write the poems if students are not yet able to write.

The following guided question activities can be done with or without the teacher, individually or in groups or "term teams."

CLASSROOM ACTIVITIES

Kindergarten: Phonological Awareness

Numerous phonological awareness activities appear in *Phonemic Awareness in Young Children: A Classroom Curriculum* (Adams, Foorman, Lundberg, & Beeler, 1998) and *Road to the Code: A Phonological Awareness Program for Young Children* (Blachman, Ball, Black, & Tangel, 2000), both published by Paul H. Brookes Publishing Co. Adams et al. included the following types of activities in *Phonemic Awareness in Young Children*.

- *Listening to Sequence of Sounds (p. 17):* Children listen to distinctive sounds that the teacher makes with household objects, such as the sound of a whistle blowing, a bell ringing, scratching, cutting with scissors, or an apple being eaten. Students first identify single sounds and then identify each one of a sequence of sounds.

- *Nonsense (p. 23):* Children close their eyes as the teacher tells a familiar story or poem but reverses or substitutes words, such as "Song a sing of sixpence" or "Baa baa purple sheep." Children are asked to detect such changes whenever they occur.

Adams et al. also described activities for analysis and synthesis (segmentation and blending) of words and for listening for two to four phonemes in a word (e.g., *pie*, two sounds; *spy*, three sounds; *spice*, four sounds).

In *Road to the Code*, Blachman et al. (2000) showed teachers how to extend phonological awareness while introducing letters corresponding with their phonemes. Students repeat alliterative sentences spoken by the teacher. For example, as children learn the letter *s*, they practice saying "Six silly, slimy, slithering snakes." Students then trace the letter in the air.

Beginning Reading

The following activities can supplement formal instruction as children learn to read.

- Have numerous alphabet books in the classroom. Read to the children. Ask them to find pictures of objects beginning with target letters. (Several excellent alphabet books are listed at the end of this chapter.)

- Purchase or make wooden or cardboard puzzles that allow children to put the letters of the alphabet in sequence.

- Have children play Go Fish for matching upper- and lowercase letters with a partner.

- Use plastic letters on the overhead projector. Ask children, "Give me words that begin with *m* /m/," as you show the letter *m* on the projector.

- See if children can recognize different forms of a letter (e.g., A, a, *a*).

- Matching visual to visual. Show the word *man*. Students circle the correct word out of four that are printed on paper (e.g., map   fan   (man) sat).

- Matching auditory to visual. Say the word *map*. Students circle the correct word out of four that are printed on paper (e.g., man   fit   fat   (map)).

- When children know several consonants and at least one vowel, make words with plastic letters on the overhead projector. Manipulate the letters to form new words. With only *s, f, t, n, g, p,* and *i*, more than 30 words, such as *it, sit, fit, pit, in, fin, pin, sin, pig, fig, nip, sip,* and *tip,* can be made. Nonwords can also be made using these letters.

- Give each child (or small group of children) a set of letters. Ask the children to find target letters. Point to one of the letters in the set and ask children if that letter comes near the beginning or near the end of the alphabet. See if children can put the set of letters in alphabetical order.

- As children begin to learn words, have them look for specific words in a story. For example, while reading "Goldilocks and the Three Bears" out loud, have children raise their hands when they hear the words *bear* and *bears*.

- Play games such as letter or word bingo. Or, play "Spin the Wheel," in which players must read the letter(s) or word(s) the dial points to.

- Read enjoyable stories such as *Horton Hears a Who* by Dr. Seuss. Ask the children to listen for the different kinds of animals that try to stop Horton from saving his friends. When done reading, ask the children to recall the animals' names and ways they tried to stop Horton.

Beginning Writing

Kindergartners can also be given formal writing activities.

- Provide a model for tracing and copying letters as they are introduced. Display an alphabet strip showing upper- and lowercase letters on the wall for children to refer to.

- Provide opportunities to draw and print using markers, crayons, and pencils at a writing area that is separate from the book area or classroom library. This writing area should be stocked with paper, writing utensils, letter stencils, and letter shapes (e.g., large plastic or cardboard letters).

- Encourage students to spell words that they know how to read.

- Use computer programs, such as Kid Pix (The Learning Company; see http://www.kidpix.com) and Kidspiration (Inspiration Software; see http://www.inspiration.com/productinfo/kidspiration/index.cfm), to give young children opportunities to match pictures and words and create stories.

WORD WISDOM: *KINDERGARTEN*

The word *kindergarten* comes from the German *kinder*, meaning *children*, and *garten*, meaning *garden*. Kindergarten was originally a place for children to prepare for formal schooling. Lessons and activities centered around play, games, music, drama, and conversation. Now, however, kindergarten is much less playful with more and more instruction taking place.

WORD WISDOM: *ALPHABET*

Firmage (1993) explained that the French introduced the word *alphabet* into England and that the word was commonly used by the 16th century: "The Old English term was 'abecede,' which by the mid-fourteenth century had shortened in Middle English to 'abece,' 'abse,' or 'ABC' " (pp. 58– 59). Long before the term came to Great Britain, alpha became the first letter of the Greek alphabet and beta the second letter.

RESOURCES FOR TEACHERS

Phonological Awareness

Adams, M.J., Foorman, B.R., Lundberg, I., & Beeler, T. (1998). *Phonemic awareness in young children: A classroom curriculum.* Baltimore: Paul H. Brookes Publishing Co.

Blachman, B.A., Ball, E.W., Black, R., & Tangel, D.M. (2000). *Road to the code: A phonological awareness program for young children.* Baltimore: Paul H. Brookes Publishing Co.

Catts, H., & Olsen, T. (1993a). *Sounds abound: Listening, rhyming, and reading.* East Moline, IL: LinguiSystems.

Catts, H., & Olsen, T. (1993b). *Sounds abound game* [Board game]. East Moline, IL: LinguiSystems.

Goldsworthy, C. (1998). *Sourcebook of phonological awareness activities: Children's classic literature.* San Diego: Singular Publishing Group.

National Reading Panel. (2000). *Teaching children to read: An evidence-based assessment of the scientific research literature on reading and its implications for reading instruction.* (NIH Publication No. 00-4754, Chapter 2). Washington, DC: U.S. Government Printing Office.

Torgesen, J., & Bryant, B. (1997). *Phonological awareness training for reading.* Austin, TX: PRO-ED.

Alphabet Books: A Few Favorites

Some of these alphabet books are out of print or hard to find, but they may be available in a local school or public library.

Anno, M. (1974). *Anno's alphabet.* New York: Thomas Y. Crowell (hardcover), Harper-Collins (softcover).

Base, G. (1986). *Animalia.* New York: Harry N. Abrams.

Bowen, B. (1991). *Antler, bear, canoe: A Northwoods alphabet year.* Boston: Little, Brown.

Cassie, B., & Pallotta, J. (1995). *The butterfly alphabet book.* Watertown, MA: Charlsbridge.

Gorey, E. (1997). *The Gashlycrumb tinies* (Reprint ed.). Orlando, FL: Harcourt.

Gustafson, S. (1990). *Alphabet soup: A feast of letters.* Chicago: Calico Books.

Jonas, A. (1990). *Aardvarks, disembark.* New York: Greenwillow Books.

Kellogg, S. (1987). *Aster Aardvark's alphabet adventures.* New York: Morrow Junior Books.

Manuelian, P.D. (1991). *Hieroglyphs from A to Z* [Book with punch-out stencils]. Boston: Museum of Fine Arts.
Musgrove, M. (1977). *Ashanti to Zulu*. New York: Dial Books.
Pallotta, J. (1995). *The flower alphabet book*. Watertown, MA: Charlsbridge. (Many other themed alphabet books by this author are available from Charlsbridge.)
Wegman, W. (1994). *ABC*. New York: Hyperion.
Wilks, M. (1986). *The ultimate alphabet*. New York: Henry Holt.
Yolen, J. (1990). *Elphabet: An ABC of elves*. Boston: Little, Brown.

Web Sites of Interest to Teachers and Parents

American Speech-Language-Hearing Association, http://www.asha.org
The International Dyslexia Association, http://www.interdys.org
Kid Pix (The Learning Company), http://www.kidpix.com
Kidspiration (Inspiration Software), http://www.inspiration.com/productinfor/kidspiration/index.cfm
Reading Rockets, http://www.readingrockets.org

Beginning Readers

Time for the Anglo-Saxon Layer of Language

Most children entering first grade eagerly await the introduction to formal reading and writing instruction. During first grade, children need to master most of the alphabetic code. Instruction on the alphabetic code focuses on pairing the sounds of the language (or phonemes) with the letters or combination of letters of the alphabet (or graphemes). In addition, students need to identify common sight words, many of them nonphonetic. When formal instruction in reading and spelling begins, teachers need to be familiar with the common Anglo-Saxon letter–sound correspondences, important irregular words, common syllable patterns, and Anglo-Saxon morphemes (base words, compound words, prefixes and suffixes).

Teachers must first find out what each child knows about the alphabet, common patterns, and related sounds. Purchase or make cards with the major orthographic patterns (i.e., consonants, vowels, consonant blends, consonant digraphs, vowel digraphs, *r*-controlled vowels). Begin with single letters. See if the child can give the letter name and the corresponding sound. Keep a checklist of what the child already knows. Many children will have picked up the letter names and even corresponding sounds for most consonants in kindergarten. If students know the sounds of most of the consonants and vowels, go on to letter combinations such as *ar*, *oo*, *oy*, *bl*, and *sh*.

Then, begin adding to what the child already knows. This is easily accomplished while working with an individual on a one-to-one basis. Follow a more specific sequence when working with groups of children. Begin with consonants; choose five or six used frequently in primers, such as *p, t, b, s, m*, and *g*. Immediately present a short vowel and beginning words for blending. Usually short /ă/ or short /ĭ/ come first. The following real words (and many others) can be read and spelled with *p, t, b, s, m*, and *a*:

am	mat	tap
at	Sam	sap
bat	Pam	map
pat	tam	tab
sat		

In addition, many nonsense words, such as *pab* or *bap*, can be created.

One logical sequence for introducing orthographic patterns, provided in *Patterns for Success in Reading and Spelling* (Henry & Redding, 1996), is as follows:

1. First, *m, l, s, t, a, p, f, c, n, b, r, j, k, i, v, g, w, d, h, u, y, z, x, o*, and *e* are introduced.

2. Next, initial blends, spelling rules, consonant digraphs, consonant blends, and other common patterns are introduced as follows: *st-, sm-, sn-, qu-*, VCE rule, *sl-, sp-, ay, sc-, sk-, -ff, -ll, -ss, -ck, sh, ee, bl-, cl-, ea, fl-, gl-, pl-, y* as long /ī/, *ch*, plural *-s, ing, ar, th* (unvoiced /th/ sound), *oy, all, th* (voiced /<u>th</u>/ sound), *br-, cr-, ow, dr-, fr-, gr-, pr-, tr-, er, oo, -ed, -ang, -ong, -ung, or, ow, wh-*, plural *-es, -ink, -ank, -onk, -unk, aw, sw-, tw-*, final blends (e.g., *-mp, -nd, -sk, -sk, -ft, -lk, -ld*), *oo, ai*, and *oa*.

3. Lessons continue with the following: three-letter blends (*spr, str, scr, spl*), *s* as /z/, *ie, ou, -tch, ea, oi, au, -dge*, soft *c* and *g, kn-, wr-, ph-, -igh, ue, ew, ear, -augh, -ough, -eigh, wor, war, ui, ey, -ind, -ild, -old, -ost, ei, gn*, and *-mb*.

4. Common syllable patterns, common suffixes and corresponding rules, compound words, common prefixes, possessives, and other plural spellings are introduced next.

CONSONANTS

Most children learn consonant graphemes and phonemes rather easily. Certain pairs of sounds, however, may be difficult for some children to discriminate. Although the sounds in each are similar, one sound is *voiced;* that is, the vocal cords vibrate. The vocal cords do not vibrate in the related but *voiceless* (or *unvoiced*) sound.

Voiced		Unvoiced	
/b/	[*bat*]	/p/	[*pat*]
/d/	[*dug*]	/t/	[*tug*]

/g/	[*goat*]	/k/	[*coat*]
/j/	[*jug*]	/ch/	[*chug*]
/v/	[*vine*]	/f/	[*fine*]
/z/	[*zip*]	/s/	[*sip*]
/<u>th</u>/	[*that*]	/th/	[*thin*]
/w/	[*wail*]	/hw/	[*whale*]

Auditory discrimination drills should be presented to children who have difficulty differentiating these sounds. For example, columns on paper can be headed with the target pair of sounds, such as /d/ and /t/. The teacher says a word containing one of the target sounds, and students repeat the word and check the appropriate column or, if able, write the word in the correct column.

VOWELS

Vowel sounds and spellings are the most difficult patterns for many students to learn. Most short vowels are rather close on the sound spectrum. For example, the short vowel sounds /ă/, /ĕ/, and /ĭ/ are especially difficult to discriminate. Therefore, it is suggested that vowel sounds not be taught in alphabetical order. Even more difficult for many than spellings for single-letter vowels are spellings for vowel digraphs such as *ee*, *ea*, *oi*, and *ou*.

Elsie Smelt (1976), an Australian educator, summarized the Hanna et al. (1971) study of spelling patterns in English (see Table 6.1) and found that 95% of the target words that contained a long /ā/ sound were spelled one of four ways: 80% were open syllable *a* (as in *baby*) or *a*-consonant-*e* (as in *made*); 9% used *ai*, usually in the middle of words (as in *pail* and *pain*); and 6% used *ay*, usually at the end. All of the words containing a short /ă/ were spelled with the letter *a*.

In these early stages, teachers should concentrate on the most productive spellings in English, not those that are used in only a handful of words. Remember, also, that word construction is cumulative. It is useful to move from two- and three-letter VC and VCV words, such as *at* and *pat*, to those with consonant blends and consonant and vowel digraphs, to two-syllable words, to affixed base words.

SPELLING RULES

Students also need to learn six categories of spelling rules. Most apply to Anglo-Saxon words and occur because of the short vowel sounds. Many teachers talk

Table 6.1.   Proportion of alternative spellings of vowel sounds

Although the most common way of writing each vowel sound is with one letter, in a comparatively small proportion of words, the vowel sound is written with two letters. Children often have difficulty knowing which vowels to use. The following calculations, compiled by Elsie Smelt (1976), were based on the Stanford Spelling Study (Hanna, Hodges, & Hanna, 1971). The study used more than "17,000 words (from a core vocabulary containing most of the words used by educated speakers and writers)" (Hanna et al., 1971, p. 80). Teach children to rely on the most commonly used letter–sound correspondences.

The sound . . .	Is written as . . .	In X% of words	Examples
/ā/	a	80	mate, vacation
	ai	9	nail
	ay	6	day
/ē/*	e	72	me, zero
	ee	10	deep
	ea	10	heat
/ī/	i	74	hide, pilot
	y	14	try
	igh	6	sigh
/ō/	o	87	hope, hobo
	oa	5	boat
	ow	5	low
/o͞o/	u	90	tune, mute, cupid
	ew	3	new
	eu	2	feud
	ue	2	due
/ă/	a	100	hat
/ĕ/	e	93	bet
	ea	4	head
/ĭ/	i	73	hid
	y	23	funny, symphony*
/ŏ/	o	95	hot
/ŭ/	u	88	hut

From Smelt, E. (1976). *Speak, spell and read English* (p. 102). Melbourne: Longman Australia; adapted by permission.

*Many dictionaries that were published before the 1980s gave the final letter y as in *funny* or *muddy* the short /ĭ/ sound. This grapheme is now pronounced more frequently as long /ē/, especially in the Midwest and West United States.

about "rules" that are actually not orthographic rules. Melvyn Ramsden cautioned teachers that "if you find an 'exception' don't blame the system—you might have got [*sic*] your 'rule' wrong" (2000, p. 11). For example, teachers often say, "When two vowels go walking, the first does the talking." Smelt (1976) found that this statement is only true 37% of the time; it works for *ai, oa, ay,* and *ee* but not for *oo, oy, ew, au,* and *aw.*

Teach these rules when students are ready for them:

1. **Silent *e* rule (VCE rule)**

   a. Silent *e* on the end of a word signals that the single vowel immediately preceding a single consonant is long as in *cube* and *vote* (i.e., the silent *e* makes the vowel "say" its name; sometimes this rule is called the "magic *e* rule").

   b. Silent *e* makes *y* say /ī/ as in *type* and *style*.

   A preceding single vowel may or may not be long before -ve. The vowels in *gave, five,* and *drove* are long; the vowels in *have, give,* and *love* are short.

2. **Doubling rule (-*ff, -ll, -ss, -zz*)**

   Double final *f, l, s,* and sometimes *z* immediately following a single vowel in a one-syllable word, as in *staff, bluff, tell, still, grass, bliss, buzz,* and *jazz*. (Common exceptions are *pal, gal, if, clef, gas, this, us, thus, yes, bus, plus,* and *quiz*. [Although *quiz* contains two vowel letters, *q* is always followed by *u* in English words so only *i* is considered a vowel in *quiz*.])

3. **Soft *c* and *g* rule**

   The letters *c* and *g* have a "soft" sound when they appear directly before *e, i,* and *y*.

   a. The letter *c* has the /s/ sound before *e, i,* and *y*, as in *cent, city,* and *cycle*.

   b. The letter *g* has the /j/ sound before *e, i,* and *y*, as in *gentle, ginger,* and *gym*. (Exceptions to the soft *g* rule do not present spelling problems because in such exceptions, *g* has its "hard" sound, as in *get, give, buggy,* and *bigger*.)

   The "hard" sounds of c, as in *cat, coat,* and *cub,* and g, as in *gas, got,* and *gum,* are taught first. Only after these are well established are the "soft" sounds and the corresponding rule introduced.

4. **The -*ck, -tch, -dge* rule**

   a. Use -*ck* to spell the /k/ sound immediately after one short vowel at the end of a one-syllable word, as in *back, clock, duck, stick,* and *deck*.

   b. Use -*tch* to spell the /ch/ sound immediately after one short vowel at the end of a one-syllable word, as in *batch, itch, stretch, Dutch,* and *notch*.

Common exceptions to the *-tch* rule, such as *such, much, rich,* and *which,* should be memorized.

c. Use *-dge* to spell the /j/ sound immediately after one short vowel at the end of a one-syllable word, as in *badge, ledge, bridge, dodge,* and *fudge.*

5. **Adding suffixes to Anglo-Saxon base words**

   a. **Drop final *-e* rule:** When a base word ends in a final *e*, drop the *e* before adding a suffix starting with a vowel (e.g., *take, taking; fine, finer; stone, stony*).

   b. **Double-letter rule:** In a one-syllable word with one short vowel (a closed syllable) ending in one consonant, double the final consonant before a suffix starting with a vowel (e.g., *-ed, -er, -ing, -y, -ish*). Do not double the final consonant before a suffix starting with a consonant (e.g., *-ful, -est, -ly, -ment, -ness*). Examples: *fit, fitted, fitful; sad, saddest, sadly; red, redder, redness;* and *ship, shipping, shipment.*

One-syllable base words containing a vowel digraph or ending in two consonants do not need to double the final consonant, as in *heat, heater* and *help, helping.* The doubling rule for polysyllabic base and root words is covered in Chapter 7.

   c. **Change final *y* to *i* rule:** When a base word ends in *y*, change the *y* to *i* before adding a suffix, unless the *y* is preceded by a vowel or unless the suffix begins with *i* (*-ing, -ish, -ist*). Examples: *cry, cried, crying; copy, copied, copyist;* and *play, player, playing.*

6. **Plural *-s* and *-es* rule**

   a. Most nouns become plural (to indicate more than one) by adding *-s* (e.g., *hat, hats; pig, pigs; girl, girls; hut, huts*).

   b. Nouns ending in *-s, -x, -z, -ch,* and *-sh* add *-es* for the plural. Students can hear the additional syllable formed by the *-es* ending (e.g., *glass, glasses; box, boxes; waltz, waltzes; lunch, lunches; wish, wishes*).

   c. Nouns ending in *y* form the plural according to the regular suffix addition rule. That is, change the final *y* to *i* and add *-es,* as in *fly, flies.* If the letter *y* follows a vowel, then keep the *y* and add *-s,* as in *boy, boys.*

   d. Exceptions exist for some nouns ending in *f* or *fe;* these change to *-ves* as in *shelf, shelves; leaf, leaves; knife, knives.*

e. Nouns ending in *o* sometimes add *-s* and sometimes add *-es* (e.g., *piano, pianos; tomato, tomatoes*). Students should check their dictionaries to be sure.

f. Some plurals are completely irregular and must be learned (e.g., *foot, feet; mouse, mice; man, men; woman, women; goose, geese; moose, moose; pants, pants; deer, deer*). Most of them can be spelled correctly by using sound sequences for clues.

Children may question the use of x versus -cks. Singular nouns usually end in x as in *tax, box, fox,* and *six.* Plural nouns or singular third-person verbs tend to end in -cks with -s as the suffix, as in *socks, locks,* he *picks,* and the chicken *pecks.*

Just as when learning a new pattern, children should have ample opportunities to read and spell numerous words fitting each rule. The teacher should make the rules concrete for students. The teacher may state the rules but also must work with students so that they practice and think about each rule. Working on the chalkboard or with transparencies is useful. For example, when discussing changing *y* to *i*, the teacher can easily erase and change the *y* to *i* if the conditions permit (e.g., *try, tried, trying*).

RECOMMENDATIONS FOR SPELLING

Many children continue to use invented spelling as they progress in the early grades. Yet, teachers need to assist students in transferring to standard spellings. Students must learn to use conventional spelling over time. During traditional spelling instruction, words are often related by meaning or by content in a story but not by orthographic structure. Knowledge of the orthographic structure and corresponding sounds provides students with specific strategies for dealing with unfamiliar words. Think of the winners of the national spelling bees. They often ask for the part of speech and the word origin to help them with their decisions.

Spelling errors are often a good estimate of reading ability in many cases. Low reading rate and poor spelling usually translate into poor reading skills. Figures 6.1 and 6.2 illustrate the types of errors found in spelling from dictation from two elementary students. These two students are poor readers and spellers. They have few strategies to work out unknown words prior to intervention. Notice also the difficulty each has with letter formation. Matt is finishing third grade and has learned cursive writing (see Figure 6.1). Notice the errors in his spellings of *box, belong, door, low, how, bring, tall, ball, ask, way,* and

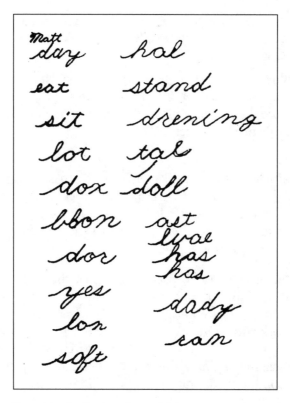

Figure 6.1. Spelling sample of a third grader.

baby. Furthermore, while reading a list of grade-appropriate words aloud, Matt makes no phonetic generalizations as he reads *Jack*, *tack*, and *sack* as *Jack*, *take*, and *snake.*

Dana repeated third grade and is now in grade 5. Unfortunately, even though she has had 3 years of cursive writing instruction, her letter formation is extremely poor as she writes *Come in on time today* from dictation. Dana wrote the cursive capital *D* in her name disjointedly by drawing two circles, a line, and an arc (see Figure 6.2). No teacher has carefully monitored Dana's cursive writing to check for correct letter formation.

Figure 6.2. Spelling sample of a fifth grader.

While introducing new patterns, dictate numerous words containing the target grapheme. Be sure students sound out the word as they write it. Say the word or phrase only once or twice. Students will get used to listening. Some students benefit by saying letter names simultaneously with the spelling, whereas other students say only the sound as they spell. Students should check each word by sounding it out. Try to monitor students as they spell and cue the children promptly when an error is made. For example, in spelling *quen* for *queen*, ask, "How do we spell /ē/ in the middle of words?" Or, in writing *quite* for *quit*, ask, "What does the final *e* do?"

Avoid scrambled-letter exercises in which words are spelled backwards, vertically rather than horizontally, or even diagonally, as such exercises are very confusing to children with reading and spelling problems. Also, giving students words that are spelled incorrectly and asking students to give correct spellings may reinforce the incorrect visual images of the words.

IRREGULAR WORDS

Students need to memorize spellings for irregular words, although multisensory techniques may still be utilized. Irregular words (sometimes called red flag, demon, maverick, or nonphonetic words) usually are irregular in the vowel spelling only. That is, the vowel sound does not carry its regular short or long sound. For example, *mother, laugh, cough,* and *prove* are all nonphonetic in the spelling of the vowel sound. The teacher provides a model on the students' papers. Students trace, copy, and then write from memory. During each step students say the letter names, not the sounds that the letters represent.

Some systems spend inordinate amounts of time on patterns that are better learned by rote. For example, Barnett called *ough* the "favorite scapegoat of critics of English orthography with its 'monstrous' 9 pronunciations" (1962, p. 83). He gave the following examples for the various sounds:

tough	thorough	cough
though	through	drought
thought	bough	hiccough

No wonder that while *ough* usually says /ô/ (as in *ought, bought, fought, thought, nought,* and *sought*), teachers may be apt to say that *ough* has many sounds! Try to concentrate on the most important and frequently used sound or sounds. Teach the other words as memory words. A leading basal series of the 1980s contained an exercise that asked children to identify all of the ways of spelling short /ĕ/ in the following words:

any	leopard	says	their
friend	end	bury	aerodrome
bread	said		

Actually, only the spellings *e* (as in *end*) and *ea* as in (*bread*) are used with any frequency for short /ĕ/.(An additional flaw of this list is that some of the vowel sounds in the words *bury, their,* and *aerodrome* are affected by /r/, meaning that children may have more difficulty hearing the short vowel sounds.) This type of instruction and practice focuses on the exceptions rather than the regularities of the English language, something that the concepts inherent in the decoding-spelling continuum hope to prevent.

As students learn new patterns, provide ample opportunities to read and spell words containing the target patterns in lists, phrases, and sentences. The resources at the end of this chapter mention lists of words found in the primary grades.

SYLLABLES

Students need additional strategies in order to read and spell polysyllabic words. Accent may be difficult for some children to hear. Encourage students to tap each syllable, using different fingers for each sound. Children can tap on the opposite fist or even on a table. Some children prefer to feel the voice box, in order to "feel" the accent (or stress), and still others like to clap each sound. Begin by having students count the syllables in their own names.

In Chapter 3, the types and rules for syllable division were presented. In the primary grades the closed (VC/CVC), open (V/CV), closed (VC/V), and consonant-*le* syllables are most common. While reading multisyllabic words, students may look for the number of vowels as a cue to the number of syllables.

Only *rhythm* and the suffix -*ism* have a pronounced syllable without a vowel.

When spelling multisyllabic words, students count syllables as they say and write the word syllable by syllable.

Students can practice by marking closed and open syllables. The diacritical marking for the short vowel sound is the breve (˘). The macron (‾) represents the long sound. Accent is usually marked with an apostrophe or a strike (') at the end of the accented syllable.

MORPHEME PATTERNS

Readers will recall that a morpheme is the smallest meaningful unit of language. Words of Anglo-Saxon origin both compound and affix. Compound words consist of two base words.

Base Words

Base words are the short meaningful words used commonly in the primary grades. Each base word is a morpheme. Teachers should point out that the meaning of the compound word is related to its constituent words or base words. Therefore, *flashlight* is related to both *flash* and *light. Blackboard* refers to a *board* that is *black.* Students enjoy generating numerous compound words, such as *football, butterfly, sailboat, shoehorn,* and *playhouse.* (See Appendix C for a list of compound words.)

Anglo-Saxon base words also affix; that is, prefixes and/or suffixes can be added to each base word. Point out that free morphemes or free base words can stand alone and that the Anglo-Saxon base words are most often free morphemes. For example, *spell* stands alone, but prefixes and suffixes can be added to this free base word, as in *misspell* and *misspelled.* (In contrast, Latin roots, which are discussed in Chapter 7, are usually bound morphemes and almost always must have a prefix and/or suffix added to make a word in English.) Remember that students do not have to completely master the letter–sound correspondences (especially the vowel digraphs) before beginning to learn spellings for the prefixes and suffixes. This is extremely important. We want to touch children with the power of word expansion and can do this by adding common affixes.

Prefixes

The first prefixes added are generally those found most frequently with Anglo-Saxon base words, such as *in-, un-, mis-, dis-, fore-, re-, de-, pre-,* and *a-.* In fact, of almost 3,000 prefixed words found in textbooks grades 3–9, words beginning with *un, re, in* (meaning *not*), and *dis* occur in more than 58% of the prefixed words (White, Sowell, & Yanagihara, 1989). Other frequently used prefixes include, in descending order, *en/em, non, in/im* (meaning *in* or *into*), *over, mis, sub, pre, inter, fore, de, trans, super, semi, anti, mid,* and *under.* Children can be given a base word and can be asked to make words with prefixes, such as with the base word *like* (e.g., *dislike, unlike*) or *read* (e.g., *reread, misread*). The prefix *a-* is one of the first uses of the schwa that students encounter. Because the base word usually retains the stress, the *a-* is unstressed; therefore, it has the schwa sound, as in *alike, around, asleep, alone, away,* and *aground.*

Suffixes

White et al. (1989) also noted that of more than 2,000 common suffixed words, *-s, -es, -ed,* and *-ing* were found in 65% of the words. Another 17% of the words used *-ly, -er (-or), -ion (-tion, -ation, -ition),* and *-ible, -able.* The following suffixes were used in 1% of the group of words studied by White et al.: *-al (-ial), -y, -ness, -ty (-ity), -ment, -ic, -ous (-eous, -ious), -en,* comparative *-er, -ive (-ative, -itive), -ful, -less,* and *-est.* Other suffixes were found in 7% of the words.

The first suffixes added are generally the inflectional endings *-s, -ed, -ing, -er, -es,* and *-est.* Inflectional endings change the number, person, or tense of the base word. Derivational endings, in contrast, are those that modify the base by adding suffixes (e.g., *care, careless, carelessness*) or by changing within the word (i.e., *song* from *sing*) and that produce an affixed word that is often a different part of speech than the base word. Examples of derivational endings include *-ly, -less, -ness, -ship, -fold,* and *-ment.* Remember that suffixes usually cause a word to be a particular part of speech. Thus, *-est* is usually an adjective ending, whereas *-ly* is an adverb ending, and *-ment* is a noun ending. While teaching suffixes, the teacher can introduce grammatical concepts such as *noun, verb, adjective,* and *adverb.*

The important suffix *-ed,* signifying past tense verbs, needs special attention because it can be pronounced three different ways. It is often a separate syllable, and because the suffix is rarely accented, the schwa sound is present. Thus, we have *heat, heated; shout, shouted;* and *squirt, squirted.* The suffix *-ed* may, however, say /t/ as in *walked, shipped, marched,* and *reached,* or it may say /d/ as in *dreamed, timed, loaned,* and *robbed.*

The teacher should begin with base words and suffixes that need no knowledge of suffix addition rules, such as *like, liked, likely; time, timely, untimely; blame, blameless, blamelessness; heat, heater;* and *stamp, stamping, stamped.* Once children learn common suffixes, usually in first and second grade, the teacher moves on to the suffix addition rules pertinent to Anglo-Saxon base words that are presented in the section on spelling rules in this chapter. Children need a great deal of practice as they work on these rules. Memory of the rule alone is not enough. The teacher should discuss the steps with the students. Here is a suggested line of questioning for dropping final *e:*

- "Here is the word *blaming.*"
- "What is the base word?" [*blame*]
- "How is it spelled?" [*b l a m e*]
- "Does it end in *e*?" [*yes*]
- "If so, does the suffix begin with a vowel?" [*yes, i*]
- "If no, just add the suffix."
- "If yes, remove the final *e* before you add the suffix." [*blāming*]

Here is a line of questioning for adding suffixes to base words ending in one vowel followed by one consonant:

- "Here is the word *big*. Let's add *-est* to this word."
- "Does the word end in one consonant preceded by one vowel?" [*yes*]
- "If yes, does the suffix begin with a vowel?" [*yes, e*]
- "If no, do not double the final consonant in the base word, as in *bigness*."
- "If yes, double the final consonant in the base word." [*biggest*]

Here are lines of questioning for adding suffixes to words ending in *y*:

- "Here is the word *play*. Let's add *-ing* to this word."
- "Is there a vowel just before the *y*?" [*yes*]
- "Do we change the *y* to *i*?" [*no*]
- "If no, add the suffix." [*play + ing = playing*]
- "Here is the word *try*. Let's add *-ed* to this word."
- "Is there a vowel before the *y*?" [*no*]
- "If no, change the *y* to *i*." [*try + ed = tried*]
- "If we were to add *-ing* to *try*, should we change the *y* to *i*?" [*no, try + ing = trying*]

Ramsden (2000) encouraged students to make webs of base words while learning to compound and affix. The teacher and students can generate words and continue to add to the web (see Figure 6.3) as new affixes and words are identified.

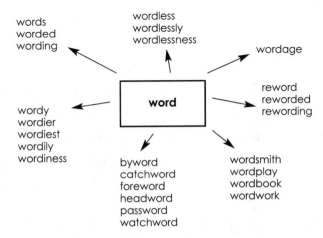

Figure 6.3. Morpheme web for the word *word*. (From Ramsden, M. [2000]. *The user's self-training manual: The essential reference for real English spelling* [Available from the author, http://perso.wanadoo. fr/melvyn/spelling/manual.html]; adapted by permission.)

Additional Topics

Third grade is really a year of transition. In most schools, this is when students begin to use cursive writing. As in the earlier grades, students need to trace and copy and practice cursive letters. When the children write from memory, you may ask them to say the sound or the name of the letter. As soon as several cursive letters have been taught, they can be joined in pairs or short words. Some linkages may prove to be difficult, especially those using bridge letters *b, o, v,* and *w,* such as *br* or *wn* in *brown,* and they should be taught explicitly. Students need practice with both upper- and lowercase letters.

Up to and during third grade, students also need to become familiar with other important concepts related to English words, such as contractions, possessives, homonyms and homographs, and antonyms and synonyms.

Contractions   Contractions are made when two words are shortened into one word marked with an apostrophe where letters have been omitted. Here are some of the main contractions:

Long form	Contraction	Long form	Contraction
it is	it's	cannot	can't
I am	I'm	do not	don't
he is, he has	he's	would not	wouldn't
she is, she has	she's	could not	couldn't
here is	here's	should not	shouldn't
where is	where's	are not	aren't
what is	what's	were not	weren't
who is	who's	had not	hadn't
I will	I'll	you are	you're
you will	you'll	we are	we're
he will	he'll	they are	they're
she will	she'll	I have	I've
we will	we'll	you have	you've
they will	they'll	we have	we've
I would	I'd	they have	they've
you would	you'd	will not	won't
he would	he'd		
she would	she'd		
we would	we'd		
they would	they'd		

The contraction *won't* is the only truly irregular contraction. An early form of *will* was *wol,* and it is assumed that *won't* came from that early form.

Have students read phrases with contractions. Also, give students dictation phrases or sentences to practice writing contractions (e.g., *she'll run, I'd like, won't open, I'm going to the movies, Don't you wish teachers wouldn't give so much homework?*)

Possessives   Nouns and pronouns often indicate ownership or possession. Usually, possessive nouns require an apostrophe (but possessive pronouns do not). Rules for possession follow:

- Add *'s* to the singular form of the noun, as in *Jane's coats, the man's hat,* and *the dog's dish.*

- Add an apostrophe after a plural ending in *s,* as in *three boys' desks, six students' tests,* and *the cats' litters* (meaning the litters of more than one cat, in contrast to *the cat's litters,* which means the litters of only one cat).

- Most pronouns are possessive pronouns and require no apostrophe to show possession, as in *his car, her house, their mother,* and *its wings* (meaning the bird's wings).

Do not use an apostrophe with the possessive pronoun *its,* as in *its dish* (meaning the *dog's dish*). Use *it's* only as the contraction of *it is,* as in *It's a nice day.*]

Homonyms and Homographs   *Homonyms* (also called *homophones*) are words that sound the same, usually have the same spelling, but differ in meaning. For example, *bank* (embankment) and *bank* (a place for money) are homonyms; so are *die* (stop living), *die* (a device for cutting/stamping objects), and *dye* (color).

Homographs are words that are spelled the same but sound different and differ in meaning. Words such as *wind* (breeze) and *wind* (to wind the clock) and *bass* (a fish) and *bass* (deep tone) are homographs.

When the teacher introduces the terms *homonym* and *homograph*, students in second and third grades can even be introduced to words of Greek origin. Students can learn the meanings of *homo* (same), *nym* (name), and *graph* (writing).

Antonyms and Synonyms   The names of other concepts, such as *antonym* (opposite name) and *synonym* (same name) also contain Greek forms. Antonyms are words that are opposite in meaning, such as *up/down, back/front, dry/wet,* and *cold/hot.* Synonyms are words carrying like meaning, such as *rain* and *precipitation.*

INTERVENTIONS FOR FLUENCY

By second and third grades, as strategies for decoding and spelling become more efficient, students will acquire greater fluency. Teachers can help promote fluency with several interventions that have been shown to be successful in helping students gain fluency.

For example, repeated readings give students multiple chances at reading a passage. First, students read silently, at slower rate, then increase rate as they become familiar with the passage. Some exercises provide lists of words to read and time the rate from day to day. Choral reading of passages may also be useful to help students to gain fluency as well as to enhance correct inflection and pauses.

Often, pretraining of targeted regular and irregular words is useful. The Slingerland (1994a, 1994b, 1996) "Preparation for Reading" exercises can be adapted to any text. The teacher selects five to seven phrases that may be difficult for students and writes them on the board or on a transparency. The teacher points to and reads each phrase as the students repeat. Next, the teacher reads a phrase and one student finds the phrase among the ones displayed, points to it, and reads it. If it is read correctly, all students repeat; if it is read incorrectly, the students remain silent and the teacher reads the phrase correctly. In the next step, the teacher asks a comprehension question, such as "Find the phrase that shows a location" or "Which phrase includes an adjective?" Again, a student responds by pointing to the phrase and reading it. Finally, a student reads the phrases again as the teacher points to them. Teachers find that the passages are read much more fluently and accurately when students have practiced the phrases prior to reading aloud.

Wolf and Katzer-Cohen (2001) discussed the RAVE-O intervention program to enhance retrieval, automaticity, vocabulary, engagement, and orthography. This program is taught in conjunction with systematic phonological analysis and blending. The program utilizes computer games to maximize rapid recognition and practice of the most frequent orthographic letter patterns. Preliminary data indicated significant gains in word attack, word identification, oral reading rate and accuracy, and passage comprehension (see Wolf, Miller, & Donnelly-Adams, 2000).

By third grade, children should continue to expand their ability to decode and spell new words. As children move to the next level of proficiency, their knowledge of word structure will grow, they will gain new strategies for reading and spelling, and their accuracy and fluency will increase. The following sample lesson provides a model for lessons that both review previously taught patterns and teach new patterns.

LESSON: CONTRASTING THE TWO SOUNDS OF THE GRAPHEME oo

Grade 2   Prerequisites: Understanding of vowel digraphs

Opening

"Today we'll review the /o͞o/ sound of oo and present an alternative sound. First we'll do our visual and auditory card drills and blend some of the cards to make syllables."

Middle

Give students a group of oo words that contain the /o͞o/ sound on an overhead transparency, the board, or a wall chart. Ask what type of pattern oo is [vowel digraph]. Have students read the words individually or in unison.

moon	croon	cool	hoop	room
scoop	groove	smooth	tooth	stool
gloom	droop	boost	stoop	boot
bloom	shoot	broom	spoon	boom
hoot	fool	spool	food	loose
soon	loon	pool	goose	

Have students spell a number of these words from dictation. Also, dictate sentences that contain some of these words.

To introduce the new sound of the spelling pattern oo, /o̮o/, have students copy, trace, and write oo on paper while sounding the new sound /o̮o/, as in book.

Show students a new list of words on the overhead, the board, or a chart:

good	shook	wool	overtook
hook	foot	undertook	cook
brook	woodpile	stood	crook
fishhook	hood	look	nook
book	took	wood	understood

Have students note similarities and differences in the old and the new lists. (The location of the vowel digraph is the same, i.e., in the middle; the sound is different.) Have students read the words from the new list. Dictate several of the words from the new list; include some of the words in phrases and sentences.

As a review, ask students to write /o͞o/ and /o͝o/ as column headings on a new piece of paper. Dictate words from either list. Students must determine in which column to place each word and then write the spelling of the word.

Closing

"Today we've worked on two sounds of the vowel digraph oo. What are they?" [/o͞o/ and /o͝o/] "Are there other ways you know how to spell the /o͞o/ sound?" [u-consonant-e as in rule, ew as in blew, ue as in true] "Are there other ways to spell the /o͝o/ sound?" [There is no other common spelling; u as in put, pull, push, bull, full, and bush is rare.]

Follow-up

"Look for words that contain the oo pattern as you read your storybook. Make a list of those words that have the /o͞o/ sound and those that have the /o͝o/ sound."

From Henry, M.K. (1990). *WORDS: Integrated decoding and spelling instruction based on word origin and word structure* (p. 13). Austin, TX: PRO-ED; adapted by permission.

CLASSROOM ACTIVITIES
AND SUGGESTED GRADE LEVELS

The following activities are suggestions for teachers to use in reinforcing the consonant and vowel patterns. The grades listed are suggested levels only; teachers may want to use the activities with students of different grades if this is more appropriate to the students' abilities.

First Grade

Introducing Sounds

Use flip charts as you introduce new sounds to make numerous words.

Initial Phoneme Substitution

Make a new word by changing the first letter of each word:

     map   __ap [*cap*]   jab   __ab [*cab*]   van   __an [*pan*]

Medial Phoneme Substitution

Read each word. Change /ă/ to /ĭ/, and read the new word:

     pan   p__n [*pin*]   fast   f__st [*fist*]   bag   b__g [*big*]

Word Sorting

Give student teams several cards with a word on each. Ask them to sort the cards by initial or final consonant, by short vowel sound, or by consonant blend versus consonant digraph.

Auditory Discrimination

Ask children to fold a piece of paper in half, lengthwise. Have them write *i* at the top of the first column and e at the top of the second column. Say a word and ask the students to write the word in the appropriate column. For example,

i	*e*
pin	pet
bit	set
fit	pen
slip	step

    Do the same for other sets of sounds that are difficult to discriminate, such as /b/ and /p/ or /ch/ and /sh/.

Finding Orthographic Patterns

Have children underline or circle the consonant blends or consonant digraphs or other orthographic categories in a list of words. For example, ask students to underline the consonant blends in the following words:

<u>bl</u>ame	pa<u>st</u>	whale [*no blends*]	thu<u>mp</u>	cla<u>sp</u>
be<u>lt</u>	<u>gr</u>ind	chick [*no blends*]	<u>spr</u>int	<u>gl</u>eam

Filling in the Blanks

Ask students to fill in the blanks with words containing a consonant digraph (or other type of target pattern):

The _____ sailed through the bay. [*ship*]
_____ the wood for the fire. [*Chop*]
Jaws was a famous _____. [*shark*]
_____ are the biggest mammals. [*Whales*]
I play _____ base on the team. [*third*]
We get wool from _____. [*sheep*]

Rhyming

Students write a word in the blank that rhymes with the target word.

I found a *hat*
just as I _____ [*sat*]
next to my _____ [*cat*]
upon a _____. [*mat*]
Can you imagine _____? [*that*]

Studying Nonphonetic Words and Other Patterns

Make wall charts or word banks for nonphonetic words, for basic sight words, for adjectives describing people, for active verbs, and so forth.

Using Pocket Charts for Spelling

Place consonants and vowels in pockets on the chart. As you dictate a word for spelling, the student places the correct card in the pocket. This is an easier cognitive task than actually writing the word.

Making Sentences with Word Cards

Make short sentences with common words provided on cards.

Spelling Short and Long Vowel Sounds

Have students read each word, then add e to the end of the word. Students read the new word.

tub__ [*tube*]	glad__ [*glade*]
scrap__ [*scrape*]	cap__ [*cape*]

Tim__ [*time*]   pet__ [*Pete*]

twin__ [*twine*]   pin__ [*pine*]

cut__ [*cute*]   grim__ [*grime*]

Finding Spelling Patterns

Students read a passage and underline the vowel digraphs (or other target pattern):

The girls and b<u>oy</u>s planned a n<u>ea</u>t picnic. When th<u>ey</u> got to the park, th<u>ey</u> pl<u>ay</u>ed before lunch. The ch<u>ee</u>se in the c<u>oo</u>ler was sp<u>oi</u>led, but th<u>ey</u> ate the <u>oa</u>tm<u>ea</u>l c<u>oo</u>kies and drank r<u>oo</u>t b<u>ee</u>r.

Second and Third Grades: Letter–Sound Correspondences

Word Sorting and Auditory Discrimination

Continue word sorting and discrimination exercises for new, more difficult patterns.

Sorting Word Cards

Give students cards with the following words on them. Ask them to read the words and put the cards in alphabetical order:

split	mask	sport	plant	nest
jungle	flower	thorn	throat	blink

Filling in the Blanks

Make silly stories that have blanks in place of the target sound, and ask children to choose the correct spelling pattern for the sound. Read the story to the children. For example, "Fill in each blank in the following passage with proper letters that make the /ch/ sound. Remember the general rule: If a short vowel comes right before the /ch/ sound, use *tch*. If two vowels or a consonant comes before the /ch/ sound, use *ch*.

"A mean, nasty, old wi__ [*witch*] lived in an old house with a crooked por__ [*porch*] at the bottom of a di__ [*ditch*]. One day she decided to make a ba__ [*batch*] of her famous wi__es [*witches*] brew. She went to her ki__en [*kitchen*] to fe__ [*fetch*] her biggest pot. She put a pin__ [*pinch*] of her secret ingredient into the pot with a bun__ [*bunch*] of her other wi__y [*witchy*] favorites. She lit the fire under her pot with a ma__ [*match*]. She stirred the brew with a cru___ [*crutch*] she had for her broken foot. She then sat on a ben___ [*bench*] and waited for her lun___ [*lunch*] to cook."

(Story by Mary Buzelli, Pittsburgh, PA; published by kind permission.)

Anglo-Saxon Sentences

Have students write three sentences in their notebooks using only one-syllable Anglo-Saxon words (e.g., *Come to the store with me; The horse jumps next to the stall; Her mom likes to cook and sew*). Then ask each student to read his or her sentence aloud.

Second and Third Grades: Syllables

Counting Syllables

Read the following words to students one by one. After you say each word, ask students to repeat the word and count the number of syllables in it.

atlas [2]	simple [2]	division [3]	population [4]
cucumber [3]	artichoke [3]	dictionary [4]	please [1]

Dividing Syllables

Ask students to divide the following words into syllables.

tennis [*ten/nis*]	mitten [*mit/ten*]	shuttle [*shut/tle*]	pilot [*pi/lot*]
thunder [*thun/der*]	basket [*bas/ket*]	helmet [*hel/met*]	music [*mu/sic*]
paper [*pa/per*]	lilac [*li/lac*]	velvet [*vel/vet*]	table [*ta/ble*]

Second and Third Grades: Morphology

Finding Base Words

Have students circle the base words in a list of compound words, such as the following:

cowboy	aircraft	flashlight	schoolyard	campground
lamppost	baseball	railroad	sailboat	boathouse

Adding Suffixes

Have students add suffixes to the following base words.

shape + ing = [shaping]   shape + ly = [shapely]

hope + less = [hopeless]   hope + ed = [hoped]

slide + ing = [sliding]   slide + er = [slider]

time + ly = [timely]   time + er = [timer]

Finding Suffixes

Have students underline the suffixes in the following words. Tell students, "Read carefully, there may be a trick or two."

glaring	basket [no suffixes]	grateful	slimmest
golden	openly	sleepy	hopefulness
dined	hundred [no suffixes]	careless	coldest

Matching Prefixes and Meanings

Have students match each prefix with its meaning.

[B]	pre-	A. not
[D]	sub-	B. before
[C]	re-	C. again
[E]	mis-	D. under
[A]	un-	E. wrong

Exploring Spelling and Meaning

Give students a word and ask guiding questions. For example, "Is the word *spell* an Anglo-Saxon base word?" [yes] "How do you know?" [It's short, and it contains a typical Anglo-Saxon pattern: final ll.] "Can you add prefixes and suffixes to this word?" [respell, misspell, spelled, misspelled, misspelling] "Why are there two s's in *misspell*?" [One is at the end of the prefix; the other is at the beginning of the base word.]

"What does *spell* mean to you?" [I spell words as I write.] "Do you know any other meanings?" [It can mean a bewitched state or trance, as in under a spell, or it can mean to add up, as in Their loss spelled chaos.]

You can do similar exercises for almost any interesting or unfamiliar word and can assign students to "term teams" to get as much information as possible.

Making Word Webs

Have children begin developing webs for base words as shown in Figure 6.3. For example, ask students to make a web for the word *spell*. Students work in teams and may come up with a web containing compound words, such as *spellbound, spellbind, spelldown,* and *spellchecker;* words with suffixes, such as *spells, spelled, speller,* and *spelling;* words with the prefix *re-,* such as *respell, respells, respelling,* and *respelled;* or words with the prefix *mis-,* such as *misspell, misspells, misspelled,* and *misspelling.*

Beginning Dictionary Usage

Students look up a variety of words for pronunciation and meaning. Students may study some words for their interesting histories. For example, ask guiding questions such as the following: "What does the word *nerd* mean to you? Do you think it is an Anglo-Saxon word? Why? Look up the word *nerd.* What did you learn about its history?" [*The word* nerd *is thought to be from a character in Dr. Seuss's 1950 book,* If I Ran the Zoo. *See the etymology on p. 1179 of the fourth edition* The American Heritage Dictionary, *2000.*]

"Look up the word *smog* to find its origin and how it came into the language." [Smog *was first recorded in 1905 at a Public Health Congress in London. In a paper titled "Fog and Smoke," the author used the term* smoky fog, *which was combined to make the term* smog.]

The word *scuba* is an acronym standing for *self-contained underwater breathing apparatus.* With this word, you can introduce students to the term *acronym.* Students can learn that the first letters of each word in a phrase or sentence make up an *acronym,* greatly shortening the phrase.

Beginning Thesaurus Activities

Encourage students to begin exploring synonyms and antonyms and the subtle differences in words. Have them think of other words that mean almost the same as *sad,* such as *unhappy, sorry, gloomy,* and *dejected.* See if students can give words that are the opposite of *sad,* such as *glad, happy,* and *joyful.*

Ask students to begin keeping their own thesaurus of words by putting each key word on an index card and adding new words as they learn

them. These cards can be kept in a pencil pouch or a recipe box for vocabulary study and writing.

Second and Third Grades: Semantics

Using Semantic Categories

Students read the words in each row and cross out the word that does not
belong. Students try to name the category of each group of words that do
belong together.

milk	cream	shirt	butter	[dairy product]
lemon	apple	grape	egg	[fruit]
bluejay	horse	robin	crow	[bird]
paper	crayon	pencil	rabbit	[writing utensil]
church	house	bus	garage	[building]
skirt	black	blue	yellow	[color]
blouse	scooter	skirt	jacket	[clothing]
car	truck	bus	jelly	[vehicle]

REINFORCEMENT AT HOME

Parents and caregivers can help with many aspects of early reading. They can
read to children or listen to children reading messages, stories, letters, e-mails,
and other text. They can ask children to find specific words as they are reading. Activities such as stamp spelling (in which students use wooden or rubber
letter stamps and an ink pad) and word games can be enjoyable activities that
reinforce reading and spelling. Parents can help children learn nonphonetic
words by asking children to spell words such as *laugh, want, through,* and *busy.*
In addition, parents can point out words and letters on street signs, billboards,
trucks, and license plates while on errands or trips. Parents and children can
search for certain letters (e.g., *q, x, z*), certain letter combinations (e.g., all
vowels, double letters), or whole words.

WORD WISDOM:
ORIGINS OF THE WORDS *READ, WRITE,* AND *SPELL*

The word *read* came from the Old English *rædan,* related to German
raāten, and was first written down in 899. The word *write* also came from Old
English *wrītan,* and was first written down in 725. Most other languages in

western Europe derived their words for *read* from the Latin *legere* (e.g., *to read* in French is *lire*). And, English is the only western European language that does not derive its word for *to write* from the Latin *scribare*.

The English word *spell* comes from Middle English *spellen,* meaning to read letter by letter. It came to English by way of the Old French *espeller,* which was of Germanic origin, and was first written down in 1325.

Source: The American Heritage Student Dictionary, 1998.

WORD WISDOM:
MORE READING AND WRITING WORDS

book   The Anglo-Saxon word for the beech tree was *boc.* Early English priests scratched a variety of symbols on the smooth bark of the beech tree.

paper   The word *paper* comes from the Egyptian rush called *papyrus* (a Latin word), from which paper was first made.

pen   The Latin word for *feather* was *penna.* In Middle English, it became *penne.* Remember that the feather, or quill, was one of the first writing utensils.

WORD WISDOM: FUN WITH WORDS

The word *fun* is an interesting one, and its meaning is changing. Traditionally, it has been a noun meaning *enjoyment* or *amusement.* Since the 1950s, *fun* has also been used as an adjective, as in *We had a fun time, The picnic was fun,* and so forth.

RESOURCES FOR TEACHERS

Bear, D.R., Invernizzi, M., Templeton, S., & Johnson, F. (2001). *Words their way* (2nd ed.). Upper Saddle River, NJ: Merrill.

Center for the Improvement of Early Reading Achievement. (2001, September). *Put reading first: The research building blocks for children learning to read. Kindergarten through third grade.* Washington, DC: Partnership for Reading (National Institute for Literacy, National Institute of Child Health and Human Development, & U.S. Department of Education). (Available from *National Institute for Literacy at ED Pubs,* P.O. Box 1398, Jessup, MD 20794-1398; 800-228-8813; e-mail: EdPubOrders@ aspensys.com; http://www.nifl/publications.html)

Henry, M.K. (1990). *WORDS: Integrated decoding and spelling instruction based on word origin and word structure.* Austin, TX: PRO-ED.

Henry, M.K., & Redding, N.C. (1996). *Patterns for success in reading and spelling.* Austin, TX: PRO-ED.

Moats, L.C. (2000). *Speech to print: Language essentials for teachers.* Baltimore: Paul H. Brookes Publishing Co.

Moats, L.C. (2003). *Speech to print workbook: Language exercises for teachers.* Baltimore: Paul H. Brookes Publishing Co.

Pinnell, G.S., & Fountas, I.C. (1998). *Word matters.* Portsmouth, NH: Heinemann.

Rome, P.D., & Osman, J.S. (1993). *Language tool kit* [Teacher's manual and cards]. Cambridge, MA: Educators Publishing Service.

Lists of One- and Two-Syllable Words

Anderson, C.W. (1980). *Workbook of resource words for phonetic reading* (Books 1–3). Lincoln, NE: Educational Tutorial Consortium. (Available from the publisher, 444 South 44th Street, Lincoln, NE 68516; 402-489-8133; http://www.etc-ne.com)

Bloom, F., & Coates, D.B. (2000). *Recipe for reading.* Austin, TX: PRO-ED.

Fry, E.B., Polk, J.D., & Fountoukidis, D.L. (1996). *The reading teacher's new book of lists* (3rd ed.). Upper Saddle River, NJ: Prentice-Hall.

Jones, T.B. (1997). *Decoding and encoding English words.* Timonium, MD: York Press.

Slingerland, B.H. (1982). *Phonetic word lists for children's use* [Catalog No. 217-W]. Cambridge, MA: Educators Publishing Service.

Slingerland, B.H. (1987). *Teacher's word list for reference* [Catalog No. 218-W]. Cambridge, MA: Educators Publishing Service.

DICTIONARIES FOR STUDENTS

Agnes, M.E. (Ed.). (1999). *Webster's new world children's dictionary* (2nd ed.) [For grades 2–7]. New York: John Wiley & Sons.

Levey, J.S. (Ed.). (1990). *Macmillan first dictionary* [For grades K–3]. New York: Simon & Schuster.

Levey, J.S. (Ed.). (2002). *Scholastic children's dictionary* [For grades 3–7]. New York: Scholastic Reference.

GAME FOR STUDENTS

Milton Bradley (a division of Hasbro). (1999). *UpWords.* East Longmeadow, MA: Author.

Advancing Readers

Time for the Latin and Greek Layers of Language

Upper elementary school students need to go beyond phonics, syllable knowledge, and simple prefixes and suffixes because word length and complexity change dramatically beyond third grade. Yet, although federal funding for reading initiatives has increased, as of 2003 most available funds target children in preschool through third grade. It cannot be assumed that by the end of third grade, children are even ready to learn all that must be learned about the structure of language as it relates to reading and spelling.

New strategies are required for decoding and spelling the multisyllabic words that upper-grade students will find in literature and in content area textbooks. The end of third grade is the time to introduce students to the Latin roots and Greek combining forms used frequently in social studies, math, and science texts. Toward the last semester of third grade, introduce some of the very common Latin roots (e.g., *form, port*) with additional prefixes and suffixes (e.g., *informal, information, formality, export, portal, important*). If third graders do not understand basic letter–sound correspondences or syllable division, these principles must be taught. Take a month or so to introduce or review the patterns in the 2 × 3 Anglo-Saxon letter–sound correspondence matrix (see Figure 3.2 in Chapter 3). Also review the common syllable division patterns before beginning to teach roots of Latin or Greek origin. You may want to introduce your students to common roots found in social studies textbooks. For example, third-grade geography books often discuss the *exports* and *imports* from numerous countries. Therefore, *port* is a logical first root to present. Words such as *export, import, imported, important, exporting, report, porter, portal,* and *transportation* can all be taught with emphasis on affixes and roots. The term *geography* is an interesting one for students to use to begin learning about Greek word roots or combining forms, with *geo* (earth) and *graph* (to write) as the main forms. Teachers of students in the upper grades can determine whether to teach the common Latin roots before introducing the Greek layer or to interweave the two.

By the time students begin to learn the Latin and Greek base elements, students are also using cursive writing. As in the primary grades, students need to trace and copy and practice cursive letters and difficult connections such as *br, ow,* and *ov.* As students write from memory, ask them to say the sound or name of each letter. As soon as several cursive letters have been taught, the letters can be joined in pairs or short words.

The Latin and Greek layers of the language provide students with concepts that are more abstract than the concepts portrayed by the words of Anglo-Saxon origin (Quirk, 1974). By learning the common Latin roots and Greek combining forms, students will begin to recognize the useful orthographic forms and understand specific meanings of these base elements as well. Learning these important patterns provides strategies for not only decoding and spelling but also for expanding expressive and receptive vocabulary. The patterns may well make mind pictures for students, making word retrieval more memorable. For example, imagining a volcano as it *erupts* or knowing someone whose appendix has *ruptured* helps students recall the meanings of the root *rupt* and words that contain it. Fortunately, words of Latin and Greek origin tend to be extremely regular; that is, they follow regular letter–sound correspondences even though the words are longer than those of Anglo-Saxon origin. Teachers need to encourage their students to become *linguaphiles* (lovers of words and language) and to begin to transfer decoding skills to literature reading and content area reading.

WORD WISDOM: *MORPH* WORDS

A *morpheme* is the smallest unit of meaning in a word.

Morphemics is the study and description of language in terms of morphemes.

A *morphemicist* is one who studies morphemics.

An *allomorph* is any variant form of a morpheme. For example, /s/ in cats, /z/ in dogs, /əz/ in horses, and /ən/ in oxen are allomorphs of the English plural morpheme. The combining form *allo* comes from the Greek word *allos,* meaning *other.*

COMMON MORPHEMES

Estimates of vocabulary knowledge vary widely. Goulden, Nation, and Read (1990) concluded that the typical educated native speaker of English has a vocabulary of approximately 17,000 words. These have been acquired at the rate of about two to three words per day. Anderson and Nagy (1992) believed that this number was greatly underestimated. They estimated that the average fifth grader may encounter more than 10,000 new words during the school year and that the average child in elementary or secondary school probably learns 2,000–3,000 words per year. By high school, he or she knows 45,000 words from the more than 88,000 word families used in elementary and secondary school. Anderson and Nagy defined *word families* as groups of words in which knowing one of the words in the family helps a reader to infer the meaning of the others when encountering them in context. For example, knowing *place* helps a reader understand *replace, replacement, misplace, placing,* and so forth. Words in English expand by compounding Anglo-Saxon base words and by adding prefixes and suffixes to Anglo-Saxon base words and to Latin roots and Greek combining forms. These affixed words prevail in content area reading.

Corson suggested that the human brain may use a coding system to process words and may not register multisyllabic words in their entirety: "Words may be analyzed by access codes into units, consisting of their bases or stems with prefixes and suffixes stripped" (1985, p. 19). He noted, also, that almost all words that are content specific (i.e., coming from science, social studies, mathematics, and other content areas), disregarding foreign phrases and slang terms, are of Latin and Greek origin. He suggested that these content-specific "specialist" words enter the child's "performance" vocabulary, if at all, at adolescence. The roots should be part of the curriculum, he recommended, because students from some social groups may not learn these in the natural environment. He stated that "for common readers, without Latin or Greek, the more serious reading becomes remote or irritating because the language of the page is not the language of the vernacular" (p. 39).

Beck, McKeown, and Kucan (2002) wrote of categories of vocabulary that they called "vocabulary tiers." Tier 1 includes basic words that rarely need to be taught, such as *hair, always, dress,* and *grass.* Tier 2 contains high-frequency words that are important for capable language learners to have in their vocabulary, such as *remorse, distinguished, capricious,* and *devious.* Low-frequency words, usually specific to an academic domain and best learned in the related content area, make up Tier 3. Such words include *isotope, photosynthesis,* and *psychologist.* Note that the words in these three tiers are of Anglo-Saxon, Latin, and Greek origin, respectively.

BEYOND PHONICS

Consider Alan, an extremely bright seventh-grade student just beginning secondary school. Alan struggled with reading and spelling in the elementary grades, but because of extremely high IQ scores, he was able to compensate for his problems and complete sixth grade with only moderate difficulty. Because of severe spelling problems, he was tested by a clinical psychologist at age 12; his paragraph writing to dictation appears in Figure 7.1. (Figure 7.2 provides the correct spelling of the passage.)

Teachers gain a rich source of information regarding a student's phonological abilities, orthographic understanding, and knowledge of corresponding rules by looking at the student's writing samples. Look at all of the clues available from Alan's spelling. Notice that Alan seemed to understand grapheme–

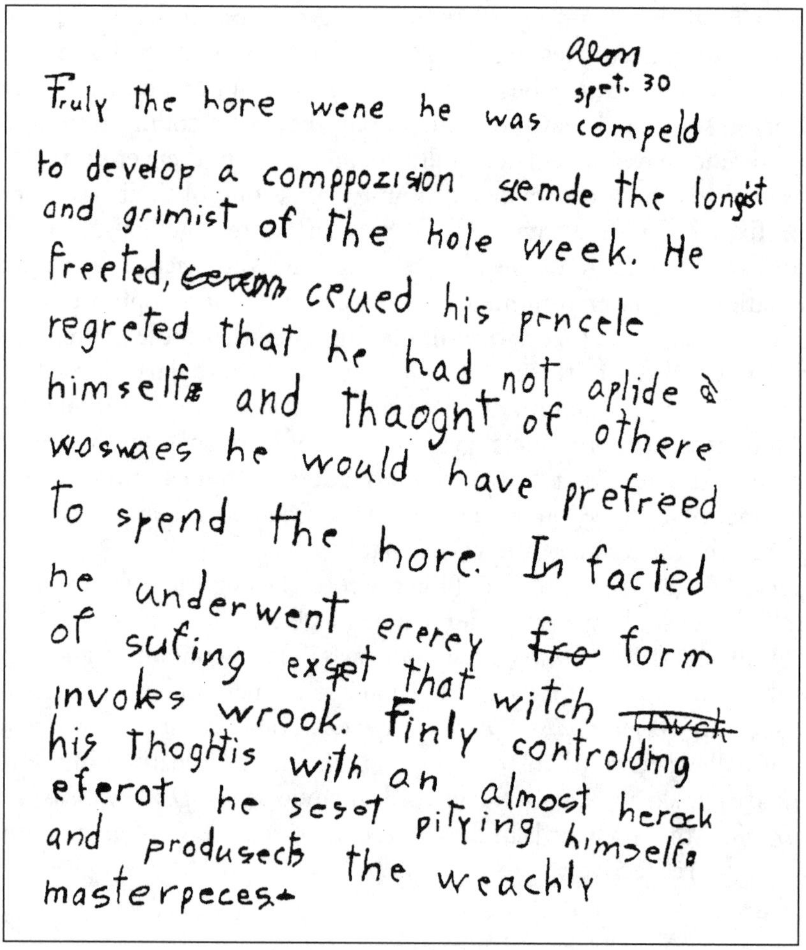
alon
spet. 30
Truly the hore wene he was compeld
to develop a comppozision semde the longist
and grimist of the hole week. He
freeted, ceued his prncele
regreted that he had not aplide
himselfe and thaoght of othere
woswaes he would have prefreed
to spend the hore. In facted
he underwent ererey form
of sufing exset that witch
involes wrook. Finly controlding
his Thoghtis with an almost herock
eferot he sesot pitying himselfe
and produsecb the weachly
masterpeces.

Figure 7.1. Spelling from dictation by Alan, a seventh-grade dyslexic student.

Truly, the hour when he was compelled to develop a composition seemed the longest and grimmest of the whole week. He fretted, chewed his pencil, regretted that he had not applied himself, and thought of other ways he would have preferred to spend the hour. In fact, he underwent every form of suffering except that which involves work. Finally, controlling his thoughts with an almost heroic effort, he ceased pitying himself and produced the weekly masterpiece.

Figure 7.2. Correct spelling of dictation paragraph. This paragraph was created and used by the late psychologist Margaret Rawson.

phoneme relationships: Some of his writing can be read phonetically (e.g., *comppozision* for *composition*, *grimist* for *grimmest*).

By the time he wrote this passage as a seventh grader, Alan had not learned many of the basic sight words needed in first and second grades, such as *hour, when, whole, ways, every, which,* and *work.* Although he did not reverse letter shapes (e.g., *b* for *d*), he did transpose the sequence of letters as in *spet.* for *Sept., exspet* for *except,* and *wrook* for *work.* Although his speaking vocabulary was outstanding, he was not consistent in his spelling: He used *-d, -de,* and *-ed* (the correct form) for the past-tense ending. The sample also shows that he did not understand the rules for suffix addition: He spelled *longest* as *longist, grimmest* as *grimist,* and *compelled* as *compeld.* Other errors include deleting a syllable, as in *sufing* (for *suffering*) and *herock* (for *heroic*).

So, where would a teacher begin instructing students with the problems that Alan showed in his writing sample? He needed some of the basic sight words, many of them nonphonetic, such as *whole, thought,* and *which.* Teachers could briefly review letter–sound correspondences and the relevant rules and then immediately begin introducing the Latin word roots and affixes.

Learning the concept of schwa would be useful for students at this point, as many of the Latin-based words contain schwa sounds as unstressed affixes are added. Understanding morphophonemic relationships, described in Chapter 3, could also benefit students with difficulties similar to Alan's. Students need to understand that as affixes are added, sounds within syllables often change but that some of the spelling patterns of the base word remain (e.g., *house, housing; know, knowledge; remedy, remediate*).

Morphological and orthographic skills are also important, especially in longer words. Teachers need to find out what their students know about morpheme patterns. One way to assess students in a classroom is to have them mark specific patterns within a list of words. A group of students can be asked to find the suffixes in words such as *imported, tractor, instructive,* and *disruption.* Or, teachers can give an individual child a card drill using common prefixes, suffixes, or Latin roots and ask the child to read the cards and explain the meaning.

Prior to teaching the Latin roots, teachers should introduce additional prefixes and suffixes that are used with Latin roots. These affixes can be taught in separate prefix and suffix units or can be introduced as the individual roots are presented.

Prefixes

In a prefix unit, the teacher reviews those prefixes mentioned in Chapter 6 (e.g., *a-*, *de-*, *dis-*, *fore-*, *in-*, *mis-*, *pre-*, *re-*, *un-*). Then other prefixes with closed syllables are taught, such as *dif-*, *dys-*, *en-*, *ex-*, *il-*, *im-*, *in-*, *mal-*, *mid-*, *non-*, *sub-*, *suc-*, *suf-*, *sug-*, *sum-*, *sup-*, *sus-*, *trans-*, and *with-*.

The prefix *dys-* is used with both Latin roots and Greek combining forms and contains the Greek-based pattern for *y* pronounced as short /ĭ/. The prefixes *syl-*, *sym-*, *syn-*, and *sys-* also contain *y* pronounced as short /ĭ/ and are usually taught along with the Greek combining forms.

Open-syllable prefixes include *bi-*, *co-*, *di-*, *e-*, *o-*, *pro-*, *tri-*, and *twi-*, as well as the previously taught *de-*, *re-*, and *pre-*. Prefixes with *r*-controlled vowels include *per-* and *fore-*, along with several of the two-syllable and chameleon prefixes described next. Two-syllable prefixes, including *ambi-*, *anti-*, *circum-*, *contra-*, *counter-*, *extra-*, *intra-*, *inter-*, *intro-*, *multi-*, *over-*, *super-*, and *ultra-*, should also be taught.

The chameleon prefixes (or assimilated prefixes) are generally taught when Latin roots are introduced. Assimilation denotes the process by which a sound is modified so that it becomes similar or identical to an adjacent or nearby sound (e.g., *inlegal* becomes *illegal*). The final letter of each of these prefixes changes depending on the first letter of the root. For example, *in-* (meaning *in* or *not*) changes to *il-* before a root beginning with *l* (e.g., *illegal*), to *ir-* before a root beginning with *r* (e.g., *irregular*), and to *im-* before a root beginning with *m*, *b*, or *p* (e.g., *immortal, imbibe, impede*). The prefix *con-* (meaning *together*) changes to variants *col-*, *cor-*, and *com-* in similar instances (e.g., *collect, correct, commute, combine, compute*). Other chameleon prefixes include *ad-* (*af-*, *ag-*, *al-*, *an-*, *ap-*, *ar-*, *as-*, *at-*), *sub-* (*suf-*, *sug-*, *sum-*, *sup-*), and *ob-* (*oc-*, *op-*). Teachers should tell their students that assimilation is formed due to *euphony* (from Greek *eu*, meaning *well*, and Greek *phon*, meaning *sound*). It sounds better!

Suffixes

Suffixes also need to be taught. In addition to those studied in Chapter 6 (i.e., *-able, -ed, -en, -er, -est, -fold, -ful, -hood, -ing, -less, -ling, -ly, -ment, -ness, -ship, -some,* and *-y*), which are used with Anglo-Saxon base words, the following suffixes need to be learned in approximately the order listed (i.e., column I prefixes are taught first, column II second, and column III last):

I	II	III
-ion (-tion, -sion)	*-ar*	*-ism*
-most	*-ability*	*-ious*
-ous	*-ible, -ibility*	*-ory*
-or	*-ize*	*-ial (-cial, -tial)*
-ess	*-ary*	*-ian (-cian)*
-ure, -ture	*-ate*	*-cious*
-dom	*-ward*	*-ation*
-ent, -ence	*-age*	*-ial (-tial)*
-an	*-al*	*-tious*
-ant, -ance	*-ify*	*-ile*
-ist	*-ity*	*-ade*
-ic	*-ee*	*-ium*
-ty	*-fy*	

(For lists of prefixes and suffixes, along with their meanings and/or grammatical information and examples of words, see Appendices D and E, respectively.)

The final spelling rule must be learned at this time:

Doubling rule (for polysyllabic base words): When a base word ends with one consonant preceded by one short vowel, double the final consonant if the final syllable in the base word is accented, as in the following examples:

- *ad/mit':* admitting, admitted (accent is on the final syllable in the base)

- *gar'/den:* gardening, gardened (accent is on the first syllable in the base, no doubling necessary)

- *con/fer':* conferring, conference (accent is on the final syllable in the base, but note the shift in accent in *conference*)

Although the past-tense forms of words such as *cancel* and *travel* traditionally have only one *l* in American English (e.g., *canceled, traveled*), newer dictionaries are giving two spellings (e.g., *canceled* or *cancelled; traveled* or *travelled*).

Here are some other interesting guidelines about suffixes:

- Use *-or* with Latin roots for nouns (as in *inventor, conductor, elevator*), but use *-ar* for adjectives (as in *popular, singular, circular*).

- Use *-or* with Latin roots (as in *spectator*), but use *-er* for Anglo-Saxon roots (as in *heater, swimmer, baker*)

- Although *-ous* and *-ess* sound alike because both are unstressed syllables that contain a schwa sound, use *-ous* for adjectives (as in *dangerous, tremendous*, and *fabulous*) and *-ess* for feminine nouns (as in *princess, hostess*, and *governess*). The similar sounding *-ice* is a noun suffix (as in *office, malice, practice*, and *apprentice*).

- Use *-est* for the comparative degree of adjectives (as in *greenest, loveliest, smallest*), but use *-ist* for people nouns (as in *dentist, pianist, socialist*)

- Although not always the case, *-able* is usually added to Anglo-Saxon base words (as in *likable, reasonable, eatable*) and *-ible* is usually added to Latin roots (as in *credible, edible, impossible*).

- Although *-ent* and *-ant*, as well as *-ence* and *-ance*, sound alike because of the schwa, *-ent* and *-ence* are used somewhat more often than *-ant* and *-ance*. If in doubt, before you check the dictionary or spell checker, use *-ent* or *-ence*. Also, the suffix *-ant* often indicates a person noun (as in *tenant, sergeant, complainant*).

When working with morphemes, be sure that students are not finding "false" morphemes in words. For example, students should not conclude that *sister* contains the comparative suffix *-er* or that *hundred* contains the past-tense suffix *-ed*. Students can consult the dictionary for etymologies together or independently to clear up confusion.

LATIN ROOTS

Teach each Latin root directly. Remember that the spelling of each Latin root is reliable in scores of words. Edmund H. Henderson reminded us that the Latin roots and Greek combining forms are stable elements of word knowledge and that "they are like the meaning characters in Chinese and Japanese.

They provide meaning efficiency for reading across a shifting surface of sound" (1990, p. 74).

As students begin to learn the Latin roots, the teacher should incorporate etymology study in the curriculum. Etymology involves the history of words and the development of the structures and meanings of words. Corson said that "marked educational improvements have been reported for children who have followed programmes focusing on the etymology and word relationship of English" (1985, p. 28). Students learn to analyze the etymology of a word by looking in the dictionary. For example, students can look up the word *inspire* in the fourth edition of *The American Heritage Dictionary* (2000). They will find an etymology that shows that the word goes back to the Latin and prefixes the root *spir* with *in-*. Teachers can ask students to use a thesaurus to find synonyms of *inspire* or can ask them to generate other words with the root *spir*.

The sequence of presentation of Latin roots is based on both the frequency of words and the regularity of spellings. The first roots learned have only one or two forms (e.g., *tract; dic, dict; stru, struct*). Next, roots with three and four variants (e.g., *duc, duce, duct; fac, fact, fect, fic*) can be learned. Two or three groups of roots can be taught in each lesson. The teacher should give ample opportunities for students to generate words and to read and spell them in lists, phrases, and sentences. (See the end of this chapter for other practice activities.)

Here is one logical sequence for presentation, reading across rows. See Appendix F for the Latin roots, their meanings, and examples of words. (Brown [1947] suggested that the 12 Latin roots marked by asterisks, along with the Greek combining forms *graph* and *ology*, provide the clues to the meaning of more than 100,000 words.)

form (to shape)	*port* (to carry)
rupt (to break or burst)	*tract* (to draw or pull)
scrib, script (to write)*	*spec, spect, spic* (to see, watch, or observe)*
stru, struct (to build)	*dic, dict* (to say or tell)
flect, flex (to bend or curve)	*mit, miss* (to send)*
fer (to bear or yield)*	*cred* (to believe)
duc, duce, duct (to lead)*	*pel, puls* (to drive or push)
vers, vert (to turn)	*pend, pens* (to hang or weigh)
fac, fact, fect, fic (to make or do)*	*jac, jec, ject* (to throw or lie)
tend, tens, tent (to stretch or strain)*	*cur, curs* (to run or go)
ped (foot)	*vid, vis* (to see)
aud (to hear or listen)	*vit, vita, viv, vivi* (to live)

leg (law)

greg (group, crowd, flock, or herd; to assemble)

capit, capt (head or chief)

spir, spire (to breathe)

cap, ceit, ceive, cep, cept, cip (to take, catch, seize, hold, or receive)*

grad, gred, gress (step, degree; to walk)

voc, vok, voke (to call)

lect, leg, lig (to choose, pick, read, or speak)

lit, liter, litera (letters)

cede, ceed, cess (to go, yield, or surrender)

ten, tain, tin, tinu (to hold)*

feder, fid, fide, feal (trust or faith)

sist, sta, stat, stit (to stand)*

cad, cas, cid (to fall or befall)

pon, pose, pound (to put, place, or set)*

cern (to separate), *cert* (to decide)

mob, mot, mov (to move)

gen, genus (race, kind, or species; birth)

cide (to kill)

cise (to cut)

plic, ply (to fold)*

Because the spellings of Latin roots are so phonetic, the teacher may present them in almost any order. The teacher may wish to determine which roots are found in the literature and textbooks that his or her students read and develop a customized sequence.

The teacher can ask students to generate morpheme webs using roots as they are presented. Ramsden (2001) illustrated this web activity (see Figure 7.3). Matrices are also good visual reinforcement for many roots. Again, Ramsden (2001) illustrated such a matrix that shows the affixes that can be added to a target root (see Figure 7.4).

The teacher should consciously direct students to the spelling–meaning connection. Remember that accent often shifts and that vowel sounds become schwa. The teacher should show the relationship of word families. For example, the teacher can help students notice that in *sign*, the *g* is not heard that but in *signal, signify,* and *signature,* the *g* gets its hard sound. Student can be asked to compare the vowel sounds in the following words: *melody, melodic,* and *melodious.* In *melody,* the *o* is pronounced as schwa; in *melodic* the *o* says short /ŏ/, and in *melodious* the *o* says long /ō/. Similar compare/contrast examples can include word pairs such as *condemn, condemnation; compete, competition; image, imagine;* and *local, locality.* Students should mark the accent and vowel sounds in each word.

The teacher should point out to students that some Latin roots require "connectives" between the root and the suffix. The *u* in *contemptuous* is a connective, as is the *i* in *solitude.* Other examples, with connectives underlined, include *mon_u_ment, famili_a_r, conspic_u_ous, conven_i_ent, ingen_i_ous,* and *editori_a_l.*

After students learn several Latin roots, the teacher connects these roots to content area reading to ensure transfer. The teacher selects phrases or sentences from a social studies text that contain words with the target roots. Students read or write the selected groups of words. (See Appendix H for content area words related to upper elementary and middle school subject areas.)

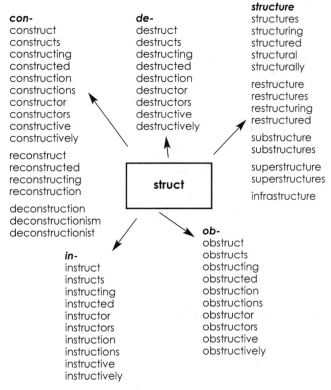

con-
construct
constructs
constructing
constructed
construction
constructions
constructor
constructors
constructive
constructively

reconstruct
reconstructed
reconstructing
reconstruction

deconstruction
deconstructionism
deconstructionist

de-
destruct
destructs
destructing
destructed
destruction
destructor
destructors
destructive
destructively

structure
structures
structuring
structured
structural
structurally

restructure
restructures
restructuring
restructured

substructure
substructures

superstructure
superstructures

infrastructure

struct

in-
instruct
instructs
instructing
instructed
instructor
instructors
instruction
instructions
instructive
instructively

ob-
obstruct
obstructs
obstructing
obstructed
obstruction
obstructions
obstructor
obstructors
obstructive
obstructively

Figure 7.3. Morpheme web for the root *struct*. (From Ramsden, M. [2000]. *The user's self-training manual: The essential reference for real English spelling* [Available from the author, http://perso.wanadoo.fr/melvyn/ spelling/manual.html]; adapted by permission.)

While working with the Latin word roots, the teacher should remember that the affixes generally contain the schwa sound. Students cannot depend only on phonological clues for decoding and spelling these multisyllabic words and must know grammatical usage as well. Remember, for example,

re de	con	struct		s ed ing
			ive	ly
de in ob sub super infra			or	s
			ion	s ism ist
			ure	s ed ing
				al	ly

Figure 7.4. Affix matrix for the root *struct*.

that in spelling the word *governess*, students need to know that both *-ous* and *-ess* say /əs/. But knowing that *-ess* is used for feminine nouns and that *governess* is a feminine noun, whereas *-ous* is used only for adjectives (e.g., *mountainous*, *adventurous*), brings students to the correct solution.

WORD WISDOM: THE INFLUENCE OF FRENCH ON ENGLISH

Many English words are influenced by the French language. For example, most words with the grapheme *ch* sounding like /sh/ come from French:

chef	cache	chenille	chamois
machine	mustache	sachet	brochure
champagne	chute	chiffon	parachute
chandelier	chivalry	nonchalant	chauvinist

Many French-based words include the grapheme *ou*:

adjourn	sojourn	journey	journal
flourish	courage	encourage	nourish
courier	couple	courtesy	courteous

The spelling pattern *eau* is also a convention from French:

flambeau	bandeau	rondeau	tableau
trousseau	bureau	chateau	plateau

In addition, the word-final *-que*, sounding like /k/, is from French:

oblique	antique	technique	pique
perique	physique	unique	critique
clique	cinque	baroque	equivoque
Basque	masque	arabesque	Romanesque
humoresque	picturesque	grotesque	

LESSON: INTRODUCING LATIN WORD ROOTS

Opening

"Today we're going to continue breaking words apart to make them easier to read and spell. We've worked on Anglo-Saxon root words and numerous prefixes and suffixes. For the next several days, we will talk about Latin roots. Who remembers what a root is?" [*The root is the main part of the word, the part to which prefixes and suffixes are added. The root usually receives the accent or stress in Latin-based words.*] "Roots are valuable not only as patterns for decoding and spelling but also for learning new vocabulary to enhance your reading, writing, listening, and speaking. Thousands of words—more than half of the words in the dictionary—come from Latin roots. Each root has a specific meaning; we change the meaning by adding prefixes and suffixes."

Middle

Write the root *rupt* on the board. Ask students to generate a number of words with *rupt* as the root. Write the words on the board. See if students can pick up the meaning of *rupt* (to break, to burst) from the words on the board. Here are some words containing *rupt:*

rupture	abruptly	erupt	eruption	eruptive
abrupt	interrupts	interrupting	interrupted	interruption
disrupt	disruptive	disrupted	corrupt	corruptible
corrupted	corrupting	corruption	irrupt	bankrupt

Add additional words containing *rupt* and affixes. For each word, have students read the word and identify the common word part (*rupt*). Have students note the placement of the root (at the beginning if there is no prefix, the end if there is no suffix, the middle if there are prefixes and suffixes).

Dictate several words containing *rupt* and sentences containing these words.

Closing

Probe for content, structure, and process. Review why learning these roots is valuable for students.

Follow-up

Have students look for words of Latin origin in newspapers or in their social studies textbook.

In a format similar to this lesson, continue to present new, frequently used roots, such as *port* (to carry); *form* (to shape); *tract* (to pull); *stru, struct* (to build); *dic, dict* (to say, tell); *flect, flex* (to bend); *mit, miss* (to send); *fer* (to bear, carry); and so forth.

From Henry, M.K. (1990). *WORDS: Integrated decoding and spelling instruction based on word origin and word structure* (p. 44). Austin, TX: PRO-ED; and Henry, M.K., & Redding, N.C. (1996). *Patterns for success in reading and spelling* (pp. 251–252). Austin, TX: PRO-ED; adapted by permission.

GREEK COMBINING FORMS

Many of the Latin roots were actually borrowed from Greek. Some of the Greek words had themselves been borrowed from the language of still earlier people, the Phoenicians. The Greek-based words in English tend to be related to math and science. Words such as *biology, geology, archaeology, physics, chemistry,* and *geography* all contain Greek combining forms, and the words used in these domains are often of Greek origin.

Teachers may want to complete the majority of Latin roots before presenting the Greek combining forms. Or, teachers may wish to teach some of the common Greek forms along with the Latin roots, especially in fifth grade, during which science and math texts begin to depend on Greek-based words as the key content words.

When introducing Greek-based words, first teach those letter–sound correspondences that are exclusive to Greek (i.e., *ph* for /f/ as in *photograph, ch* for /k/ as in *chemotherapy,* and *y* for /ĭ/ as in *symphonic*). Other Greek-based letter combinations include *y* as long /ī/ as in *hydrogen, ps* as in *psychology, rh* as in *rhinoceros, pn* as in *pneumonia, pt* as in *pterodactyl,* and *mn* as in *mnemonic.* If a word begins with *x,* students can assume it is from Greek, as in *xylophone* and *Xerxes.*

Because Greek-based word parts compound, the parts are usually called *combining forms.* Some teachers, however, use the term *root,* which is fine as long as the term is used consistently. Note also that some teachers use the term *prefix* for Greek combining forms that appear at the beginnings of words (e.g., *auto, tele*) and the term *suffix* for those forms appearing at the ends of words (e.g., *ology, logue*). Again, this is fine as long as the terms are applied consistently.

Give approximately four to six Greek combining forms in any lesson. This way, scores of words can be generated from each combining form. A possible sequence for presenting the Greek combining forms, based primarily on grade level and frequency, follows, reading across rows:

phon, phono (sound)

gram, graph (written or drawn)

tele (distant)

micro (small or minute)

therm, thermo (heat or hot)

scope (to watch or see)

biblio (book)

geo (earth)

pol, polis, polit (city; method of government)

derm (skin)

chron, chrono (time)

hyper (over, above, or excessive)

phys (nature)

path (feeling, suffering, or disease)

lex (word)

mega (large or great)

meta (beside, after, later, or beyond)

kine, cine (movement)

the, theo (god)

mania (madness, frenzy, abnormal desire, or obsession)

ast, astro (star)

archae, arche, archi (primitive or ancient)

photo (light)

auto (self)

logy (study; from *logos, logue* [speech or word])

meter, metr (measure)

bio (life)

hydr, hydra, hydro (water)

cracy, crat (rule)

metro (mother city; measure)

dem, demo (people)

hypo (under)

cycl, cyclo (wheel or circle; circular)

chrom (color)

techn (skill, art, or craft)

psych (mind or soul)

gno, gnosi (know)

mech (machine)

arch (chief or ruler)

phil, phila, phile, philo (love or affinity for)

soph (wisdom or cleverness)

phobia, phobic; phobe (irrational fear or hatred; one who fears-hates)

andr, anthr (man)

A combined unit on Latin- and Greek-based number words is recommended for the upper-grade students, as the terms appear over and over in math and science textbooks at this level. (See the section in Appendix D called "Number Prefixes from Latin and Greek" for the related number words.)

LESSON: INTRODUCING GREEK COMBINING FORMS

Opening

"Today we will switch from working on words of Latin origin to learning words of Greek origin. You may remember that these words are often used in science classes and textbooks. Different people use different terms to describe the Greek word parts. In some dictionaries and books they are called *roots*, in some they are called *combining forms*, in others some Greek-based word parts are known as *prefixes* and *suffixes*. We will call them all *combining forms* because usually there are two parts of equal stress and importance that are combined, almost as in the Anglo-Saxon compound words. Some of the parts come only at the beginning of a word, and others come at the end. Some forms can be used in either position."

Middle

On the board, write a number of word parts. Point out that some parts usually come at the beginning or at the end of words. Among the first combining forms to be learned are *auto, phono, photo, biblio, hydro, hyper, tele, chron, chrom, arch, phys, psych, micro, peri, bi, semi, hemi, mono, meta, mega, metro, philo, soph, theo, techni, graph, gram, meter, ology, sphere, scope, crat, cracy,* and *polis.*

Alert students to the Greek letter–sound correspondences that prevail in these combining forms, such as *ph; ch; y* as medial vowel; silent *p* in *ps, pt,* and *pn*; and, rarely, *rh, mn,* and *x* that sounds like /z/.

Have students generate Greek-based words such as the following:

chronometer	perimeter	microscope	hyperactive
physiology	physician	periscope	archeology
bibliography	physiologist	telescope	phonograph
telegraph	zoology	autograph	architect
autobiography	metropolis	metropolitan	hemisphere
hydrogen	philosophy	philharmonic	theology
psychology	pterodactyl	pneumonia	metaphysics

Have students read words from flip charts or from word lists that you have prepared.

Dictate a number of words with Greek word parts for students to spell.

Closing

Review the terminology and origin of these Greek combining forms. Let students know that in the next lesson, they will deal with the specific meaning of many of these combining forms.

Follow-up

Have students look in their science textbooks for words that contain Greek combining forms. Continue to teach several specific combining forms in following lessons. The format will remain the same. See Appendix G for the Greek combining forms, their meanings, and examples. Also, provide plenty of practice in working with content area words as found in Appendix H.

From Henry, M.K. (1990). *WORDS: Integrated decoding and spelling instruction based on word origin and word structure* (p. 47). Austin, TX: PRO-ED; and Henry, M.K., & Redding, N.C. (1996). *Patterns for success in reading and spelling* (pp. 281–284). Austin, TX: PRO-ED; adapted by permission.

PRACTICE READING AND SPELLING LONGER WORDS

As students read unfamiliar words, the teacher should ask the students to try to identify the language origin. Next, they should look for the morpheme units (e.g., prefixes, roots, and suffixes; combining forms). If students cannot find morphemes in a word or find morphemes but still cannot read the entire word, students should break the word into syllables using the common syllable division options. If syllable division does not work or works for only part of the word, students should use letter–sound correspondences to read the word.

ACTIVITIES TO REINFORCE LATIN- AND GREEK-BASED MORPHEMES

The following are examples of activities that are designed for students to reinforce their familiarity with Latin- and Greek-based morphemes.

Matching Prefixes and Meanings

Have students match prefixes and their meanings:

trans-	[B]	A. forward
pro-	[A]	B. across
mid-	[E]	C. under
non-	[F]	D. out
sub-	[C]	E. between
ex-	[D]	F. not

ultra-	[C]	A. between
contra-	[E]	B. around
intro-	[D]	C. beyond
inter-	[A]	D. inward
intra-	[F]	E. against
circum-	[B]	F. within

Matching Suffixes and Meanings

Students match suffixes and their parts of speech.

-or	[C]	A. adverb
-ess	[D]	B. adjective
-ist	[E]	C. noun
-ly	[A]	D. feminine noun
-ous	[B]	E. noun, person

Finding Morphemes in Words

Students read the following words and list the root and any prefixes and/ or suffixes. Analyze the following Latin-based words for word structure and pronunciation.

Word	Prefix(es)	Root	Suffix(es)
reflection	[re]	[flect]	[ion]
disrupted	[dis]	[rupt]	[ed]
attractive	[at]	[tract]	[ive]
collective	[col]	[lect]	[ive]
subtracting	[sub]	[tract]	[ing]
prescriptions	[pre]	[script]	[ion, s]
reconstructionist	[re, con]	[struct]	[ion, ist]
pendant	[no prefixes]	[pend]	[ant]
congregation	[con]	[greg]	[ation]
inspector	[in]	[spect]	[or]

Finding Latin Roots

Have students underline the Latin word roots in the following words:

nonde_script_	in_struc_tive	con_vert_ible	confe_rence_
at_tract_ive	ad_vers_ary	unin_tent_ionally	con_duct_or
ex_pell_ed	_spect_acular	re_flect_ion	con_ject_ure

Matching Roots and Meanings

Students match the Latin root with the letter of the correct meaning:

[C]	rupt	A. to say or tell
[F]	spect	B. to breathe
[A]	dict	C. to break or burst
[E]	flect	D. to pull
[B]	spire	E. to bend
[D]	tract	F. to see

Matching Words and Meanings

Ask students to match the correct meaning with each word containing the root dic, dict (meaning to say or tell)

[F]	malediction	A. an absolute ruler
[D]	benediction	B. to express the opposite
[B]	contradict	C. to point out
[G]	prediction	D. a blessing
[A]	dictator	E. a reference book for words
[C]	indicate	F. a curse
[E]	dictionary	G. something foretold

Defining Roots

Students write the Latin root that corresponds with each of the following:

to pull [tract]	to build [struct]
to write [scribe or script]	to bend [flect or flex]
to see [spect]	to break [rupt]
to hear [aud]	to run [cur or curs]
to stretch [tend or tens]	to turn [vert or vers]
to believe [cred]	to bear [fer]

Identifying Affixes

Ask students to underline the prefixes and circle the suffixes in the following passage.

The active conductor took the elevator to the fifth floor. There he walked briskly to the composer's attractive apartment. Mr. Musician, the conductor, was furious that Mr. Composition had forgotten to deliver the latest manuscript to the auditorium for the rehearsal.

Mr. Music(ian:) "How can the orchestra possib(ly) play this piece at tonight('s) perform_ance? We have been <u>un</u>able to <u>re</u>hearse. The violin(ist)s are fum(ing,) the trombon(ist)s are seeth(ing,) and the <u>percussion(ist)s</u> are almost <u>in</u>sane."

Mr. Composit(ion:) "The lat(est) correct(ion)s have been <u>includ(ed)</u> in this fin(al) draft. Your music(ian)s are so talent(ed) and <u>precoci(ous)</u> they can play anything. Take this fold(er) contain(ing) the <u>sym</u>phony and leave me (a)lone!"

Finding Target Morpheme Cards

Using 3 × 5 cards with prefixes, roots, and suffixes on them, ask students to find target cards, such as the cards that mean *before, against, build, turn,* and so forth (*pre, ante, struct, vert*).

Using Words in Context

Ask students to write each word in a sentence:

exports	[*The United States exports grain to many countries.*]
bankrupt	[*Numerous companies may go bankrupt during a recession.*]
transformed	[*The darkness transformed our memory of the forest.*]

Filling in the Blanks

Ask students to fill in the missing word in each sentence with the best word from the following choices:

interrupted	information	formality	convertible
spectators	supported	report	formula

My _____ card had mostly As.   [*report*]

My sister _____ our telephone conversation.   [*interrupted*]

The building was _____ by heavy beams.   [*supported*]

Give me new _____ on the research.   [*information*]

I have a new yellow _____.   [*convertible*]

The _____ cheered at the football game.   [*spectators*]

Substituting Latin-Based Words

For each italicized word or phrase, students choose a substitute term from the three choices given. This substitute term should contain a Latin-based root.

My *teacher* helped the principal at lunchtime.

  informer   [*instructor*]   reporter

Turn in your *research paper* tomorrow.

  [*manuscript*]   prescription   protractor

Sign the *business agreement* soon.

  [*contract*]   inscription   export

He had a new mathematical *equation* to study.

  informal   conductor   [*formula*]

Adding Suffixes

Review the doubling rule for polysyllabic base words. Ask students to underline the accented syllable in the following base words, and write the word with the given suffix added:

con<u>struct</u> + ed [*constructed*]   com<u>mit</u> + ee [*committee*]

ex<u>pel</u> + ing [*expelling*]   ad<u>mit</u> + ance [*admittance*]

<u>gov</u>ern + or [*governor*]   <u>sum</u>mon + ed [*summoned*]

pre<u>vent</u> + ive [*preventive*]   for<u>bid</u> + en [*forbidden*]

Identifying Language of Origin

Have students identify the origin languages (Anglo-Saxon, Latin, or Greek) of the following words:

philharmonic [*Greek*]   psychology [*Greek*]

extraction [*Latin*]   hopelessness [*Anglo-Saxon*]

introspective [*Latin*]   laughing [*Anglo-Saxon*]

bookish [*Anglo-Saxon*]   manufactured [*Latin*]

expeditious [*Latin*]   hydrophobia [*Greek*]

Finding Greek Combining Forms

Students circle the Greek combining forms in the following words:

chronology   microscope   telegraph   hydrosphere

polygon   monogram   thermometer   philosophy

Matching Combining Forms

Students match the letter of the correct meaning with the Greek combining form.

[F]	*micro*	A. sound
[G]	*ology*	B. life
[D]	*auto*	C. look or see
[J]	*graph, gram*	D. self
[I]	*therm*	E. distant
[E]	*tele*	F. small
[B]	*bio*	G. study
[A]	*phon, phono*	H. water
[C]	*scope*	I. heat
[H]	*hydro*	J. written or drawn

Identifying Parts of Speech

Ask students to give the part of speech (noun, verb, or adjective) for each word:

geology [*noun*]   geologist [*noun*]
geologize [*verb*]   geologizer [*noun*]
geologizing [*noun*]   geologic [*adjective*]
geological [*adjective*]   geologically [*adverb*]
geologian [*noun*]

Making Words

Give pairs of children a Greek-based word with two combining forms, such as *biology*. Have the students identify the two combining forms, *bio* and *logy;* give the forms' meanings; and make words with those two forms.

biology

bio (life)   *logy* (study of)
biosphere   geology
biodegradable   dermatology
biochemistry   phonology
biography   zoology
autobiography   pathology
                                     mythology

Finding Words in Context

Astro is a Greek combining form meaning *star.* Ask students to find as many *astro* words as possible in their science book, in the dictionary, or on the Internet. [*astrophysics, astrochemistry, astrobiology, astrogeology, and so forth*]

Making Morpheme Webs

Ask students to draw a web for the root *rupt,* using the blank web shown in Figure 7.5 as a model. Students should use as many prefixes and suffixes as they can. This can be a group or individual activity.

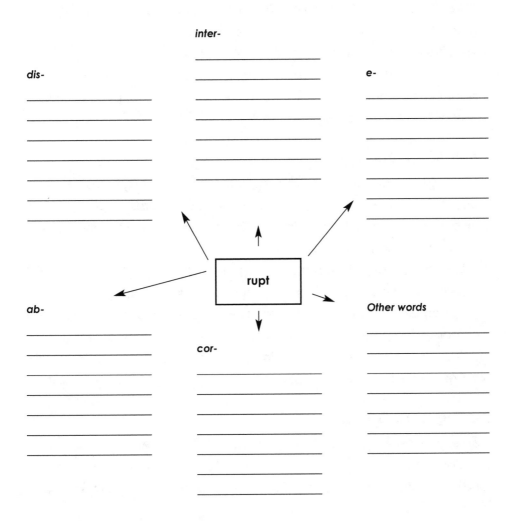

Figure 7.5.   Blank morpheme web for the root *rupt.*

Brainstorming Greek-Based Words

Students write as many words containing each Greek combining form as they can. This can be a group or solo activity.

micro

chron

photo

Guided Questioning

Have students answer the following types of questions about words of interest:

photosynthesis: "What is the word's origin? [*Greek*] What are the clues?"
[*The letters* ph *saying* /f/ *and* y *saying* /ĭ/] "What do you think this word means? What is the dictionary definition?"

interruption: "What is the word's origin?" [*Latin*] "What are the clues?" [*prefix* inter-, *root* rupt, *suffix* -ion] "What is the meaning?" [*a hindering or stopping of some action by someone breaking in*] "What is the literal definition?" [*to break between*]

Contrasting Meaning

Have children contrast word pairs, as in the following examples. Students should try to figure out the meaning of the target words and can check their answers by using the dictionary. This is a good activity for small groups of students working together.

"Describe a person with *megapods* and *megadonts*." [*A person with megapods and megadonts has large feet and large teeth.*]

"Compare the behavior of an *extrovert* and an *introvert*." [*An extrovert is outgoing and gregarious, whereas an introvert turns inward.*]

"How do *intrastate* and *interstate* highways differ?" [*Intrastate highways exist within a state, whereas interstate highways run between states.*]

Playing Word Games

Games are useful for reinforcing concepts learned. Activities based on popular games such as Bingo, Concentration, Jeopardy!, Wheel of Fortune, and Charades can be adapted to practice with word roots and combining forms.

WORD WISDOM: THE LETTER *i* AS CONSONANT /y/

When the letter *i* comes after *ll* or word-medial *l* or *n*, the *i* is often pronounced as the consonant sound /y/:

alien	familiar	civilian	peculiar
billiards	million	billion	trillion
bunion	companion	onion	union

RESOURCES FOR TEACHERS

Bebko, A.R., Alexander, J., & Doucet, R. (n.d.). *LANGUAGE!: Roots* (2nd ed.). Longmont, CO: Sopris West.

Blanchard, C. (n.d.). *Word root series* (Level A: grades 4–6, Level B: grades 7 to adult). Pacific Grove, CA: Critical Thinking Books and Software.

Ehrlich, I. (1988). *Instant vocabulary* (Reissue ed.). New York: Pocket Books.

Fifer, N., & Flowers, N. (1990). *Vocabulary from classical roots.* Cambridge, MA: Educators Publishing Service.

Henry, M.K. (1990). *WORDS: Integrated decoding and spelling instruction based on word origin and word structure.* Austin, TX: PRO-ED.

Henry, M.K., & Redding, N.C. (1996). *Patterns for success in reading and spelling.* Austin, TX: PRO-ED.

Johnson, K., & Bayrd, P. (1998). *Megawords series.* Cambridge, MA: Educators Publishing Service.

Marcellaro, E.G., & Ostrovsky, G.R. (1988). *Verbal vibes series.* Sacramento, CA: Lumen Publications.

Michaels, B., & Laurita, R.E. (Eds.). *The Spelling Newsletter.* (Available from the editors, Post Office Box 1326, Camden, ME 04843)

Morgan, K. (2002). *Dynamic roots.* Albuquerque, NM: Morgan Dynamic Phonics.

Quinion, M. (2002). *Ologies and isms: Beginnings and endings of words.* Oxford, England: Oxford University Press.

Rome, P.D., & Osman, J.S. (2000). *Advanced language tool kit* [Teacher's manual and cards]. Cambridge, MA: Educators Publishing Service.

Steere, A., Peck, C.Z., & Kahn, L. (1971). *Solving language difficulties.* Cambridge, MA: Educators Publishing Service.

Wimer, D.B. (1994). *Word studies: A classical perspective. Vol. 1: Prefixes + roots + suffixes.* Richmond, VA: Author. (Available from the author, Post Office Box 5362, Richmond, VA 23220)

Dictionaries and Thesauri

The American Heritage Student Dictionary (for grades 6–9). (1998). Boston: Houghton Mifflin.

The American Heritage Student Thesaurus (for grades 7–10). (1999). Boston: Houghton Mifflin.

Barnhart, R.K. (Ed.). (1988). *The Barnhart dictionary of etymology.* New York: The H.W. Wilson Company.

Bollard, J.K. (1998). *Scholastic children's thesaurus.* New York: Scholastic.

Crutchfield, R.S. (1997). *English vocabulary quick reference: A comprehensive dictionary arranged by word roots.* Leesburg, VA: LexaDyne Publishing. (Also available on-line: http://www.quickreference.com/order.htm)

Halsey, W.D. (Ed.). (2001). *Macmillan dictionary for children.* New York: Simon & Schuster.

Latimer, J.P., & Nolting, K.S. (2001). *Simon & Schuster thesaurus for children* [ages 9–12]. New York: Simon & Schuster.

Web Sites

Critical Thinking Books and Software, www.criticalthinking.com

Explore English Words by Focusing on Words, www.wordexplorations.com

Morgan Dynamic Phonics, www.dynamicphonics.com

World Wide Words, www.worldwidewords.org/index.htm

GAME FOR STUDENTS

Johnson, P.F. (1999). *Word Scramble 2.* East Moline, IL: LinguiSystems.

Competent Readers

Extending the Latin and Greek Layers of Language

Many teachers and curriculum developers believe that reading instruction is the purview of the elementary school. Yet, many students need further strategies to analyze and comprehend more difficult words found in their high school and college textbooks and literature. Langer (2001) found that 60% of twelfth graders could not interpret or analyze text in more than superficial ways, according to the 1998 National Assessment of Educational Progress. The students were unable to make inferences or to understand figurative language. A California State University (2002) report on English and math proficiency noted that almost half of first-time freshmen admitted under normal admission standards in the fall of 2000 needed remediation in English. The students came from many ethnicities; unfortunately, no data were available on the number of students whose first language was not English.

Langer urged us to embrace Vygotsky's sociocultural framework, where learning occurs "within an environment in which both [teacher and student] can participate in thoughtful examination and discourse about language and content" (2001, p. 839). Langer noted the importance of providing students with challenging literary tasks, along with explicit teaching of skills. She found that in those English classrooms that performed highest, students learned how

---

Except where noted otherwise, the dictionary definitions in the activities in this chapter are paraphrased from *The American Heritage Dictionary* (2000).

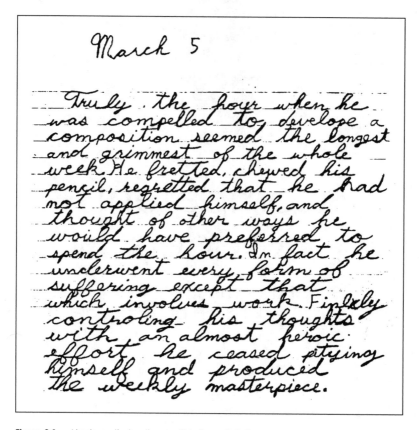

Figure 8.1.   Alan's postinstruction spelling from dictation.

language works in context: "[Students] were learning grammar, spelling, vo-cabulary, and organizational structure—sometimes in context but also with carefully planned activities that focused directly on the structure and use of language" (p. 856).

Remember Alan, whose seventh-grade writing sample is presented in the preceding chapter. After little more than 5 months' instruction, one hour per week, in the common affixes, Latin roots, and Greek combining forms, Alan provided another writing sample from dictation (see Figure 8.1).

During instruction, Alan did not work on these words directly; instead, he learned the important orthographic structures and rules. Beginning with a re-view of letter–sound correspondences and syllable patterns, Alan immediately began learning about affixes and roots. Notice also that Alan learned to use cur-sive writing. Using cursive was part of the instruction, and he balked at this ini-tially. Alan learned the linguistic information presented in preceding chapters. He also learned other less common Latin roots and Greek combining forms.

LESS COMMON LATIN ROOTS

After having learned the more common Latin affixes and roots and Greek combining forms suggested in Chapter 7, students are ready for less common forms. Such less common Latin roots include the following:

civ (citizen)

claim, clam (to declare, call out, or cry out)

claus, clois, clos, clud, clus (to shut or close)

corp, corpor (body)

crea (create)

dent (tooth)

dorm (to sleep)

fin, finis (end)

flu, fluc, fluv, flux (flowing)

forc, fort (strong)

grat, gre (thanks; pleasing)

grav, gravi (heavy)

hab, habit (to have or live)

hum, human (earth, ground, or man)

intellect, intellig (power to know and think)

join, junct (to join)

jud, judi, judic (judge)

jur, jus (law)

liber, liver (free)

lic, licit (permit)

loc, loqu (to speak)

luc, lum, lus (light)

matr, matri (mother)

numer (number)

patr, pater (father)

pict, picto (paint)

plac, plais (please)

plu, plur, plus (more)

portio (a part or a share)

poten, poss (power)

prim, prime (first)

punct (point or dot)

put (to think)

rect, recti (straight or right)

rog, roga (to ask or beg)

sat, satis (enough)

sign, signi (to sign, mark, or seal)

simil, simul (like or resembling)

sume, sump (to take, use, or waste)

tact, tag, tang, tig, ting (to touch)

tempo, tempor (time)

trib (to pay or bestow)

tui, tuit, tut (to guard or teach)

ultima (last)

vac (empty)

vale, vali, valu (strength, worth, or valor)

ver, veri (true or genuine)

vore (to devour)

Lesson formats for these roots are the same as presented in earlier chapters.

ACTIVITIES RELATED TO LESS COMMON LATIN ROOTS

Older students require more intellectually challenging activities to reinforce concepts and patterns. For example, older students may do some of the following.

Studying Shakespeare

Study the words of William Shakespeare. These words are notable for surviving for more than 400 years. Shakespeare used Anglo-Saxon words such as *lonely* and *bump* but also introduced Latin-based words such as *assassination, accommodation, reliance, dexterously, submerged,* and *obscene* and the Greek words *apostrophe* and *misanthrope* and many others (Klausner, 1990). Students can look for unfamiliar words in the works of Shakespeare and investigate their origin and meaning.

Comparing/Contrasting

Have students compare/contrast *luxuriant* and *luxurious.* "How are these words similar in meaning?" [*Both contain the root* luxor, *meaning* excess; *both are adjectives.*] "How are they different?" [Luxuriant *means* characterized by rich or profuse growth, *whereas* luxurious *means* fond of or given to luxury.]

Compare/contrast *ingenious* and *ingenuous.* What are their similarities? [*Both are adjectives.*] How do they differ? [*Although the roots look alike, they are different; therefore meaning differs.* Ingenious *comes from the Latin* ingenium *and means* inborn talent marked by inventive skill, imagination, or cleverness, *whereas* ingenuous *comes from Latin* ingenuus, *meaning* lacking in cunning or artless.]

Creating Word Webs

Have students make webs of words related to newly learned Latin roots such as *dent, poten,* or *dorm.*

Using Thematic Units

Thematic units provide students with listening, speaking, reading, and writing opportunities based on numerous topics. Teachers in the secondary grades can plan thematic units that enhance knowledge of Latin roots and Greek combining forms. For example, teachers might facilitate units on the environment, on citizenship, or on other topics related to Latin roots, such as the branches of government. (Several types of thematic units are discussed later in this chapter.) Students can read in their social studies textbook about the *judicial, legislative,* and *executive* branches and can identify the origin of these words and their meanings. [*All are Latin;* judicial *comes from* judic, *meaning* judge; legislative *comes from* legis, *meaning* law, *and* lator, *meaning* bearer *or* proposer; *and* executive *comes from* sequi, *meaning* to follow.] As students continue reading and complete further research, they can identify other words of Latin or Greek origin.

LESS COMMON GREEK COMBINING FORMS

Other Greek combining forms less common than those presented in Chapter 7 also require instruction. They include

drome, dromos (course or running)

dyn, dynamo (power, strength, or force)

eco (house or home)

ecto (outside, external, or beyond)

helio (sun)

hema, hemo (blood)

hypn, hypno (sleep)

lith, litho (stone)

log, logo, logue (speech or word; *logy,* meaning *study,* comes from this word family)

macro (large, long, or great)

morph (form, shape, or structure)

neo (new or recent)

nym, onym (name)

ortho (straight, correct, or upright)

pan (all)

phyll (leaf or leaves)

pneumon, pneuma (breath or lung)

proto (earliest, original, or first in time)

saur (lizard or serpent)

stereo (solid, firm, or hard)

zo, zoo (animal)

Not only will learning the Latin and Greek word parts enhance reading and spelling, but it will also enhance performance on SATs and other verbal achievement tests. (See Appendix H for words found in middle school and high school social studies and psychology textbooks.)

WORD WISDOM: A UNIQUE GREEK LETTER COMBINATION

The Greek grapheme *ph* is sometimes found before *th*. Usually, the *ph* and *th* occur in separate syllables, as in *diphthong, diphtheria, ophthalmology, exophthalmos, naphtha,* and *aphtha,* and are pronounced as /f/ and /th/, respectively. Sometimes, however, *ph* is followed by *th* in the syllable, especially in words denoting chemicals or disease, such as *phthalic, phthalein,* and *phthisic.* In this latter group of words, the letters *phth* are pronounced either as /th/ or as /t/.

ACTIVITIES RELATED TO
LESS COMMON GREEK COMBINING FORMS

Older students need activities to reinforce their learning of the less common Greek combining forms, much as they do for learning the less common Latin roots. The following activities provide opportunities for this kind of practice with Greek combining forms.

Adding Words to a Bulletin Board

Design bulletin boards where students can add words that contain the primary word parts listed on the boards. For example, Pete Bowers built a bulletin board with his fourth-grade students to show words containing the Greek combining form *graph* (see Figure 8.2).

Bowers used whole-class and individual brainstorming sessions with his students. Using dictionaries, students were able to come up with an amazing number of words that use the Greek form *graph:* 92 different words using 15 prefixes and 18 suffixes. The students studied the meanings of all the words. Students added rare words, found in a variety of texts, on a separate "challenge" list. These words included *paragraphic, graphitic, biogeography, biostratigraph,* and *orthograph.* (Can you guess the meaning of these words by looking at their parts?) Mr. Bowers sent a letter to parents describing the *graph* bulletin board and how it was formed. He encouraged students to explain this word work to their parents.

Exploring -*nym* Words

The Greek combining forms *nym* and *onym* mean *name.* Have students find as many words as possible ending in *nym* or *onym.* Ask them to use their dictionaries to define and give examples of the following words.

acronym   [*A word formed from the initial letters of a name or phrase, such as RADAR from **r**adio **d**etecting **a**nd **r**anging and WAC from **W**omen's **A**rmy **C**orps*]

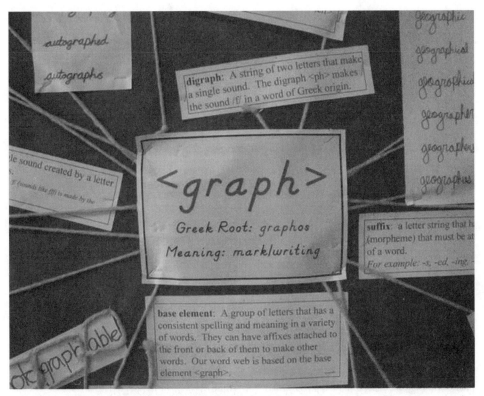

Figure 8.2. Part of Pete Bowers's class bulletin board of *graph* words. Students found 92 *graph* words using 15 prefixes and 18 suffixes. (Used by kind permission of Pete Bowers)

eponym [*A person whose name is or is thought to be the source of the name of something, such as a city or era. Romulus is the eponym of Rome.*]

pseudonym [*A fictitious name, especially a pen name. Samuel Clemens used the pseudonym Mark Twain.*]

antonym [*A word having a meaning opposite to that of another word. Hot and cold, tall and short, and sweet and sour are antonyms.*]

synonym [*A word having the same or nearly the same meaning as another word or words. Large and big, as well as run and jog, are synonyms.*]

paronym [*A cognate; a word derived from the same root as another; for example,* heal *is a paronym of* health.]

homonym [*One of two or more words that have the same sound and often the same spelling but differ in meaning; a synonym of the term* homophone. Bank, *a place where money is kept, and* bank, *an embankment, are homonyms.*]

tautonym   [*A scientific name in which the genus and the species names are the same. For example, the scientific name for one kind of green-finch is* Chloris chloris, *the bank swallow is* Riparia riparia, *the black rat is* Rattus rattus, *and the gorilla is* Gorilla gorilla.]

numeronyn   [*A telephone number that spells a word or words. For example, to purchase tickets for Stanford University athletic events, dial 1-800-BEATCAL. CAL denotes the rival University of California–Berkeley Bears.*]

Studying Unfamiliar Words

Select an unfamiliar word, such as *pterodactyl*. Ask students guiding questions such as the following.

"Analyze the word *pterodactyl*. What is its origin?" [*Greek*] "How do you know?" [*The* pt *and* y *for short* /ĭ/ *are clues; the word sounds scientific.*] "What are the two combining forms?" [ptero *and* dactyl] "What are the meanings of *ptero* and *dactyl*?" [Ptero *means* wing, *and* dactyl *means* digit *or* finger.] "In what subject area might you find this word?" [*history, archaeology, paleontology*] "Can you find other related words?" [*pterosaur, pteranodon, pteropod, dactylitis, dactylology, and so forth*]

Comparing/Contrasting *dermatology* and *psychology*

Have students compare/contrast the words *dermatology* and *psychology*. [*Both contain* ology, *meaning* study of, *as one combining form. The first combining forms differ; one is* derma, *meaning* skin, *and the other is* psych, *meaning* mind.] "What word origin do they share?" [*Greek*] "How are the words related?" [*Both are medical terms; both deal with people.*]

Exploring the Term *euphemism*

Have students analyze the word *euphemism*. "What is its part of speech?" [*noun*] "What is its meaning?" [*A mild, indirect, or vague term used in place of one considered harsh, blunt, or offensive*] "What are its parts and their meaning?" [Eu *means* good, pheme *means* speaking, *and* ism *is a noun suffix.*] "Give examples of several euphemisms." [pass away *for* die, sanitation worker *for* garbage collector, budget *for* cheap, reception centers *for* concentration camps in World War II]

Exploring the Term *etymology*

"What is the meaning of the term *etymology?* Find the etymology of the word *etymology.*"

Studying Manias and Phobias

Older students are often intrigued with learning *mania* and *phobia* words. See if students can figure out the meaning of the following manias:

Anglomania	monomania	bibliomania	pyromania
demonomania	dipsomania	Gallomania	kleptomania
theomania	logomania	melomania	

See how many of these phobias students can identify before checking in the dictionary. Students enjoy doing this type of exercise in teams.

arachnophobia	chromophobia	hydrophobia	pyrophobia
ichthyphobia	scriptophobia	agoraphobia	claustrophobia
kenophobia	tachophobia	Anglophobia	thermophobia
astrophobia	cyclophobia	limnophobia	toxiphobia
microphobia	verbophobia	auroraphobia	verminophobia

(See The Phobia List, http://www.phobialist.com, compiled by Fredd Culbertson, for more phobias.)

WORD WISDOM: INTERESTING *gram* WORDS

Common metric measures, such as kilogram and milligram, contain the Greek combining form *gram;* other *gram* words relate to written language:

pictogram: Images representing objects or ideas rather than words. Egyptian hieroglyphs are pictograms.

logogram (also called *ideogram*):   A sign or character representing a word. Chinese writing consists of logograms.

phonogram: A written character or symbol representing a common sound (e.g., *b* is a phonogram representing the phoneme /b/)

anagram: A word or phrase made by transposing or rearranging the letters of another word or phrase. For example, *dirty room* is an anagram for *dormitory.* Can you think of anagrams for *the Morse code* or for *slot machines*? [*here comes dots* and *cash lost in 'em*]

isogram: A word without repeated letters

pangram: A sentence that makes use of all the letters of the alphabet (from the Greek *pan*, meaning *all*, and *gram*, meaning *something written*). The most well-known pangram is the one used to study the typewriter or computer keyboard: *The quick brown fox jumps over a lazy dog.* Others include *By Jove, my quick study of lexicography won a prize* and *Pack my box with five dozen liquor jugs.*

epigram   A short expression or observation (often a poem) that is usually witty

WORD WISDOM: PALINDROMES

A *palindrome* is any word or phrase that is spelled the same forward and backward. *Palindrome* comes from the Greek combining forms *palin*, meaning *again* and *backwards*, and *dromos*, meaning *course* or *running*. Here are some palindromes:

deed	level	redder	noon	reviver
peep	Eve	civic	toot	Madam

must sell at tallest sum	senile felines	Anna
evil olive	never odd or even	Renner

Try to find other palindromes. Barbara Kingsolver's book *The Poisonwood Bible* has one character who speaks only in palindromes!

WORD WISDOM: PORTMANTEAU WORDS

The term *portmanteau* comes from the name of a large traveling case for carrying clothes. The term *portmanteau word* was invented by Lewis Carroll and can be found in *Alice Through the Looking Glass.* Portmanteau words are words formed by merging the sounds and meanings of two separate words. Common portmanteau words and their components include the following:

brunch	breakfast and lunch
chortle	chuckle and snort

bit	binary and digit
smog	smoke and fog
motel	motor and hotel
splatter	splash and spatter
squish	squirt and swish
squawk	squall and squeak
blurt	blow and spurt

THEMATIC UNITS

Thematic units are useful for integrating several content areas as students read, write, and speak on a variety of related topics. Several examples of possible units follow.

Calendar Unit

Students themselves often raise the question "Why are the last 4 months of the year, actually the 9th, 10th, 11th, and 12th months, named September, October, November, and December, the roots of which mean 7, 8, 9, and 10, respectively?" This question leads to some interesting research for the students to find out why, indeed. In their research they will find that the Roman calendar consisted of 10 months and 304 days. In 702 B.C.E., two more months were added, with Januarius as the first month and Februarius as the last month.

Julius Caesar, in 46 B.C.E., developed the Julian calendar of 12 months with January as the first month, February second, and so forth. The current Gregorian calendar, introduced in 1582 C.E., was modified slightly to add a leap year, but the order of months remained the same. This calendar is used throughout most of the world.

This unit examines interesting historical, mathematical, and linguistic concepts. Subunits based on the names of months and the days of the week can be designed. In English, the names of the months retain their Roman origin. Students can learn the Roman origins for the names of the months, such as Janus, god of beginning and endings, for January; Mars, the god of war, for March; Augustus, the first Roman emperor (who was originally called Sextilius), for August (the 6th month of the Roman calendar); and so forth.

The Romans associated a cycle of 7 days with the sun, the moon, and the five known planets (i.e., Sunday comes from *dies solis,* meaning *sun's day;* Monday comes from *dies lunae,* meaning *moon's day;* Saturday comes from *dies Saturni,* meaning *Saturn's day).* The other days of the week are based on Germanic names for Mars, Mercury, Jupiter, and Venus (i.e., Tuesday from *Tiw's day,* Wednesday from *Woden's day,* Thursday from *Thor's day,* and Friday from *Frigg's day).*

Unit on *An Exaltation of Larks*

Provide each student with a copy of *An Exaltation of Larks: The Ultimate Edition* by James Lipton (1968/1993). Lipton provided terms denoting crowds or flocks of animals, such as an *exaltation* of larks, a *herd* of swine, a *skulk* of foxes, a *nye* of pheasants, a *swarm* of eels, and a *gam* of whales. Most of these collective terms came to us from the 15th century, during the time of Middle English. Students can work in groups or individually study these terms. Lipton's book also includes terms for people, places, things, professions, sports, and medicine.

Dictionary Unit

Introduce high school students to a variety of dictionaries and reference sources. Have students look for similarities and differences in pronunciation, definition, and so forth. For example, use the word *bury* or *burial* as the target word. Various dictionaries list different pronunciations and meanings for each of these words. See, for example, *Webster's II New College Dictionary* (1995), *World Book Millennium 2000: The World Book Dictionary* (2000), and *Webster's Third New International Dictionary* (1981).

Ask students to read *The Professor and the Madman: A Tale of Murder, Insanity, and the Making of the Oxford English Dictionary,* by Simon Winchester (1998). This outstanding book tells the remarkable story of the writing of the *Oxford English Dictionary* and two of the extraordinary men who made it possible. Students will become immersed in new words, etymology, and an amazing tale.

Mythology Unit

Students can study Greek, Roman, German, and Scandinavian mythology. They can find the etymology of the word *mythology.* Students can define the common term in the term's root word, *myth*. Students can find the names of gods and goddesses prevalent in mythology, such as Dionysus, the Greek god of wine and grape growing; Vulcan, the Roman god of fire and craftsmanship; Frija, the Germanic goddess of marriage and fertility; and Thor, the Norse god of thunder. Students can research the battles, the objects of art, the symbols, and other key elements of these mythical tales.

Word Analysis in Advanced Thematic Units

Thematic units at this more advanced level contain words from all three major language origins. As students read and investigate, they can categorize the words in text as to the language of origin. For example, a unit on prehistoric times may include the following words:

Anglo-Saxon	*Latin*	*Greek*
earthquake	ancestors	tectonics
embedded	evolution	anthropology
hunter	extinct	geologist
tar pit	culture	archaeology
Stone Age	aggregate	dinosaur
spearhead	minerals	pterodactyl
toolmaker	volcano	technology
imprint	fossilize	paleoarchaeology

Other activities related to reading and spelling include looking up unknown words in a textbook's glossary or the dictionary; writing reports; reading supplemental texts; developing a time line; and contrasting related terms, such as *anthropologist, archaeologist,* and *paleoarchaeologist*.

NEW WORDS ENTERING THE ENGLISH LANGUAGE

Barnett noted that "it is clear that the English language in America today differs from that of the past primarily with respect to its vocabulary" (1965, p. 15). He observed that "its underlying architecture remains the same, and its mechanisms of inventions and expansion have not changed" (p. 15). The same is true today. New words and phrases are being coined, but they generally use familiar word parts or are proper names that become familiar due to world events. An examination of the fourth edition of *The American Heritage Dictio-*

nary (2000) reveals that many newly invented words have actually been formed by extension of the use of Latin and Greek word parts.

For example, Soukhanov (1995) described *compunication*, "a coupling of the technologies for transmission and manipulation of information" (p. 293), and *criticality*, "an item of hardware or a system on a spacecraft or on the rocket launching the spacecraft, for which there is no backup, the loss of failure of which will result in a catastrophic accident involving the loss of crew, craft, and payload" (p. 294). In these two terms, bases are combined or suffixes are added to form new words.

Barnett stated that "throughout the long history of the English tongue, the challenge of new concepts and experiences has repeatedly forced new words into being" (1965, p. 15). While learning more about the structure of written English and gaining new strategies for both reading and spelling words from *abecedarian* to *zymosis*, students will enhance their academic and personal success.

CONCLUSION

In writing this book, I hope I have conveyed the joys of learning to read and write words in the English language. When teachers and their students understand some of the historical forces influencing the development of English, they find that English is not a language of exceptions, but rather is a stable and learnable language. As Ramsden stated so well, "The English spelling system is tidy, behaves itself and has a high degree of order" (2000, p. 6).

The structure of the majority of English words is based on historical events and influences from the origin languages, primarily Anglo-Saxon, Latin, and Greek. I strongly encourage teachers to move beyond phonics at the Anglo-Saxon layer of language, to the Latin affixes and roots and Greek combining forms that are used in upper elementary and secondary texts. Without learning the contributions of the Latin and Greek languages, students will be unable to read text much beyond the primary grade level.

As teachers present the letter–sound correspondences, affixes, roots, and combining forms, students need numerous opportunities to read and spell words. Just as in learning to play a musical instrument or a new sport successfully, students need extensive practice while learning to read and spell. My hope is that this book gives teachers and tutors the background necessary to teach decoding and spelling, along with effective instructional strategies and activities for student practice.

RESOURCES FOR TEACHERS AND STUDENTS

See also the resources at the end of Chapter 7.

Calendar Unit

Burns, M. (1987). The calendar story. In V.A. Arnold & C.B. Smith (Eds.), *Tapestries* (pp. 528–537). New York: Macmillan.

Calendar. (2002). *Columbia encyclopedia* (6th ed., pp. 421–422). New York: Columbia University Press. (Also available online at http://www.bartleby.com/65/ [choose "Search:" and select "Entry Words," type "calendar" in the box to the right, and click "Go"])

Calendars. (1992). *The new encyclopedia Britannica* (5th ed., Vol. 2, p. 741).

Calendars. (2002). *World book* (Vol. 3, pp. 28–32). Chicago: World Book.

Unit on *An Exaltation of Larks*

Lipton, J. (1993). *An exaltation of larks: The ultimate edition* (Rev. ed.). New York: Penguin. (Original work published 1968)

Dictionary Unit

Winchester, S. (1998). *The professor and the madman: A tale of murder, insanity, and the making of the Oxford English Dictionary.* New York: HarperCollins.

High school students can use almost all college and adult dictionaries. One possible dictionary for the transition from children's to adult dictionaries is
Merriam-Webster's intermediate dictionary. (1999). Springfield, MA: Merriam-Webster.

Mythology Unit

Cotterell, A. (1989). *The Macmillan illustrated encyclopedia of myths and legends.* New York: Macmillan.

Graves, R. (1988). *The Greek myths.* Mount Kisco, NY: Moyer Bell.

Mythology. (2002). *World book* (Vol. 13, pp. 973–990). Chicago: World Book.

Vinge, J.D. (1999). *The Random House book of Greek myths.* New York: Random House.

Web Sites

Explore English Words by Focusing on Words, www.wordexplorations.com
A.Word.A.Day Home Page, www.wordsmith.org/awad/index.html
The WordsWorth Compendium, www.dictionary-thesaurus.com

References

Abbott, S., & Berninger, V. (1999). It's never too late to remediate: A developmental approach to teaching word recognition. *Annals of Dyslexia, 49,* 223–250.

Adams, M.J. (1990). *Beginning to read: Thinking and learning about print.* Cambridge, MA: The MIT Press.

Adams, M.J., Foorman, B.R., Lundberg, I., & Beeler, T. (1998). *Phonemic awareness in young children: A classroom curriculum.* Baltimore: Paul H. Brookes Publishing Co.

The American heritage dictionary (4th ed.). (2000). Boston: Houghton Mifflin.

The American heritage student dictionary. (1998). Boston: Houghton Mifflin.

American Speech-Language-Hearing Association. (2002). *How does your child hear and talk?* Retrieved January 3, 2003, from http://www.asha.org/speech/development/dev_milestones.cfm

Anderson, R.C., Hiebert, E.H., Scott, J.A., & Wilkinson, I.A.G. (Eds.). (1985). *Becoming a nation of readers: The report of the Commission on Reading.* Washington, DC: National Academy of Education, Commission on Education and Public Policy.

Anderson, R.C., & Nagy, W.E. (1992). The vocabulary conundrum. *American Educator, 16*(4), 14–18, 44–47.

Arnbak, E., & Elbro, C. (2000). The effects of morphological awareness training on the reading spelling skills of young dyslexics. *Scandinavian Journal of Educational Research, 44*(3), 229–251.

Ayto, J. (1999). *Twentieth century words.* New York: Oxford University Press.

Badian, N. (1997). Dyslexia and the double deficit hypothesis. *Annals of Dyslexia, 47,* 69–87.

Ball, E.W. (1993). Phonological awareness: What's important and to whom? *Reading and Writing, 5*(2), 141–160.

Balmuth, M. (1982). *The roots of English.* Timonium, MD: York Press.

Balmuth, M. (1992). *The roots of phonics.* Timonium, MD: York Press.

Barnett, L. (1962, March 2). The English language. *LIFE, 52*(9), 74–77, 79–80, 83.

Barnett, L. (1964). *The treasure of our tongue.* New York: Alfred A. Knopf.

Barnett, L. (1965). History of the English language. *LIFE Educational Reprints,* Reprint 54.

Barnhart, R.K. (Ed.). (1988). *The Barnhart dictionary of etymology.* New York: H.W. Wilson Company.

Bear, D. (1992). The prosody of oral reading and stage of word knowledge. In S. Templeton & D. Bear (Eds.), *Development of orthographic knowledge and the foundations of literacy: A memorial Festschrift for Edmund H. Henderson* (pp. 137–186). Mahwah, NJ: Lawrence Erlbaum Associates.

Beck, I.L., McKeown, M.G., & Kucan, L. (2002). *Bringing words to life.* New York: Guilford Press.

Berninger, V.W. (2000). Dyslexia the invisible, treatable disorder: The story of Einstein's Ninja turtles. *Learning Disability Quarterly, 23*(3), 175–195.

Berninger, V.W., Nagy, W.E., Carlisle, J., Thomson, J., Hoffer, D., Abbott, S., Abbot, R., Richards, T., & Aylward, E. (in press). Effective treatment for dyslexics in grades 4–6: Behavioral and brain evidence. In B. Foorman (Ed.), *Preventing and remediating reading disabilities: Bringing science to scale.* Timonium, MD: York Press.

Blachman, B.A., Ball, E.W., Black, R., & Tangel, D.M. (2000). *Road to the code: A phonological awareness program for young children.* Baltimore: Paul H. Brookes Publishing Co.

Blok, H., Oostdam, R., Otter, M.E., & Overmaat, M. (2002). Computer-assisted instruction in support of beginning reading instruction: A review. *Review of Educational Research, 72*(1), 101–130.

Bodmer, F. (1944). *The loom of language.* New York: W.W. Norton.

Bowers, P.G., Sunseth, K., & Golden, J. (1999). The route between rapid naming and reading progress. *Scientific Studies in Reading, 3*(1), 31–53.

Bowers, P.G., & Wolf, M. (1993). *A double-deficit hypothesis for developmental reading disorders.* Paper presented at the biennial meeting of the Society for Research in Child Development, New Orleans.

Brady, S., & Moats, L. (1997). *Informed instruction for reading success: Foundations for teacher preparation* [A position paper of The International Dyslexia Association]. Baltimore: The International Dyslexia Association.

Brown, J.I. (1947). Reading and vocabulary: 14 master words. In M.J. Herzberg (Ed.), *Word study, 1–4.* Springfield, MA: G & C Merriam.

Bruck, M., & Waters, G.S. (1990). An analysis of the component spelling and reading skills of good readers–good spellers, good readers–poor spellers, and poor readers–poor spellers. In T.H. Carr & B.A. Levy (Eds.), *Reading and its development: Component skills approaches* (pp. 161–206). San Diego: Academic Press.

Butler, K.G., & Silliman, E.R. (2002). *Speaking, reading and writing in children with learning disabilities.* Mahwah, NJ: Lawrence Erlbaum Associates.

Calfee, R.C., & Baldwin, L.S., Chambliss, M., Curley, R., Henry, M., Munson, R., Ramey, D.R., et al. (1981–1984). *The book: Components of reading instruction.* Unpublished manuscript, Stanford University, California.

Calfee, R.C., & Henry, M.K. (1986). Project READ: An inservice model for training classroom teachers in effective reading instruction. In J.V. Hoffman (Ed.), *The effective teaching of reading: Research into practice* (pp. 199–229). Newark, DE: International Reading Association.

Calfee, R.C., Henry, M.K., & Funderburg, J.A. (1988). A model for school change. In S.J. Samuel & P.D. Pearson (Eds.), *Building exemplary reading programs and initiating change* (pp. 120–141). Newark, DE: International Reading Association.

California State University. (2002). *Percentage of freshmen's proficiency in English and math increases after completing courses at CSU.* Retrieved January 6, 2003, from http://www.calstate.edu/PA/news/remedial02.shtml

Carlisle, J.F. (1987). The use of morphological knowledge in spelling derived forms by learning-disabled and normal students. *Annals of Dyslexia, 37*, 90–108.

Carlisle, J.F. (1995). Morphological awareness and early reading achievement. In L.B. Feldman (Ed.), *Morphological aspects of language processing* (pp. 189–209). Mahwah, NJ: Lawrence Erlbaum Associates.

Carney, E. (1994). *A survey of English spelling.* London: Routledge.

Catts, H., & Kamhi, A. (1999). *Language and reading disabilities.* Needham Heights, MA: Allyn & Bacon.

Chall, J.S. (1967). *Learning to read: The great debate.* New York: McGraw-Hill.

Chall, J.S. (1983). *Stages of reading development.* New York: McGraw-Hill.

Chall, J.S., & Popp, H.M. (1996). *Teaching and assessing phonics.* Cambridge, MA: Educators Publishing Service.

Chall, J.S., & Squire, J.R. (1991). The publishing industry and textbooks. In R. Barr, M. L. Kamil, P. Mosenthal, & P.D. Pearson (Eds.), *Handbook of reading research* (Vol. 2, pp. 120–146). New York: Longman.

Cicci, R. (1995). *What's wrong with me?: Learning disabilities at home and school.* Timonium, MD: York Press.

Claiborne, R. (1983). *Our marvelous native tongue: The life and times of the English language.* New York: Times Books.

Cooper, E.K., Blackwood, P.E., Boeschen, J.A., Giddings, M.G., & Carin, A.A. (1985). *HBJ SCIENCE* (Purple ed.). Orlando, FL: Harcourt.

Corson, D. (1985). *The lexical bar.* Oxford: Pergamon Press.

Coulmas, F. (1996). *The Blackwell encyclopedia of writing systems.* Malden, MA: Blackwell Publishers.

Denckla, M., & Rudel, R. (1976). Rapid automatized naming (R.A.N.): Dyslexia differentiation from other learning disabilities. *Neuropsychologia, 14,* 471–479.

DeStefano, J.S. (1972). *Some parameters of register in adult and child speech.* Louvain, Belgium: Institute of Applied Linguistics.

Dickinson, D.K. (2001). Putting the pieces together: Impact of preschool on children's language and literacy development in kindergarten. In D.K. Dickinson & P.O. Tabors (Eds.), *Beginning literacy with language: Young children learning at home and school* (pp. 257–287). Baltimore: Paul H. Brookes Publishing Co.

Dickinson, D.K., & Tabors, P.O. (Eds.). (2001). *Beginning literacy with language: Young children learning at home and school.* Baltimore: Paul H. Brookes Publishing Co.

Downing, J. (1979). *Reading and reasoning.* New York: Springer-Verlag.

Ehri, L.C. (1985). Effects of printed language acquisition on speech. In D.R. Olson, N. Torrance, & A. Hildyard (Eds.), *Literacy, language, and learning* (pp. 333–367). Cambridge, England: Cambridge University Press.

Ehri, L.C. (1987). Learning to read and spell words. *Journal of Reading Behavior, 19,* 5–31.

Ehri, L. (1989). The development of spelling knowledge and its role in reading acquisition and reading disability. *Journal of Learning Disabilities, 22,* 356–365.

Ehri, L. (1991). Development of the ability to read words. In R. Barr, M. Kamil, P. Mosenthal, & P.D. Pearson (Eds.), *Handbook of reading research* (Vol. 2, pp. 383–417). New York: Longman.

Ehri, L. (1998). Research on learning to read and spell: A personal-historical perspective. *Scientific Studies in Reading, 2*(2), 97–114.

Ehri, L., & Soffer, A.G. (1999). Graphophonemic awareness development in elementary students. *Scientific Studies in Reading, 3*(1), 1–30.

Elbro, C., & Arnbak, E. (1996). The role of morpheme recognition and morphological awareness in dyslexia. *Annals of Dyslexia, 46,* 209–240.

Elkind, J. (1998). Computer reading machines for poor readers. *Perspectives, 24*(2), 9–14.

Felton, R.H. (1993). Effects of instruction on the decoding skills of children with phonological-processing problems. *Journal of Learning Disabilities, 26*(9), 583–589.

Fernald, G.M., & Keller, H. (1921). The effect of kinaesthetic factors in the development of word recognition in the case of non-readers. *Journal of Educational Research, 4,* 355–377.

Fielding-Barnsley, R. (1999). How preschools can contribute to identifying and helping children at risk for dyslexia. *Perspectives, 25*(4), 6–9.

Firmage, R.A. (1993). *The alphabet ABECEDARIUM.* Boston: David R. Godine.

Flavell, J. (1985). *Cognitive development* (2nd ed.). Upper Saddle River, NJ: Prentice-Hall.

Foorman, B.R., Francis, D.J., Beeler, T., Winikates, D., & Fletcher, J.M. (1997). Early interventions for children with reading problems: Study designs and preliminary findings. *Learning Disabilities, 8,* 63–71.

Forrest-Pressley, D.L., & Waller, T.G. (1984). *Cognition, metacognition, and reading.* New York: Springer-Verlag.

Frith, U. (Ed.). (1980). *Cognitive processes in spelling.* London: Academic Press.

Fromkin, V., & Rodman, R. (1998). *An introduction to language* (6th ed.). Orlando, FL: Harcourt.

Gillingham, A., & Stillman, B.W. (1956). *Remedial training for children with specific disability in reading, spelling and penmanship* (5th ed.). Cambridge, MA: Educators Publishing Service.

Gillingham, A., & Stillman, B.W. (1997). *The Gillingham manual: Remedial training for children with specific disability in reading, spelling and penmanship* (8th ed.). Cambridge, MA: Educators Publishing Service.

Goodman, K. (1967). Reading: A psycholinguistic guessing game. *Journal of the Reading Specialist, 6*(1), 126–135.

Goodman, K. (1976). Reading: A psycholinguistic guessing game. In H. Singer & R. Ruddell (Eds.), *Theoretical models and processes of reading* (2nd ed., pp. 497–508). Newark, DE: International Reading Association.

Gough, P.B., & Tunmer, W.E. (1986). Decoding, reading, and reading disability. *Remedial and Special Education, 7*(1), 6–10.

Goulden, R., Nation, P., & Read, J. (1990). How large can a receptive vocabulary be? *Applied Linguistics, 11*(4), 341–363.

Groff, P. (1971). *The syllable: Its nature and pedagogical usefulness.* Portland, OR: Northwest Regional Educational Laboratory.

Hammill, D.D., Mather, N., Allen, E.A., & Roberts, R. (2002). Using semantics, grammar, phonology, and rapid naming tasks to predict word identification. *Journal of Learning Disabilities, 35*(2), 121–136.

Hanna, P.R., Hodges, R.E., & Hanna, J.S. (1971). *Spelling: Structure and strategies.* Boston: Houghton Mifflin.

Hart, B., & Risley, T.R. (1995). *Meaningful differences in the everyday experience of young American children.* Baltimore: Paul H. Brookes Publishing Co.

Henderson, E.H. (1990). *Teaching spelling* (2nd ed.). Boston: Houghton Mifflin.

Henderson, L. (1982). *Orthography and word recognition in reading.* London: Academic Press.

Henderson, L. (1985). Toward a psychology of morphemes. In A.W. Ellis (Ed.), *Progress in the psychology of language* (Vol. 2, pp. 15–72). Mahwah, NJ: Lawrence Erlbaum Associates.

Henry, M.K. (1988a). Beyond phonics: Integrated decoding and spelling instruction based on word origin and structure. *Annals of Dyslexia, 38,* 259–275.

Henry, M.K. (1988b). Understanding English orthography: Assessment and instruction for decoding and spelling. *Dissertation Abstracts International, 48,* 2841A. (University Microfilms No. 8800951)

Henry, M.K. (1989). Children's word structure knowledge: Implications for decoding and spelling instruction. *Reading and Writing: An Interdisciplinary Journal, 2,* 135–152.

Henry, M.K. (1990). *WORDS: Integrated decoding and spelling instruction based on word origin and word structure.* Austin, TX: PRO-ED.

Henry, M.K. (1993). Morphological structure: Latin and Greek roots and affixes as upper grade code strategies. *Reading and Writing, 5*(2), 227–241.

Henry, M.K. (1997). The decoding/spelling curriculum: Integrated decoding and spelling instruction from pre-school to early secondary school. *Dyslexia, 3*, 178–189.

Henry, M.K. (1998). *Just the facts series: Multisensory teaching.* Baltimore: The International Dyslexia Association.

Henry, M.K. (1999). A short history of the English language. In J.R. Birsh (Ed.), *Multisensory teaching of basic language skills* (pp. 119–140). Baltimore: Paul H. Brookes Publishing Co.

Henry, M.K., Calfee, R.C., & Avelar-LaSalle, R.A. (1989). A structural approach to decoding and spelling. In S. McCormick & J. Zutell (Eds.), *Thirty-eighth yearbook of the National Reading Conference* (pp. 155–163). Chicago: National Reading Conference.

Henry, M.K., & Redding, N.C. (1996). *Patterns for success in reading and spelling.* Austin, TX: PRO-ED.

Henshilwood, C.S., d'Errico, F., Yates, R., Jacobs, Z., Tribolo, C., Duller, G.A.T., Mercier, N., Sealy, J.C., Valladas, H., Watts, I., & Wintle, A.G. (2002). Emergence of modern human behavior: Middle stone age engravings from South Africa. *Science, 295*, 1278–1280.

Holdaway, D. (1986). The visual face of experience and language: A metalinguistic excursion. In D.B. Yaden, Jr., & S. Templeton (Eds.), *Metalinguistic awareness and beginning literacy* (pp. 65–78). Portsmouth, NH: Heinemann.

King, D.H. (2000). *English isn't crazy!* Timonium, MD: York Press.

Klausner, J.C. (1990). *Talk about English: How words travel and change.* New York: Thomas Y. Crowell.

Krensky, S. (1996). *Breaking into print: Before and after the invention of the printing press.* Toronto: Little, Brown.

Langer, J.A. (2001). Beating the odds: Teaching middle and high school students to read and write well. *American Education Research Journal, 38*(4), 837–880.

Lederer, R. (1991). *The miracle of language.* New York: Pocket Books.

Liberman, I.Y. (1973). Segmentation of the spoken word and reading acquisition. *Bulletin of the Orton Society, 23*, 65–77.

Liberman, I.Y., & Liberman, A.M. (1990). Whole language vs. code emphasis: Underlying assumptions and their implications for reading instruction. *Annals of Dyslexia, 40*, 51–78.

Liberman, I.Y., & Mann, V. (1981). Should reading instruction vary with the sex of the child? In A. Ansara, N. Geschwind, A. Galaburda, M. Albert, & N. Gartrell (Eds.), *Sex differences in dyslexia* (pp. 151–167). Baltimore: The International Dyslexia Association.

Liberman, I.Y., & Shankweiler, D. (1991). Phonology and beginning reading: A tutorial. In L. Rieben & C.A. Perfetti (Eds.), *Learning to read: Basic research and its implications* (pp. 3–17). Mahwah, NJ: Lawrence Erlbaum Associates.

Liberman, I.Y., Shankweiler, D., Fischer, F.W., & Carter, B. (1974). Explicit syllable and phoneme segmentation in the young child. *Journal of Experimental Child Psychology, 18*, 201–212.

Lipton, J. (1993). *An exaltation of larks: The ultimate edition* (Rev. ed.). New York: Penguin. (Original work published 1968)

Logan, R.K. (1986). *The alphabet effect.* New York: St. Martin's Press.

Lyon, G.R. (1995). Research initiatives in learning disabilities: Contributions from scientists supported by the National Institute of Child Health and Human Development. *Journal of Child Neurology, 10*, 120–126.

Lyon, G.R. (1996). The future of children: Learning disabilities. *Special Education for Students with Disabilities, 6*(1), 54–76.

Lyon, G.R. (1999). In celebration of science in the study of reading development, reading difficulties, and reading instruction: The NICHD perspective. *Issues in Education: Contributions from Educational Psychology, 5*, 85–115.

Lyon, G.R., Fletcher, J.M., & Barnes, M.C. (2003). Learning disabilities. In E.J. Mash & R.A. Barkley (Eds.), *Child psychopathology* (2nd ed., pp. 520–588). New York: Guilford Press.

Male, M. (2003). *Technology for inclusion* (4th ed.). Boston: Allyn & Bacon.

Manguel, A. (1996). *A history of reading.* New York: Viking.

McIntyre, C., & Pickering, J. (1995). *Clinical studies of multisensory structured language education for students with dyslexia and related disorders.* Salem, OR: International Multisensory Structured Language Education Council.

Moats, L. (1994). The missing foundation in teacher education: Knowledge of the structure of spoken and written language. *Annals of Dyslexia, 44,* 81–102.

Moats, L.C. (1995). *Spelling: Development, disability, and instruction.* Timonium, MD: York Press.

Moats, L.C. (2000). *Speech to print: Language essentials for teachers.* Baltimore: Paul H. Brookes Publishing Co.

Moats, L.C. (2003). *Speech to print workbook: Language exercises for teachers.* Baltimore: Paul H. Brookes Publishing Co.

National Reading Panel. (2000). *Teaching children to read: An evidence-based assessment of the scientific research literature on reading and its implications for reading instruction* (NIH Publication No. 00-4754). Washington, DC: U.S. Government Printing Office.

Nist, J. (1966). *A structural history of English.* New York: St. Martin's Press.

Orton, J.L. (1966). The Orton-Gillingham approach. In J. Money (Ed.), *The disabled reader: Education of the dyslexic child.* Baltimore: Johns Hopkins University Press.

Orton, S.T. (1937). *Reading, writing, and speech problems in children.* New York: W.W. Norton.

Paulesu, E., Démonet, J.-F., Fazio, F., McCrory, E., Chanoine, V., Brunswick, N., Cappa, S.F., Cossu, G., Habib, M., Frith, C.D., & Frith, U. (2001). Dyslexia: Cultural diversity and biological unity. *Science, 291,* 2165–2167.

Perfetti, C. (1984). Reading acquisition and beyond: Decoding includes cognition. *American Journal of Education, 93,* 40–60.

Perfetti, C. (1985). *Reading ability.* New York: Oxford University Press.

Perfetti, C. (1986). Continuities in reading acquisition, reading skill and reading disability. *Remedial and Special Education, 7(1),* 11–21.

Pratt, C., & Grieve, R. (1984). The development of metalinguistic awareness: An introduction. In W. Tunmer, C. Pratt, & M. Herriman (Eds.), *Metalinguistic awareness in children* (pp. 2–11). New York: Springer-Verlag.

Pressley, M. (1998). *Reading instruction that works: The case for balanced teaching.* New York: The Guilford Press.

Quirk, R. (1974). *The linguist and the English language.* London: Arnold.

Ramsden, M. (2001). *The user's self-training manual: The essential reference for real English spelling* (Available from the author, http://perso.wanadoo.fr/melvyn/spelling/manual.html)

Raskind, M. (1998). Assistive technology for individuals with learning disabilities: How far have we come? *Perspectives, 24(2),* 20–26.

Read, C. (1971). Pre-school children's knowledge of English phonology. *Harvard Educational Review, 41(1),* 1–34.

Reid, J.F. (1966). Learning to think about reading. *Educational Research, 9,* 56–62.

Sampat, P. (2001, May–June). Last words. *World-Watch,* 34–40.

Scanlon, D.M., & Vellutino, F.R. (1996). Prerequisite skills, early instruction and success in first grade reading. *Mental and Developmental Disabilities Research Reviews, 2,* 54–63.

Scarborough, H. (1998). Early identification of children at risk for reading disabilities: Phonological awareness and some other promising predictors. In B. Shapiro, P. Accardo, & A. Capute (Eds.), *Specific reading disability: A view of the spectrum* (pp. 75–119). Timonium, MD: York Press.

Seidenburg, M.S., & McClelland, J.L. (1989). A distributed developmental model of word recognition and naming. *Psychological Review, 96*(4), 523–568.

Singson, M., Mahony, D., & Mann, V. (2000). Reading ability and sensitivity to morphological relations. *Reading and Writing: An Interdisciplinary Journal, 12,* 191–218.

Slingerland, B.H. (1994a). *Basics in scope and sequence of a multi-sensory approach to language arts for specific language disability children: A guide for primary teachers* (Book 2, Rev. ed.). Cambridge, MA: Educators Publishing Service.

Slingerland, B.H. (1994b). *A multi-sensory approach to language arts for specific language disability children: A guide for elementary teachers* (Book 3, Rev. ed.). Cambridge, MA: Educators Publishing Service.

Slingerland, B.H. (1996). *A multi-sensory approach to language arts for specific language disability children: A guide for primary teachers* (Book 1). Cambridge, MA: Educators Publishing Service.

Smelt, E. (1976). *Speak, spell and read English.* Melbourne: Longman Australia.

Snow, C.E., Burns, M.S., & Griffin, P. (Eds.). (1998). *Preventing reading difficulties in young children.* Washington, DC: National Academy Press.

Soukhanov, A.H. (1995). *Word watch: The stories behind the words of our lives.* New York: Henry Holt & Co.

Stahl, S.A., & Miller, P.D. (1989). Whole language and language experiences approaches for beginning reading. *Review of Educational Research, 59,* 87–116.

Stanback, M.L. (1992). Syllable and rime patterns for teaching reading: Analysis of a frequency-based vocabulary of 17,602 words. *Annals of Dyslexia, 42,* 196–221.

Stanovich, K.E. (1980). Toward an interactive-compensatory model of individual differences in the development of reading fluency. *Reading Research Quarterly, 16,* 32–71.

Stanovich, K.E. (1986). Matthew effects in reading: Some consequences of individual differences in the acquisition of literacy. *Reading Research Quarterly, 21,* 360–407.

Stanovich, K.E. (1996). Romance and reality. *The Reading Teacher, 47,* 280–291.

Stanovich, K.E., West, R.F., & Feeman, D.J. (1981). A longitudinal study of sentence context effects in second-grade children: Tests of an interactive-compensatory model. *Journal of Experimental Child Psychology, 32,* 185–199.

Steere, A., Peck, C.Z., & Kahn, L. (1971). *Solving language difficulties.* Cambridge, MA: Educators Publishing Service.

Tangel, D.M., & Blachman, B.A. (1995). Effect of phoneme awareness instruction on the invented spelling of first-grade children: A one-year follow-up. *Journal of Reading Behavior, 27,* 153–185.

Templeton, S. (1986). Metalinguistic awareness: A synthesis and beyond. In D.B. Yaden, Jr., & S. Templeton (Eds.), *Metalinguistic awareness and beginning literacy* (pp. 293–309). Portsmouth, NH: Heinemann.

Templeton, S. (1995). *Children's literacy: Contexts for meaningful learning.* Boston: Houghton Mifflin.

Templeton, S., & Morris, D. (2002). Theory and research into practice: Questions teachers ask about spelling. *Reading Research Quarterly, 34,* 102–112.

Torgesen, J.K. (2000). Individual differences in response to early intervention in reading: The lingering problem of treatment resisters. *Learning Disability Research and Practice, 15,* 55–64.

Torgesen, J.K., Wagner, R.K., & Rashotte, C.A. (1997). Prevention and remediation of severe reading disabilities: Keeping the end in mind. *Scientific Studies in Reading, 1*(3), 217–234.

Treiman, R. (1993). *Beginning to spell: A study of first-grade children.* New York: Oxford University Press.

Tunmer, W.E., & Herriman, M. (1984). The development of metalinguistic awareness: A conceptual overview. In W. Tunmer, C. Pratt, & M. Herriman (Eds.), *Metalinguistic awareness in children* (pp. 12–35). New York: Springer-Verlag.

Venezky, R. (1999). *The American way of spelling.* New York: Guilford Press.

Webster's new universal unabridged dictionary (2nd ed.). (1983). New York: Simon & Schuster.

Webster's third new international dictionary. (1981). Springfield: Merriam-Webster.

Webster's II new college dictionary. (1995). Boston: Houghton Mifflin.

West, R.F., & Stanovich, K.E. (1978). Automatic contextual facilitation in readers of three ages. *Child Development, 49,* 717–727.

West, T. (1998). Words to images: Technological change redefines educational goals. *Perspectives, 24*(2), 27–31.

Westbrook, A. (2002). *Hip hoptionary.* New York: Harlem Moon-Broadway.

White, T.G., Sowell, J., & Yanagihara, A. (1989). Teaching elementary students to use word-part clues. *The Reading Teacher, 42,* 302–308.

Winchester, S. (1998). *The professor and the madman: A tale of murder, insanity, and the making of the Oxford English Dictionary.* New York: HarperCollins.

Wise, B.W. (1998). Computers and research in learning disabilities. *Perspectives, 24*(2), 4–6.

Wise, B.W., Olson, R.K., & Ring, J. (1997). Teaching phonological awareness with and without the computer. In C. Hulme & M. Snowling (Eds.), *Dyslexia: Biology, cognition and intervention* (pp. 254–275). London: Whurr Publishers.

Wolf, M. (1991). Naming speed and reading: The contribution of the cognitive sciences. *Reading Research Quarterly, 26*(2), 123–141.

Wolf, M., & Katzer-Cohen, T. (2001). Reading fluency and its intervention. *Scientific Studies in Reading, 5*(3), 211–239.

Wolf, M., Miller, L., & Donnelly-Adams, K. (2000). Retrieval, Automaticity, Vocabulary Elaboration, Orthography (RAVE-O): A comprehensive fluency-based reading intervention program. *Journal of Learning Disabilities, 33,* 375–386.

World Book millennium 2000: The World Book dictionary. (2000). Chicago: World Book.

Yaden, D.B., Jr., & Templeton, S. (1986). Metalinguistic awareness: An etymology. In D.B. Yaden, Jr., & S. Templeton (Eds.), *Metalinguistic awareness and beginning literacy* (pp. 3–10). Portsmouth, NH: Heinemann.

Appendices

Surveys of Language Knowledge

The following surveys of language knowledge are intended to help teachers become aware of their own strengths and weaknesses. The surveys vary in difficulty and may challenge even experienced teachers who may already have a strong background in language structure. A word of caution, however: The questions and the way they are posed require a deeper and more explicit level of knowledge than many "teacher tests" that are used to test superficial knowledge of phonics. Critics have argued that such knowledge is not required to teach reading. Those professionals who have deepened their knowledge, however, will be better at explaining concepts, individualizing instruction, choosing examples, and making language study come alive even for children who are struggling.

From Moats, L.C. (2003). *Speech to print workbook: Language exercises for teachers* (pp. 1–10). Baltimore: Paul H. Brookes Publishing Co.; adapted by permission.

Answers appear at the end of Appendix A.

BRIEF SURVEY OF LANGUAGE KNOWLEDGE

Phoneme Counting

Count the number of speech sounds or phonemes that you perceive in each of the following spoken words. Remember, the speech sounds may not be equivalent to the letters. For example, the word *spoke* has four phonemes: /s/, /p/, /ō/, and /k/. Write the number of phonemes to the right of each word.

thrill	ring	shook
does	fix	wrinkle
sawed	quack	know

Syllable Counting

Count the number of syllables that you perceive in each of the following words. For example, the word *higher* has two syllables, the word *threat* has one, and the word *physician* has three. Write the number of syllables to the right of each word.

cats	capital	shirt
spoil	decidedly	banana
recreational	lawyer	walked

Phoneme Matching

Read the first word in each line and note the sound that is represented by the underlined letter or letter cluster. Then select the word or words on the line that contain the same sound.

1. pu<u>sh</u>   although   sugar   duty   pump
2. w<u>eigh</u>   pie   height   raid   friend
3. doe<u>s</u>   miss   nose   votes   rice
4. in<u>t</u>end this   whistle baked   batch
5. ri<u>ng</u>   sink   handle   signal pinpoint

From *Speech to Print Workbook: Language Exercises for Teachers* by Louisa Cook Moats.
Copyright © 2003 by Paul H. Brookes Publishing Co. • www.brookespublishing.com • 1-800-638-3775
Do not reproduce without permission of Paul H. Brookes Publishing Co.

Recognition of Sound–Symbol Correspondence

Find in the following words the letters and letter combinations that correspond to each speech sound in the word. For example, the word stress has five phonemes, each of which is represented by a letter or letter group: s / t / r / e / ss. Now try these:

b e s t	f r e s h	s c r a t c h
t h o u g h	l a u g h e d	m i d d l e
c h i r p	q u a i n t	

Definitions and Concepts

Write a definition or explanation for each of the following:

Vowel sound (vowel phoneme)

Consonant digraph

Prefix

Inflectional (grammatical) morpheme

Why is phonemic awareness important?

How is decoding skill related to reading fluency and comprehension?

COMPREHENSIVE SURVEY
OF LANGUAGE KNOWLEDGE (FORM A)

1. From the list below, find an example of each of the following (answer will be a word or part of a word):

   Inflected verb

   Compound noun

   Bound root

   Derivational suffix

   Greek combining form

   peaches   incredible   slowed   although   shameful

   bicycle   neuropsychology   sandpaper   vanish

2. For each word in the following list, determine the number of syllables and the number of morphemes:

	Syllables	Morphemes
bookworm		
unicorn		
elephant		
believed		
incredible		
finger		
hogs		
telegram		

3. A closed syllable is one that _____.

   An open syllable is one that _____.

4. How many speech sounds are in the following words?

sigh	thrown	scratch
ice	sung	poison
mix	shrink	know

5. What is the third speech sound in each of the following words?

   joyful   should   patchwork

   tinker   rouge   talk

   square   start   shower

   protect

6. Underline the schwa vowels:

   telephone   along   imposition

   addenda   precious   unless

7. Underline the consonant blends (not all words have blends):

   knight   napkin   springy

   climb   squished   first

   wreck

8. Underline the consonant digraphs (not all words have digraphs):

   spherical   numb   thought

   church   shrink   whether

9. When is *ck* used in spelling?

10. What letters signal that *c* is pronounced /s/?

11. List all of the ways you know to spell long /ō/.

12. List all of the ways you know to spell the consonant sound /f/.

13. When adding a suffix to a word ending with silent *e*, what is the spelling rule?

14. How can you recognize an English word that came from Greek?

COMPREHENSIVE SURVEY
OF LANGUAGE KNOWLEDGE (FORM B)

What is your professional role at present?

How many years have you taught?

What is your most advanced degree?

1. From the list below, find an example of each of the following (answer may be a word or part of a word):

   Inflected verb

   Compound noun

   Bound root

   Derivational suffix

revise	already	carpetbag	trilogy
released	behind	complexity	flower

2. For each word in the following list, determine the number of syllables and the number of morphemes:

	Syllables	Morphemes
caterpillar		
attached		
contracts		
butter		
spring		
preacher		
telemeter		

3. How many speech sounds (phonemes) are in the following words?

exit	flung	boil	sledge
thrash	shocks	through	gnawed

4. Underline the schwa vowels:

   amend   complicate   correlation

   alumnus   compare   position

5. Underline the consonant blends (not all words have blends):

   autumn   gnaw   square   burst

   cloak   shepherd   twang

6. Underline the consonant digraphs (not all words have digraphs):

   asphyxiate   thigh   shrunk

   nimble   chunk   whistle

7. When is *tch* used in spelling?

8. What letters signal that *g* is pronounced /j/?

9. List all of the ways you know to spell long /ōo/.

10. List all of the ways you know to spell the consonant sound /k/.

11. Why does *bible* have one *b* and *bubble* have two?

12. If a child writes the word *dress* as *JRS*, what hypotheses can you make about the child's approach to spelling?

13. Describe the sound, spelling, and meaning structure of this word: *metamorphosis*

ANSWERS FOR THE
SURVEYS OF LANGUAGE KNOWLEDGE

Brief Survey: Phoneme Counting

Number of speech sounds or phonemes:

thrill [4]	ring [3]	shook [3]
does [3]	fix [4]	wrinkle [5]
sawed [3]	quack [4]	know [2]

Brief Survey: Syllable Counting

Number of syllables:

cats [1]	capital [3]	shirt [1]
spoil [1 or 2]	decidedly [4]	banana [3]
recreational [5]	lawyer [2]	walked [1]

Brief Survey: Phoneme Matching

1. pu<u>sh</u> [sugar]

2. w<u>eigh</u> [raid]

3. doe<u>s</u> [nose]

4. in<u>t</u>end [baked]

5. ri<u>ng</u> [sink]

Brief Survey:
Recognition of Sound–Symbol Correspondence

The letters and letter combinations that correspond to each speech sound:

b / e / s / t	f / r / e / sh	s / c / r / a / tch
th / ough	l / au / gh / ed	m / i / dd / le
ch / i / r / p	q / u / a i / n / t	

Brief Survey: Definitions and Concepts

A vowel sound (vowel phoneme) is an open speech sound that is the nucleus of a syllable.

A consonant digraph is a letter combination corresponding to one unique sound.

A prefix is a morpheme (meaningful part), usually of Latin origin, that is added before a root and that changes the meaning of the whole word.

An inflectional (grammatical) morpheme is a grammatical ending added to a verb, adjective, or noun that changes the number, degree, or tense of the word but does not change the meaning of the word.

Phonemic awareness is one (but not the only) necessary skill in learning to read an alphabetic writing system.

The ability to decode words accurately will not of itself support good reading. In addition to decoding, one needs to read words fluently so that attention can be relegated to comprehension.

Comprehensive Survey (Form A)

1. Inflected verb [*slowed*]

    Compound noun [*sandpaper*]

    Bound root [*cred, cyc, psych*]

    Derivational suffix [*-ful, -ible*]

    Greek combining form [Any of the following are correct: *neuro, psych, ology*]

2.

	Syllables	Morphemes
bookworm	2	2
unicorn	3	2
elephant	3	1
believed	2	3
incredible	4	3
finger	2	1
hogs	1	2
telegram	3	2

3. A *closed syllable is one that contains a short vowel and ends in one consonant. An open syllable is one that contains a long vowel sound spelled with one vowel letter that ends the syllable.*

4. Number of speech sounds in the following words:

sigh [2]	thrown [4]	scratch [5]
ice [2]	sung [3]	poison [5]
mix [4]	shrink [5]	know [2]

5. The third speech sound in the following words:

joyful	/f/	should	/o͝o/	patchwork	/ch/
tinker	/ng/	rouge	/zh/	talk	/k/
square	/w/	start	/ŏ/	shower	/w/
protect	/ō/				

6. Schwa vowels:

tel<u>e</u>phone	<u>a</u>long	imp<u>o</u>siti<u>o</u>n
<u>a</u>ddend<u>a</u>	prec<u>iou</u>s	<u>u</u>nless

7. Consonant blends:

knight [*none*]	napkin [*none*]	<u>spr</u>ingy
<u>cl</u>imb	<u>squ</u>ished	fir<u>st</u>
wreck [*none*]		

8. Consonant digraphs:

<u>sph</u>erical	numb [*none*]	<u>th</u>ought
<u>ch</u>ur<u>ch</u>	<u>sh</u>rink	<u>wh</u>e<u>th</u>er

9. *The spelling ck is used when a /k/ sound follows a stressed, short sound.*

10. Letters that signal that c is pronounced /s/: e, i, or y following the c.

11. Ways to spell long /ō/: o, oa, ow, oe, o-e (o-consonant-e), ough

12. Ways to spell the consonant sound /f/: f, ff, gh, ph

13. When adding a suffix to a word ending with silent e, the spelling rule is: *Drop the e if the suffix begins with a vowel; keep the e if the suffix begins with a consonant.*

14. *An English word that came from Greek might have ph for /f/, ch for /k/, or y for /i/; it is likely to be constructed from two or more combining forms; and it is likely to be a mythological (myth), scientific (chlorophyll), or mathematical (dyscalculia) term.*

Comprehensive Survey (Form B)

1. Inflected verb [*released*]

    Compound noun [*carpetbag*]

    Bound root [Any of the following are correct: *vis, lease, ready, complex, logy, flower*]

    Derivational suffix [*ity*]

2.

	Syllables	Morphemes
caterpillar	4	1
attached	2	3
contracts	2	3
butter	2	1
spring	1	1
preacher	2	2
telemeter	4	2

3. Number of speech sounds (phonemes) in the following words:

    exit [4]   flung [4]   boil [3]   sledge [4]

    thrash [4]   shocks [4]   through [3]   gnawed [3]

4. Underline the schwa vowels:

    <u>a</u>mend   complic<u>a</u>te   corr<u>e</u>lati<u>o</u>n

    <u>a</u>lumn<u>us</u>   c<u>o</u>mpare   p<u>o</u>siti<u>o</u>n

5. Consonant blends:

    autumn [*none*]   gnaw [*none*]   <u>squ</u>are   bur<u>st</u>

    <u>cl</u>oak   shepherd [*none*]   <u>tw</u>ang

6. Consonant digraphs:

as<u>ph</u>yxiate	<u>th</u>igh	<u>sh</u>runk
nimble [*none*]	<u>ch</u>unk	<u>wh</u>istle

7. *The spelling* tch *is used when a* /ch/ *sound follows a stressed, short vowel.*

8. Letters that signal that *g* is pronounced /j/: *e, i,* or *y* following the *g* (exception: *get, give, gynecologist*)

9. Ways to spell long /o͞o/: *u, oo, ou, oe, ue, ew, ough, o, u-e (u-consonant-e)*

10. Ways to spell the consonant sound /k/: *k, -ck, c, -que, kh*

11. *The first syllable in* bible *is open (it ends in a long vowel). The last syllable is* -ble. *The first syllable in* bubble *is closed (it ends with the consonant* b *):* bub + ble = bubble.

12. *The child is showing the beginnings of phonetic spelling but does not yet have conventional use of symbols to represent speech sounds. He or she has phoneme awareness but does not have complete knowledge of grapheme–phoneme correspondence.*

13. *The word* metamorphosis *has five syllables, 11 phonemes, and two morphemes (*meta + morphosis*). It is of Greek origin (clues are the Greek combining form* meta, *the fact that it is a scientific word, and the use of* ph *to spell the* /f/ *sound. The word means* transformation, *and the morphemes in the word mean* change *and* form.

Nonphonetic Rote Memory Word Lists

Approximately 150 commonly used words have nonphonetic spellings, primarily in the vowel sounds. These words need to be rote memorized for both reading and spelling. List A includes those words that should be taught in first and second grades. List B includes those words that should be taught by third or fourth grade. Students should memorize 3–5 words at a time. Students should write the words, saying the letter names (not the sounds represented by the letters) out loud as they form the letters. Frequent review is necessary for reading and spelling accuracy.

Groups of words that contain similar letter–sound correspondences (or similar patterns) should be taught together as suggested.

Sources: Henry, M.K., & Redding, N.C. (1996). *Patterns for success in reading and spelling.* Austin, TX: PRO-ED. Rome, P.D., & Osman, J.S. (1993). *Language tool kit* [Teacher's manual and cards]. Cambridge, MA: Educators Publishing Service.

LIST A

a	are	could	door
again	bear	do	friend
against	been	does	from
always	both	done	give
any	come	don't	goes
gone	one	sure	want
guess	only	talk	was
guest	other	tear	wear
guide	pear	the	were
guy	people	their	what
have	pretty	there	where
hour	pull	they	which
live	push	though	who
love	put	through	whom
much	rich	to	whose
nothing	said	too	would
of	says	toward	you
off	should	two	your
often	son	very	youth
once	such	walk	

Groups to Be Taught Together

once	could	to	bear
one	should	too	pear
only	would	two	tear
			wear
who	such	you	
whom	much	your	
whose	rich	youth	
	which		

LIST B

among	build	clothes	enough
another	built	cough	eye
blood	busy	debt	flood
break	buy	double	floor
broad	calf	doubt	four
fourth	listen	sew	trouble
front	many	soft	truth
gauge	month	some	usual
great	move	steak	Wednesday
group	muscle	straight	whole
guard	ninth	sugar	wolf
half	ocean	swore	won
heart	pint	sworn	wore
hearth	prove	thorough	worn
height	rough	tough	

honest
honor
iron
island
laugh

Groups to Be Taught Together

great	rough	guard	heart
break	tough	guess	hearth
steak	enough	guest	
		guide	calf
blood	hour	guy	half
flood	honest		
	honor	group	
wore		soup	
worn	double		
swore	trouble		
sworn			

Compound Words

Compound words can be read when students have learned most consonant and vowel patterns. The teacher explains that two short words of Anglo-Saxon origin often combine, or compound, to form a new word that is based on the meanings of the two constituent words. Students should try to generate as many compound words as they can before reading words listed in this appendix.

ACTIVITIES USING COMPOUND WORDS

The compound words in this appendix can be used in the activities mentioned in Chapter 6. The compound words can also be used in the following activities.

Phonological Awareness: Syllable Deletion

Ask students to say a compound word and then ask them to delete one part of it. For example, "Say *skywalk*. Now say it without *sky*," or "Say *housecoat*. Now say it without *coat*."

Adding Words to a Bulletin Board

Have children add new compound words to a bulletin board of compound words. The words can be divided into categories such as the ones used in this appendix.

Compound Invention

Ask children to invent new compound words and draw pictures representing the words.

Discussion

Discuss with students how meaning of the constituent words in a compound relate to its meaning.

An excellent source of word lists for compound words and other important patterns is Jones, T.B. (1997). *Decoding and encoding English words: A handbook for language tutors.* Timonium, MD: York Press.

COMPOUND WORDS

People

grandchild	stepmother	dogcatcher	cowboy
grandparent	stepfather	salesperson	skycap
grandmother	stepson	bodyguard	statesman
grandfather	stepdaughter	housekeeper	bookworm
housemother	schoolgirl	stagehand	scatterbrain

Animals

butterfly	bluebird	starfish
blackbird	snowbird	shellfish

Actions

slipstitch	sleepwalk	sleighride

Objects

bookbag	shoebox	pillowcase	checkbook
lunchbox	shoelace	tablecloth	blackberry
blackboard	snowshoe	wallpaper	blueberry
chalkboard	snowball	hardware	spitball
floorboard	snowboard	stepladder	slingshot
skateboard	flashlight	snapshot	trapdoor
mailbox	housecoat	turntable	chairlift

Games

baseball	football	basketball	tetherball

Buildings/Places

classroom	lighthouse	airport	waterfall
boardroom	treehouse	graveyard	riverhead
stockroom	smokehouse	campground	headwall
playground	smokestack	campfire	skywalk
playhouse	haystack	skyline	sweatshop
warehouse	railroad	seawall	

Vehicles

sailboat	motorbike	airplane	shipwreck
speedboat	motorcycle	spacecraft	truckload
motorboat	steamship		

Abstract Concepts

trademark	homesick	homework	grandstand
showtime	humpback	paperwork	northwest
seasick	horseback	viewpoint	southeast

Weather

sunrise	starlight	sandstorm	rainstorm
sunset	whirlwind	thunderstorm	earthquake

Prefixes

The prefixes in this appendix are listed alphabetically, not in order of presentation. See Chapters 6 and 7 for logical sequences of presentation. In most cases, numerous other words containing the target prefixes can be added to these lists. Prefixes generally have specific meanings, and these are given after the prefix in parentheses. The prefixes in this appendix are of Latin origin unless marked otherwise. (Number prefixes are listed at the end of this appendix.) Suffixes can be added to many of the words in this appendix.

PREFIXES

a- (*on or in; to;* Anglo-Saxon and Latin)

abeam	across	alone	around
abed	adrift	along	aside
abet	afire	aloud	asleep
abide	afoot	among	aswarm
abound	ahead	amuse	await
above	alight	anoint	awake
abroad	alike	apart	away
abut	alive	arise	awoke

The prefix *a-* can also mean *without* or *not* as in *amoral* and *asocial.*

ab- (*from or away*)

abdicate	ablation	abrupt	absorption
abdication	ablative	abscess	abstain
abduct	ablution	abscissa	abstinence
abduction	abnegate	absence	abstract
aberration	abnegation	absent	abuse
abjection	abrade	absentee	abusive
abjuration	abrasion	absenteeism	
abjure	abrogate	absorb	

ad- (*to, toward, in, or near*)

adapt	adhesion	administrator	advent
adaptation	adhesive	admiration	adverb
adapter	adjacent	admire	adverse
adaptive	adjectival	admirer	advertise
addict	adjective	admission	advertisement
address	adjunct	admit	advertiser
adduct	adjust	admonish	advice
adduction	administer	adopt	advise
adhere	administration	advance	adviser
adherence	administrative	advantage	advisor

Variants of *ad-*

ac- (used before roots beginning with *c, k,* or *q*)

accede	accolade	account	accustomed
accelerant	accommodate	accountant	acknowledge
accelerate	accommodation	accretion	acquaint
accent	accompany	accrual	acquaintance
accept	accomplice	accrue	acquiesce
access	accomplish	accumulate	acquire
accessory	accord	accuracy	acquisition
accident	accordance	accurate	acquit
acclaim	accost	accuse	acquittal

af- (used before roots beginning with *f*)

affair	affiliate	afflict	affright
affect	affiliation	affliction	affront
affection	affinity	affluent	affusion
affectation	affirm	afflux	
affidavit	affix	afford	

ag-   (used before roots beginning with *g*)

agglomerate	aggrandize	aggression	aggrieved
agglutinate	aggravate	aggressive	
aggrade	aggregate	aggressor	

al-   (used before roots beginning with *l*)

allegation	alleviate	allot	allure
allege	alliance	allotment	allusion
allegiance	alliterate	allow	alluvial
allegory	alliteration	allowance	
allergic	allocate	alloy	
allergy	allocation	allude	

an-   (used before roots beginning with *n*)

annex	annotate	annul
annexation	announce	annulment
annihilate	announcement	annunciate

 The prefix *an-* can also mean *without* or *not* as in *anhydride*.

ap-   (used before roots beginning with *p*)

appall	append	applicant	apprehend
apparatus	appendage	application	apprehension
apparent	appendicitis	applicator	apprentice
apparition	appendix	apply	apprise
appeal	apperceive	appoint	approach
appear	appertain	apportion	appropriate
appearance	applaud	apposite	approve
appease	applause	appraisal	approximate
appellate	appliance	appreciate	approximation
appellation	applicable	appreciation	

ar-   (used before roots beginning with *r*)

arraign	arrangement	arrest	arrogant
arraignment	array	arrival	
arrange	arrears	arrogance	

as-   (used before roots beginning with *s*)

assail	assessment	assimilation	assortment
assault	assessor	assist	assuage
assemble	asset	assistance	assume
assembler	assiduous	assistant	assumption
assembly	assign	associate	assurance
assent	assignation	association	assure
assert	assignment	assonance	
assess	assimilate	assonant	

at-   (used before roots beginning with *t*)

attach	attend	attire	attribute
attachment	attention	attitude	attribution
attack	attenuate	attorney	attrition
attain	attenuation	attract	attune
attainment	attest	attraction	
attempt	attestation	attractive	

ambi-   (*both*)

ambidextrous	ambiguous	ambivalent
ambiguity	ambivalence	ambiversion

ante-   (*before*)

ante	antecessor	antefix	anteroom
antebellum	antechamber	antemeridian	anteversion
antecede	antechoir	antenatal	anteverted
antecedence	antedate	antependium	
antecedent	antediluvian	antepenultimate	

anti-   (*opposite or against*)

antiabortion	anticlerical	anti-intellectual
antiaircraft	anticlimax	antilock
antiallergic	anticoagulant	antimagnetic
antiantibody	anticonvulsant	antimony
antianxiety	anticrime	antinoise
antiapartheid	antidepressant	antipope
antiart	antifeminist	antismog
antibiotic	antifreeze	antismoking
antibody	antihero	antisocial
anticancer	antihistamine	
antichoice	anti-inflammatory	

be- (*completely, thoroughly, or excessively;* used as an intensive; Anglo-Saxon)

becalm	bedraggled	beguiling	besotted
became	befoul	belabor	betray
becloud	befriend	belay	betrayal
become	befuddle	belittle	betrayer
bedeck	begrudge	beloved	between
bedevil	beguile	beset	

bene- (*well or good*)

benediction	beneficent	benefit	benevolent
benefactor	beneficial	benevolence	

circum- (*around or about*)

circumambulate	circumference	circumlocute	circumspect
circumcise	circumfix	circumlocution	circumstance
circumcision	circumflex	circumnavigate	circumstantial
circumduct	circumfluent	circumpolar	circumvent
circumduction	circumfuse	circumscribe	circumvention

con- (*together, with, joint, or jointly*)

concatenate	condole	confrontation	considerate
concatenation	conduct	confuse	consideration
concave	conduction	confusion	consolation
conceit	conductor	congest	console
concentrate	confection	congestion	consonant
concentration	confectioner	congregate	conspire
concentric	confederacy	congress	constellation
concern	confederate	congressional	constitute
concert	confer	congruent	constitution
concise	confess	conjecture	constrain
conclave	confessor	conjunction	constraint
conclude	confide	connect	construct
conclusion	confidant	connection	construction
concord	confident	connotation	consult
concrete	confiscate	connote	consultant
concur	conflict	conscript	consultation
condemn	conform	conscription	consume
condemnation	conformance	consecrate	consummate
condense	conformist	consecration	consummation
condition	confront	consider	contact

contain	contraction	contribute	conversation
containment	contracture	contribution	converse
continuation	contraption	convene	conversion
continue	contrary	convention	convert
contract	contrast	converge	convince

Variants of *con-*

co- (usually used before a vowel or *h*)

co-anchor	coexist	coherent	cooperate
co-author	cohabit	cohesion	coordinate
coeducation	cohere	cohesive	copilot
coerce	coherence	cohort	

col- (used before roots beginning with *l*)

collaborate	collateral	collector	collision
collaboration	colleague	college	colloquium
collaborator	collect	collegiate	colloquy
collapse	collection	collide	collude
collate	collective	collinear	collusion

com- (used before roots beginning with *m*, *b*, or *p*)

combat	commitment	comparison	compliment
combatant	committee	compartment	complimentary
combative	commode	compassion	compose
combination	commodious	compatible	composer
combine	communal	compatriot	composition
command	commune	compel	comprehend
commander	Communism	compendium	comprehension
commandment	community	compensate	compress
commence	commutation	compete	compression
commencement	commutative	competence	comprise
commentate	commute	competition	compulsion
commentator	compact	compilation	compunction
commerce	compaction	compile	computation
commercial	companion	complain	compute
commiserate	companionship	complainant	computer
commiseration	company	complaint	
commission	comparable	complement	
commit	compare	complementary	

cor- (used before roots beginning with *r*)

corrade	correspondence	corroborate	corrupt
correlate	correspondent	corrode	corruption
correspond	corrigible	corrosion	

contra- (*against, opposite, contrasting*)

contraband	contradict	contrapuntal
contrabass	contradiction	contravene
contrabassoon	contrapositive	contravention

counter- (*contrary, opposite*)

counterargument	counterexample	counterpart
counterattack	counterfeit	counterplea
counterbalance	counterfeiter	counterplot
counterblow	counterforce	counterpoint
countercharge	counterintelligence	counterproposal
countercheck	counterintuitive	counterrevolution
counterclaim	countermand	countersue
counterclockwise	countermarch	counterterrorism
counterculture	countermeasure	
counterdemonstration	counterpane	

de- (*down or away from*)

debark	declaim	defeat	deflection
debarkation	decline	defect	defog
debate	decode	defection	deform
debrief	decoding	defenestrate	delight
debug	decompose	defenestration	depilatory
decamp	decomposition	defer	deplace
decampment	deduce	deferral	deplane
decay	deduct	defile	deport
decease	deduction	deflect	deportation

dis- (*not, absence of, or apart*)

disability	disclose	disgrace	dislike
disable	discount	dishonest	dislodge
disarm	discuss	dishonesty	disorder
disband	discussion	dishonor	displace
disbar	disfavor	disinterest	disposal
discharge	disfigure	disjoint	dispose

dispute dissolve distend distrust
disrupt distal distention
disruption distance distract
dissolution distant distraction

Variant of *dis-*

dif- (used before roots beginning with *f*)

differ difficult diffident diffuse
different difficulty diffract diffusion
differentiate diffidence diffraction diffusive

dys- (*bad or difficult*; Latin from Greek)

dyscalculia dysgraphia dysphagia dysthymia
dysenteric dyskinesia dysphasia dystonia
dysentery dyslexia dysphonia dystrophy
dysfunction dyslexic dysplasia
dysfunctional dyspepsia dyspnea
dysgenic dyspeptic dysrhythmia

ex- (*out*)

exact excuse expeditious explosion
exalt execute expel explosive
exaltation execution expense export
example executive expensive exportation
excavate executor experience exporter
excavation exemplify experiential express
exceed exempt experiment expression
excel exemption experimentation expressive
excellency exercise experimenter expulsion
excellent exhilarate expert extant
excelsior exhilaration expertise extend
except exist expiration extension
exchange existential expire extensive
excise exit explain extensor
excision expand explanation extent
excite expatriate explicate extract
excitement expect explication extraction
exclude expectorant explode extricate
exclusive expectorate exploration extrication
exclusivity expedite explore
excursion expedition explorer

The prefix ex- is usually pronounced /ĕgz/ when followed by a vowel or silent *h* and /ĕks/ when followed by a consonant.

Variant of *ex-*

e-

ebullient	elapse	erase	evaluate
eclectic	elect	erect	evaluation
eclipse	electric	erode	evaporate
edict	electron	eruct	event
effluent	elide	erupt	eviscerate
egress	elision	evacuate	evoke
eject	emit	evacuation	

fore- (*before;* Anglo-Saxon)

forearm	forefather	foreman	foreshadow
forebear	forefoot	foremast	foreshock
forebode	forego	foremost	foresight
forebrain	foregone	forename	forestall
forecast	foreground	forepaw	foretell
forecaster	forehand	forepeak	forethought
foreclose	forehead	forereach	forewarn
foreclosure	foreleg	forerunner	foreword
forecourt	forelimb	foresail	
foredeck	forelock	foresee	

in- (*in, on, or toward*)

inbreed	incise	incrimination	indicate
incandescence	incision	incriminatory	indication
incandescent	incite	incubate	indict
incarcerate	inclination	incubation	indictment
incarceration	incline	incubator	individual
incarnate	include	incumbency	induce
incarnation	inclusion	incumbent	inductance
incentive	inclusive	incur	induction
inception	income	indebted	indulge
incident	incorporate	indeed	indulgent
incinerate	incorporation	indent	infect
incineration	increase	indentation	infection
incinerator	incriminate	indenture	infer

inference	innovate	inspect	intensive
infield	innovation	inspection	intent
inflate	innovative	inspector	intention
inflation	innovator	inspire	intrude
ingrained	input	inspiration	intrusion
ingredient	inquire	install	inure
ingress	inquisition	installation	invent
inhabit	inquisitive	institute	invention
inhabitant	insect	institution	inventive
inherent	insert	instruct	inventor
inhibit	insertion	instruction	inversion
inhibition	inset	insult	invert
inject	inside	insurance	invest
injection	insider	insure	investment
inlay	insist	insurer	invitation
innate	insistence	intense	invite

Variants of *in-* (*in, on, or toward*)

il- (used before roots beginning with *l*)

illuminate	illumine	illustration	illustrious
illumination	illustrate	illustrative	

im- (used before roots beginning with *b*, *m*, or *p*)

imbibe	impale	import	imprint
immerge	impalement	important	imprison
immerse	impart	importer	imprisonment
immigrant	impeach	impose	improve
immigrate	impeachment	imposition	improvement
immigration	implant	impress	
imminence	implantation	impression	
imminent	implore	impressive	

ir- (used before roots beginning with *r*)

irradiate	irrigate	irrupt
irradiation	irrigation	irruptive

in- (*not*)

inability	inactive	inadequate	inappreciative
inaccuracy	inactivity	inadvertent	inarticulate
inaccurate	inadequacy	inadvisable	inartistic

inattentive	indecent	ineptitude	insensibility
inattentiveness	indecision	inexact	insensible
incapable	indecisive	infant	insensitive
incognito	indelible	infantile	insensitivity
incognizant	independence	infelicitous	insignificance
incomparability	independent	infinite	insignificant
incomparable	indestructible	infinity	insolent
incomplete	indifference	infirm	insolvency
incompletion	indifferent	infirmary	insolvent
incompliant	indignity	infirmity	insufficiency
inconclusive	indirect	inharmonious	insufficient
inconsiderate	indiscreet	injustice	insupportable
inconsideration	ineffective	innocence	intrepid
inconsistent	ineffectiveness	innocent	invalid
incorrupt	inelastic	inobservant	invariable
incurability	inelasticity	inorganic	involuntary
incurable	ineluctable	insane	
indecency	inept	insanity	

Variants of *in-* (*not*)

il- (used before roots beginning with *l*)

illegal	illegible	illicit	illusion
illegality	illegitimacy	illiteracy	illusory
illegibility	illegitimate	illiterate	

im- (used before roots beginning with *b*, *m*, or *p*)

imbalance	immodest	impatient	impingement
imbecile	immoral	impeccable	implement
immaterial	immorality	impedance	implementation
immature	immortal	impede	implication
immaturity	immortality	impel	imply
immediacy	immovable	impenetrability	impossible
immediate	immune	impenetrable	impossibility
immemorial	immunity	imperfect	improper
immense	impair	impersonal	impulse
immethodical	impairment	impertinent	impure
immiscible	impartial	imperturbable	imputation
immitigable	impartiality	impetuous	impute
immobile	impassability	impetus	
immoderate	impassable	impinge	

ir-   (used before roots beginning with *r*)

irrational	irrelevant	irresistible	irretrievable
irreclaimable	irreligious	irresoluble	irreverent
irreconcilable	irremovable	irresolute	irritate
irreducible	irreparable	irrespective	irritation
irregular	irreplaceable	irresponsible	
irregularity	irreproachable	irresponsive	

inter-   (*between*)

interact	interject	interrelate
interaction	interjection	interrelation
interactive	interlace	interrelationship
interbreed	interlope	interrogate
intercede	interloper	interrogation
intercept	intermediary	interrogative
interception	intermediate	interrogator
intercession	intermix	interrupt
interchange	interpersonal	interruption
interchangeability	interplay	intersect
interchangeable	interpolate	intersection
intercom	interpolation	interstate
intercontinental	interpose	interstice
interdict	interposition	intervene
interdiction	interpret	intervention
interest	interpretation	interview
interfere	interpreter	interviewee
interference	interregnum	interviewer

intra-   (*within*)

intracellular	intramural	intraocular	intrastate
intradermal	intramuscular	intrapersonal	intravenous

intro-   (*in or inward*)

introduce	introjection	introspect	introversion
introduction	intromission	introspection	introvert
introject	intromit	introspective	

mal- (*bad or badly; abnormal*)

maladaptation	malcontent	malevolent	malodorous
maladaptive	maldistribution	malfeasance	malpractice
maladjusted	malediction	malfeasant	malversation
maladjustment	maleficence	malformation	
maladminister	maleficent	malfunction	
malapropism	malevolence	malnutrition	

mid- (*middle*; **Anglo-Saxon**)

midline	midsection	midterm	midwinter
midnight	midshipman	midtown	
midpoint	midstream	midway	
midriff	midsummer	midweek	

mis- (*bad or badly; wrong or wrongly*; **Anglo-Saxon and Latin**)

misadventure	miscreant	mismatch	mistaken
misbecome	misdirect	misname	mistook
misbehave	misfire	misplace	mistreat
misbelieve	misgive	misprint	mistrial
miscall	mishandle	misread	misuse
miscast	mishap	misspell	
mischief	mishear	misspent	
miscount	mislead	mistake	

multi- (*many or much*)

multicellular	multilevel	multiply
multicolor	multilingual	multiport
multidirectional	multimedia	multipurpose
multifaceted	multimillionaire	multiracial
multifamily	multinational	multisensory
multifold	multinuclear	multisport
multiform	multiparty	multistage
multigenerational	multiped	multistory
multilateral	multiplex	multivariable
multilayered	multiplication	multivitamin

non-   (*not or negative*)

nonconformist	nonfood	nonreader	nonstop
nondairy	nonhero	nonsense	non-union
nondrinker	nonjuror	nonskid	nonverbal
nonfat	nonperson	nonstick	

ob-   (*down, against, or facing; to*)

obituary	obligation	obsequious	obsession
object	oblige	observation	obsolescence
objectification	obliterate	observe	obsolete
objectify	obliteration	observer	obstreperous
objection	oblong	obsess	obverse

The prefix ob- can also be used as an intensive, as in obfuscate.)

Variants of *ob-*

oc-   (used before roots beginning with *c*)
occult

of-   (used before roots beginning with *f*)
offense   offer

op-   (used before roots beginning with *p*)

opponent	opposition	oppression	oppressor
oppose	oppress	oppressive	opprobrium

per-   (*through or completely;* also used as an intensive)

perceive	perfume	perpetuity	persuade
perception	perfuse	perplex	persuader
percolate	perfusion	perquisite	persuasion
percolation	perjure	persecute	persuasive
percussion	perjurer	persecution	pertain
percussive	perjury	persecutor	perturb
perennial	permeate	perseverance	pervade
perfect	permeation	perseverate	pervasive
perfection	permission	perseveration	pervasiveness
perform	permissive	persevere	
performance	permit	persist	
performer	perpetual	persistence	

post- (*after, behind, or following*)

postclassical	posthypnotic	postmark	postscript
postdate	postimpressionism	postmortem	postwar
posthaste	postlude	postpone	

pre- (*before or earlier*)

preamble	prediction	prejudice	presentiment
prearrange	predictor	prejudicial	preservation
precaution	predispose	preliminary	preservative
precede	predominance	premeditate	preserve
precinct	predominant	premeditation	preserver
precipice	predominate	premix	presold
precipitate	prefabricate	prename	pretend
precipitation	prefabrication	prepackage	pretest
precipitous	prefabricator	preparation	pretext
precise	prefer	prepare	prevail
precision	preferable	preparedness	prevalence
preclude	preference	prepay	prevalent
precognition	preferential	preplan	prevent
precondition	preflight	prerecord	preventative
precursor	preform	prescribe	prevention
predate	preheat	prescription	preview
predetermine	prehistorical	presell	
predicament	prehistory	present	
predict	prejudge	presenter	

pro- (*forward, earlier, or prior to*)

problem	production	profuse	pronounce
problematic	productive	profusion	pronunciation
procedural	profane	program	proscribe
procedure	profanity	programmatic	proscription
proceed	profess	progress	protect
process	profession	progression	protection
procession	professional	progressive	protector
proclaim	professionality	proliferate	protectorate
proclamation	professor	prologue	protest
procure	professorial	promise	protestation
procurement	profile	promote	protester
procurer	profit	promoter	proverb
produce	profiteering	promotion	provide
producer	profligate	pronoun	provider

| province | provision | provoke |
| provincial | provocation | |

re- (*back or again;* also used as an intensive)

rebind	reformation	release	respond
rebirth	reformer	relegate	respondent
rebound	refrain	relieve	responder
rebuild	refresh	relinquish	restain
rebuke	refreshment	relocate	restoration
rebut	refusal	remain	restorative
rebuttal	refuse	remand	restore
recall	regain	remark	restorer
recapture	regard	remission	restrain
recast	regardless	remit	restrict
recent	regress	remittance	restriction
reciprocal	regression	remote	restrictive
reciprocation	rehearsal	removal	restructure
reciprocity	rehearse	remove	retell
reclaim	reinforce	renounce	rethink
recollection	reinforcement	renunciation	retire
record	reinvest	reorder	retirement
recount	reinvestment	repay	retouch
recover	reissue	repel	retrace
recuperate	reject	repellent	retract
recuperation	rejection	replace	retraction
refer	rejoice	replacement	retrain
reference	rejoin	reprint	return
referential	rejuvenate	reproach	reversal
refine	rejuvenation	reproachful	reverse
refinement	relapse	reproduce	reversion
reflect	relate	reproduction	revert
reflection	relation	reproductive	revival
reflective	relationship	require	revive
reflector	relative	resign	rewrite
reflex	relativity	resignation	rework
reflexive	relax	respect	
reform	relaxation	respectful	

se- (apart or aside, without)

secede	sedate	segregate	separation
secession	sedation	segregation	sever
seclude	sedition	segregationist	several
secrecy	seditious	select	severe
secret	seduce	selection	severity
secrete	seducer	selective	
secure	seduction	selector	
security	seductive	separate	

sub- (under, beneath, or below; secondary)

subaltern	subjugate	subscribe	substrate
subalternate	subjugation	subscription	substruction
subclass	subjunctive	subsequent	subterminal
subcontract	sublease	subserve	subterranean
subcontractor	submarine	subservient	subtract
subdivide	submerge	subside	subtraction
subdivision	submission	subsidiary	suburb
subdue	submissive	subsidy	suburban
subgroup	submit	subsist	suburbanite
subhuman	subnormal	subsoil	subversion
subject	suboceanic	substage	subversive
subjection	subordinate	substitute	subvert
subjective	subplot	substitution	subway

Variants of sub-

suc- (used before roots beginning with c)

succeed	succession	succinct	succumb
success	successive	succor	

suf- (used before roots beginning with f)

suffer	sufficiency	suffrage	suffusion
sufferable	sufficient	suffragist	
sufferance	suffix	suffuse	

sug- (used before roots beginning with g)

suggest	suggestible	suggestion	suggestive

sup-   (used before roots beginning with *p*)

supplant	supply	suppose	suppressive
suppliant	support	supposition	suppressor
supplicant	supporter	suppress	
supplication	supportive	suppression	

sus-   (used before roots beginning with *p* or *t*)

suspect	suspense	suspicious	sustenance
suspend	suspension	suspire	
suspenders	suspicion	sustain	

syn-   (*together or with;* Greek)

synagogue	synchronous	syncretism	synecdoche
synapse	syncline	syndicate	synergy
synchronic	syncopate	syndication	synthetic
synchronize	syncopation	syndrome	

Variants of syn-

syl-   (used before roots beginning with *l*)

syllabary	syllabicate	syllabus	syllogism
syllabic	syllable	syllepsis	

sym-   (used before roots beginning with *b*, *m*, or *p*)

symbiosis	symmetry	symphony	symptomatic
symbol	sympathetic	symphysis	symptomize
symbolize	sympathy	symposium	
symmetrical	symphonic	symptom	

trans-   (*across or beyond*)

transact	transcription	translate	transportation
transaction	transfer	translation	transporter
transcend	transference	translator	transpose
transcendence	transfix	transmission	transposition
transcendental	transform	transmit	transverse
transcribe	transformation	transpire	
transcriber	transformer	transport	

un- (*to undo or reverse;* Anglo-Saxon and Latin)

unarm	unearth	unlash	unseat
unbend	unfold	unlatch	unsnarl
unbind	unglue	unlearn	unstick
unchain	unhand	unload	unwrap
unclothe	unhitch	unlock	unyoke
uncoil	unlace	unpack	unzip

un- (*not or opposite of;* Anglo-Saxon and Latin)

unable	uneasy	unlawful	unskilled
unabridged	unfair	unlike	unsound
unasked	unfaithful	unlucky	unthinkable
unaware	unfit	unmanly	untruthful
unawares	unfounded	unmindful	unusual
unbidden	unhappy	unpaid	unwilling
uncertain	unhealthy	unready	unwise
unclean	unjust	unrest	
undaunted	unkempt	unruly	
undying	unknown	unsafe	

NUMBER PREFIXES FROM LATIN AND GREEK

1

uni- (Latin)

unicorn	unicycle	uniform	universe

mono- (Greek)

monochromatic	monocycle	monolith	mononucleosis
monochrome	monodynamic	monolithic	monopoly
monochronic	monogram	monologue	
monocle	monograph	monomania	

See Appendix G for more *mono-* words.

2

bi- (Latin)

biannual	biceps	biennium	binocular
bicameral	bicycle	bifocals	biplane
bicentenary	bidirectional	bifurcate	bipolar
bicentennial	biennial	bifurcation	

duo- (Latin)

dual	duality	duo	duopoly
dualism	duet	duologue	

di- (Greek)

dichromatic	diode	dipole
digraph	dioxide	

3

tri- (Latin/Greek)

triangle	triceratops	triennial	triplicate
triangular	tricycle	trigonometry	tripod

ter- (Latin)

tercentenary	tercentennial	tercet	tertiary

4

quadr-, quar- (Latin)

quadrangle	quadrennium	quart	quartile
quadrangular	quadruped	quarter	
quadrennial	quadruple	quartet	

tetra- (Greek)

tetracycline	tetragonal	tetrameter
tetragon	tetrahedron	

5

quint- (Latin)

quintet	quintile	quintuple	quintuplet

pent- (Greek)

pentadactyl	pentagonal	pentarchy
pentagon	pentameter	pentathlon

6

sex- (Latin)

sextant	sextet	sextuple

hex- (Greek)

hexagon	hexagram	hexameter	hexidecimal
hexagonal	hexahedron	hexane	

7

sept- (Latin)

September	septet	septilateral	septuagenarian

hept- (Greek)

heptagon	heptagonal	heptameter	heptarchy

8

octa-, octo- (Latin/Greek)

octagon	octet	octogenarian
octagonal	October	octopus

9

nona-, nove- (Latin)

nonagenarian	nonagonal	novena
nonagon	November	

10

dec-, deca-, deci- (Latin/Greek)

decade	decathlon	decennium	decimate
decagon	December	decigram	decimation
decagonal	decennial	decimal	decimeter

100

cent- **(Latin)**

| cent | centennial | centigram | centipede |
| centenary | centigrade | centimeter | century |

hect- **(Greek)**

hectare   hectogram   hectometer

1,000

mille- **(Latin)**

| millenary | millennium | millipede |
| millennial | million | |

kilo- **(Greek)**

| kilobyte | kiloliter | kilowatt |
| kilogram | kilometer | |

10,000

myria- **(Greek)**

myriad   myriameter

million

mega- **(Greek; *mega* also means *large*)**

megabyte   megameter   megawatt

 See Appendix G for more *mega-* words.

billion

giga- **(Greek)**

gigabyte   gigacycle   gigahertz   gigameter

trillion

tera- **(Greek)**

terahertz   terameter

quadrillion

peta- **(Greek)**

petameter

quintillion

exa- **(Greek)**

exameter

REFERENCES

The American heritage dictionary (2nd ed.). (1982). Boston: Houghton Mifflin.
The American heritage dictionary (4th ed.). (2000). Boston: Houghton Mifflin.
Random House unabridged dictionary (2nd ed.). (1993). New York: Random House.

Suffixes

Suffixes are word parts added to the end of a base element that is usually of Anglo-Saxon or Latin origin. Some suffixes have specific meanings and usually place a word in a specific part of speech; other suffixes do not. Because suffixes are usually unstressed, the vowel sound is likely to be schwa. The suffixes listed in this appendix appear in thousands of words and are of Latin origin unless marked otherwise. The meaning and/or part of speech are given for each suffix. The suffixes appear in alphabetical order, not order of presentation. See Chapter 7 for a logical sequence of presentation. Students need to learn suffixes for both reading and spelling. Prefixes and additional suffixes can be added to some of the words in this appendix.

-able (able, can do; adjective; generally used with Anglo-Saxon base words)

allowable	definable	flammable	notable
answerable	desirable	floatable	observable
approachable	disputable	forgivable	organizable
approvable	dissolvable	honorable	passable
arguable	drinkable	hospitable	payable
bearable	eatable	improvable	portable
believable	employable	jumpable	preservable
buyable	enjoyable	kissable	readable
charitable	excitable	likable	realizable
comfortable	explainable	lovable	reasonable
creditable	exportable	mendable	receivable
deceivable	fixable	movable	recognizable

regrettable	retrievable	storable	testable
remarkable	returnable	suitable	trainable
removable	sailable	supportable	valuable
repairable	sinkable	swimmable	weavable
repayable	sizable	tastable	workable
respectable	smellable	taxable	
retractable	solvable	teachable	

The related suffix *-ability* (*-able* + *-ity*) can be added to many of the same base elements to make nouns (e.g., *teachable, teachability; floatable, floatability; remarkable, remarkability*).

Variant of *-able*

   -ible (*able, can do*; **adjective; primarily used with Latin roots**)

accessible	credible	forcible	reprehensible
collapsible	destructible	illegible	repressible
compatible	edible	intelligible	resistible
comprehensible	eligible	legible	responsible
convertible	expressible	perceptible	reversible
corrigible	extendible	possible	sensible
corruptible	flexible	reducible	terrible

The related suffix *-ibility* can be added to many of the same base elements to make nouns (e.g., *credible, credibility; responsible, responsibility; possible, possibility*)

-ade (*result of action*; **noun**)

accolade	cascade	escapade	masquerade
ambuscade	cavalcade	esplanade	palisade
balustrade	charade	gallopade	promenade
barricade	colonnade	lemonade	renegade
blockade	crusade	marinade	serenade
brigade	escalade	marmalade	stockade

-age (*collection, mass, relationship*; **noun**)

acreage	bandage	cooperage	foliage
anchorage	beverage	courage	herbage
appendage	brokerage	dockage	leafage
baggage	coinage	drainage	leakage

leverage	parsonage	salvage	storage
lineage	passage	savage	trackage
linkage	personage	selvage	truckage
luggage	pilgrimage	sewage	vicarage
mileage	plumage	shrinkage	village
moorage	postage	soakage	voyage
package	poundage	steerage	wreckage
parentage	ravage	stoppage	

-al, -ial (*relating to or characterized by;* **adjective**)

abdominal	elemental	menial	proportional
acquittal	emotional	mental	rational
adverbial	eternal	millennial	recessional
alluvial	external	minimal	recital
ancestral	federal	monarchal	regional
baptismal	final	moral	remedial
baronial	formal	mortal	retinal
betrayal	fractional	nasal	retrieval
biennial	frontal	national	reversal
binomial	functional	natural	ritual
cardinal	funeral	nocturnal	seasonal
causal	general	nominal	sensational
centennial	gradual	normal	several
collegial	guttural	occasional	skeletal
colloquial	horizontal	octagonal	spinal
colonial	hymnal	optional	spiritual
confessional	institutional	ordinal	spousal
conjugal	internal	original	subliminal
correctional	intestinal	ornamental	supplemental
criminal	journal	parochial	taxidermal
denial	labial	pastoral	terminal
dental	liberal	paternal	terrestrial
dermal	literal	perennial	territorial
developmental	manual	personal	thermal
devotional	marginal	pictorial	universal
diagonal	marital	plural	visional
disposal	maternal	polynomial	visual
doctoral	mayoral	primordial	
editorial	medical	principal	
educational	medicinal	professional	

Variants of *-ial*

-cial   (used after base elements ending in *c*)

artificial	facial	judicial	racial
beneficial	financial	official	social
commercial	glacial	provincial	special

-tial   (usually used after base elements ending in *t*)

celestial	differential	initial	prudential
circumstantial	experiential	martial	substantial
credential	inferential	potential	

-an   (*relating to;* adjective or noun)

American	Cuban	Lutheran	suburban
Anglican	epicurean	Minnesotan	urban
cosmopolitan	European	Republican	veteran

Variant of *-an*

-ian

agrarian	Bostonian	humanitarian	Yugoslavian
Appalachian	Canadian	Italian	
Armenian	centenarian	Norwegian	
Australian	civilian	vegetarian	

-ant   (*action or state;* noun)

accountant	consultant	informant	servant
adjutant	contestant	irritant	stimulant
annuitant	decongestant	lieutenant	supplicant
attendant	disinfectant	merchant	tenant
claimant	expectorant	peasant	
complainant	immigrant	Protestant	

-ant   (adjective)

abundant	dominant	flippant	relevant
arrogant	dormant	gallant	tolerant
brilliant	elegant	hesitant	truant
buoyant	exorbitant	incessant	vibrant
discordant	expectant	intolerant	
distant	extravagant	militant	

The suffix -*ance* is related to the suffix -*ant* and can be added to many of the same base elements to form nouns (e.g., *tolerant, tolerance; brilliant, brilliance; dominant, dominance*). The related suffix -*ancy* also forms nouns (e.g., *militancy, accountancy, compliancy*).

-*ar* (adjective; used with Latin roots)

angular	muscular	singular	vernacular
cellular	particular	solar	vestibular
circular	peculiar	spectacular	vulgar
familiar	polar	stellar	
glandular	popular	tubular	
globular	rectangular	vascular	
molecular	secular	vehicular	

Some common nouns end in -*ar* (e.g., *beggar, molar, hangar, sugar, liar, burglar, cellar, pillar, collar, vinegar, cigar, scholar, registrar*), but note that these -*ar* spellings do not always denote the suffix -*ar*.

-*ard* (one habitually or excessively in a specified condition; Anglo-Saxon/German; noun)

coward	drunkard	laggard

-*ary* (relating to, place where; noun)

anniversary	emissary	missionary	statuary
apothecary	estuary	mortuary	subsidiary
aviary	formulary	notary	summary
beneficiary	glossary	obituary	syllabary
boundary	granary	plenipotentiary	topiary
commissary	infirmary	reliquary	tributary
dictionary	judiciary	secretary	visionary
dispensary	mercenary	seminary	vocabulary

-*ary* (adjective)

arbitrary	cautionary	contrary	customary
binary	confectionary	coronary	dietary

disciplinary	military	proprietary	sedentary
documentary	momentary	reactionary	sedimentary
elementary	monetary	revolutionary	stationary
extraordinary	necessary	rudimentary	temporary
fiduciary	ordinary	salivary	veterinary
honorary	plenary	salutary	voluntary
imaginary	preliminary	sanitary	
literary	primary	secondary	

-ate   (cause or make; verb)

affiliate	dictate	illustrate	repudiate
ambulate	dominate	infiltrate	retaliate
appropriate	enunciate	initiate	speculate
approximate	eradicate	mediate	stimulate
associate	estimate	mutilate	stipulate
coagulate	exfoliate	operate	substantiate
decimate	hesitate	percolate	vaccinate
dedicate	hibernate	radiate	vacillate
deviate	hydrate	relate	ventilate

-ate   (adjective)

adequate	collegiate	desolate	moderate
alternate	compassionate	desperate	private
appellate	confederate	determinate	separate
appropriate	considerate	immediate	temperate
articulate	corporate	legitimate	ultimate

 The vowel sound in the suffix -ate is usually long /ā/ when the affixed word is a verb (e.g., as in appropriate, meaning to set aside). When the affixed word is an adjective, the vowel sound in the suffix is usually schwa (e.g., as in appropriate, meaning fitting the situation).

-cide   (kill; noun)

autocide	herbicide	matricide	sororicide
biopesticide	homicide	parenticide	suicide
fratricide	infanticide	patricide	uxoricide
fungicide	insecticide	pesticide	vermicide
germicide	liberticide	regicide	

The suffix -*cide* and the root *cise*, meaning *to cut*, come from the same Latin root, *caedere*.

-cy   (*state, condition, or quality*; noun)

bankruptcy	policy	secrecy

Variant of -*cy*

-acy

accuracy	conspiracy	intimacy	papacy
adequacy	delicacy	legitimacy	pharmacy
advocacy	diplomacy	literacy	piracy
candidacy	efficacy	lunacy	privacy
celibacy	inaccuracy	obstinacy	supremacy

-dom   (*quality, realm, office, or state*; Anglo-Saxon; noun)

boredom	dukedom	kingdom	stardom
chiefdom	earldom	martyrdom	wisdom
Christendom	freedom	popedom	
clerkdom	heirdom	serfdom	

-ed   (Anglo-Saxon; past participle of regular verb)

(pronounced /əd/ after a base element ending in *d* or *t*)

belted	fitted	herded	sighted
blasted	founded	inspected	stranded
blinded	fretted	knotted	stunted
bonded	funded	lifted	tinted
branded	gifted	minded	unfounded
disrupted	handed	pointed	vaulted
erupted	headed	ragged	
exploded	heated	sanded	

(pronounced /d/ after a base element ending in a voiced consonant)

armed	drowned	gleaned	stewed
called	famed	hinged	swelled
canned	fledged	opened	tailed
clubbed	frowned	rubbed	
curved	garbed	screamed	

(pronounced /t/ after a base element ending in an unvoiced consonant)

backed	fixed	hooked	mixed
boxed	fleeced	laughed	offed
cropped	flipped	locked	peaked
crushed	flounced	marked	voiced
cursed	forced	matched	
dished	helped	milked	

The suffix -*ed* can be added to many hundreds of other words of Anglo-Saxon, Latin, and Greek origin.

-ee (*one who receives the action;* **noun [person]**)

absentee	divorcee	internee	releasee
addressee	employee	licensee	trustee
appointee	endorsee	nominee	Yankee
committee	escapee	payee	
confirmee	examinee	pledgee	
deportee	grantee	referee	
devotee	guarantee	refugee	

-eer (*one associated with;* **noun [person]**)

auctioneer	commandeer	mountaineer	privateer
balladeer	electioneer	musketeer	profiteer
buccaneer	engineer	mutineer	volunteer
charioteer	gazetteer	pioneer	

-en (*made of or to make;* **Anglo-Saxon; verb; primarily used with Anglo-Saxon base words**)

blacken	enliven	lighten	thicken
cheapen	flatten	loosen	tighten
dampen	freshen	ripen	toughen
darken	harden	roughen	waken
deepen	hasten	soften	weaken
enlighten	lengthen	strengthen	widen

-en (**Anglo-Saxon; adjective**)

barren	drunken	mistaken	spoken
broken	frozen	olden	sullen

-en (*made of;* Anglo-Saxon; adjective)

earthen	leaden	silken	woolen
golden	oaken	wooden	

-ence (action, state, or quality; noun)

circumference	confluence	dissidence	reference
conference	difference	independence	resilience
confidence	diffidence	interdependence	

-ency (*action, state, or quality;* noun)

deficiency	emergency	urgency
efficiency	fluency	

-ent (*referent;* noun)

accident	decedent	incident	resident
adolescent	delinquent	incumbent	student
agent	dependent	patient	
constituent	dissident	referent	

-ent (adjective)

absorbent	diligent	inconsistent	negligent
affluent	emergent	indulgent	obedient
beneficent	evident	innocent	resilient
candescent	excellent	intelligent	reticent
confident	exigent	latent	silent
convenient	existent	lenient	sufficient
convergent	fluent	magnificent	transparent
decadent	imminent	malevolent	urgent
dependent	incident	munificent	violent

The suffixes -ence and -ency are related to the suffix -ent and can be added to many of the same base elements to form nouns (e.g., *dependent, dependence, dependency; resident, residence, residency*).

-er (*one who; that which;* noun; primarily used with Anglo-Saxon base words)

archer	banker	catcher	counter
baker	boxer	clipper	dancer

diner	keeper	prowler	stationer
fiddler	lodger	rancher	swimmer
fighter	logger	roaster	talker
financier	looter	runner	teller
gambler	manager	scribbler	tracker
hanger	marker	shipper	walker
hauler	milker	skater	washer
healer	miner	skier	watcher
heater	performer	smoker	
helper	picker	splasher	
informer	pitcher	sprinkler	

-er (adjective [comparative degree]; primarily used with Anglo-Saxon base words; see -est for superlative degree adjectives)

bigger	eager	older	smaller
blacker	fatter	redder	sweeter
bolder	flatter	safer	taller
clearer	greener	shorter	wetter
cloudier	happier	simpler	
colder	hotter	skinnier	
drier	muddier	slimmer	

-ery (relating to, quality, or place where; noun)

bakery	demagoguery	nunnery	stationery
bindery	embracery	nursery	stitchery
bravery	flattery	pottery	tannery
confectionery	hatchery	refinery	treachery
cookery	imagery	rookery	trickery
creamery	knavery	slavery	witchery
crockery	millinery	sorcery	

-ese (related to; noun or adjective)

Burmese	journalese	Portuguese	Vietnamese
Cantonese	legalese	Siamese	
Chinese	novelese	Taiwanese	
Japanese	Pekingese	Tonkinese	

-ess (feminine; noun)

actress	goddess	leopardess	sculptress
authoress	governess	lioness	songstress
countess	heiress	mayoress	tigress
duchess	hostess	murderess	waitress
empress	huntress	princess	

-est (adjective [superlative degree]; see **-er** for comparative degree adjectives)

biggest	fastest	hottest	reddest
cloudiest	fleetest	longest	slowest
deepest	greenest	muddiest	warmest

 The suffix -est can be added to most adjectives.

-ette (*small or diminutive;* noun)

banquette	dinette	navette	statuette
barrette	gazette	novelette	usherette
bassinette	layette	palette	wagonette
brunette	maisonette	pianette	
cigarette	marionette	rosette	

-fold (*related to a specified number or quantity;* noun)

fiftyfold	manyfold	tenfold	twofold
hundredfold	multifold	thousandfold	

-ful (*full of or full;* Anglo-Saxon; adjective; primarily used with Anglo-Saxon base words)

armful	forgetful	plateful	thankful
awful	fretful	plentiful	truthful
bashful	frightful	restful	useful
beautiful	gainful	rightful	wasteful
boastful	grateful	sackful	willful
bountiful	harmful	shameful	wishful
careful	helpful	spiteful	wonderful
doubtful	hopeful	spoonful	wrongful
faithful	mouthful	tactful	youthful
fitful	painful	tasteful	

-fy, -ify (*make;* verb)

beautify	electrify	identify	pacify
certify	falsify	intensify	personify
classify	fortify	justify	prettify
deify	gentrify	liquefy	purify
dignify	glorify	magnify	putrefy
diversify	gratify	modify	qualify
edify	horrify	notify	quantify

rarefy	signify	stupefy	unify
reify	simplify	terrify	vilify
satisfy	specify	testify	

The Latin roots *fac*, *fact*, *fect*, and *fic* are related to the suffixes *-fy* and *-ify*.

-hood   (condition, state, or quality; Anglo-Saxon; noun)

babyhood	fatherhood	livelihood	priesthood
boyhood	girlhood	manhood	sainthood
brotherhood	knighthood	motherhood	sisterhood
childhood	likelihood	neighborhood	womanhood

-ian (-cian)   (one having a certain skill or art; noun [person])

academician	magician	patrician	rhetorician
diagnostician	mathematician	Phoenician	statistician
electrician	metaphysician	phonetician	tactician
geometrician	musician	physician	theoretician
Grecian	obstetrician	politician	
logician	optician	practician	

In these words ending in *-cian*, *c* is the final letter of the base element and *-ian* is the suffix, but this pattern is often taught as *-cian*.

-ic   (of, pertaining to, or characterized by; adjective)

academic	geometric	music	ritualistic
agnostic	gigantic	mystic	romantic
arithmetic	hectic	narcotic	rustic
automatic	historic	naturalistic	scientific
civic	hypnotic	optimistic	seismic
classic	hypothetic	Pacific	Slavic
diagnostic	impressionistic	parasitic	socialistic
diplomatic	linguistic	patriotic	solipsistic
eccentric	logarithmic	philharmonic	specific
egotistic	logistic	pluralistic	stoic
elastic	magic	poetic	stylistic
enthusiastic	materialistic	politic	symbolic
epileptic	microscopic	public	

-ile   (*relating to, suited for, or capable of;* noun)

automobile	locomobile	quartile	textile
domicile	missile	quintile	
juvenile	percentile	reptile	

-ile   (*relating to, suited for, or capable of;* adjective)

agile	fragile	mobile	versatile
ductile	futile	nubile	
facile	hostile	prehensile	
fertile	immobile	sterile	

-ine   (*nature of;* noun)

(usually pronounced /ĭn/)

discipline	intestine	saccharine
heroine	medicine	

(pronounced /ēn/)

aquamarine	figurine	magazine	vaccine
chlorine	gasoline	mezzanine	wolverine
citrine	glassine	submarine	
citrulline	glycine	tambourine	

-ine   (*nature of;* adjective)

(usually pronounced /īn/)

alkaline	clandestine	feline	piscine
aquiline	divine	leonine	porcine
bovine	elephantine	murine	serpentine
canine	equine	ovine	taurine

(usually pronounced /ĭn/)

crystalline	genuine	peregrine
feminine	masculine	

(usually pronounced /ēn/)

Benedictine	pristine

-ing   (*action, process, or art;* noun)

dancing	gathering	swimming
drawing	skipping	swashbuckling

-ing **(present participle of verb; adjective)**

believing   seeing   thinking

Many hundreds of other words contain the suffix *-ing*.

-ion (-sion) **(*act of, state of, or result of;* noun)**

(usually pronounced /shən/ when final syllable of base element has a short vowel sound)

admission	depression	mansion	recession
apprehension	expansion	pension	regression
concession	expression	possession	submission
confession	expulsion	procession	suspension
convulsion	extension	progression	tension

(usually pronounced /zhən/ when final syllable of base element has a long vowel sound)

abrasion	erosion	intrusion	submersion
adhesion	exclusion	invasion	vision
cohesion	excursion	persuasion	
diversion	infusion	seclusion	

In these words ending in *-sion*, *s* is the final letter of the base element and *-ion* is the suffix, but this pattern is often taught as *-sion*.

-ion (-tion) **(*act of, state of, or result of;* noun)**

(pronounced /shən/)

abdication	ammunition	celebration	condensation
abstraction	appreciation	certification	condition
acquisition	attention	circulation	congregation
adaptation	authorization	citation	construction
addition	aviation	collection	contention
adoption	cancellation	commendation	continuation
ambition	causation	composition	correlation

creation	extraction	medication	relation
decimation	federation	meditation	replication
declaration	fertilization	modernization	reputation
dedication	flirtation	modulation	reservation
deduction	flotation	mortification	resignation
delegation	formulation	nation	revocation
depletion	foundation	navigation	rotation
deportation	frustration	negotiation	salivation
derivation	glorification	notification	satisfaction
description	gradation	numeration	segregation
desolation	graduation	nutrition	sensation
devotion	habitation	objection	situation
diction	identification	obstruction	sophistication
dislocation	implication	population	stipulation
disposition	incubation	position	strangulation
disruption	indication	prediction	subjection
distraction	inflation	preparation	subtraction
distribution	inhalation	preposition	suffocation
domination	inhibition	prescription	susurration
duplication	injection	presentation	syllabication
edition	insertion	preservation	syndication
education	inspiration	presumption	tabulation
elation	instruction	probation	temptation
election	intention	projection	termination
elevation	interruption	proportion	traction
equation	intoxication	provocation	tradition
eructation	introduction	qualification	transition
evacuation	investigation	quotation	trepidation
examination	invitation	radiation	vacation
exception	invocation	recommendation	validation
exhalation	justification	recreation	variation
expectation	location	reduction	ventilation
explication	lubrication	reflection	vibration
exploration	mediation	regulation	violation

In these words ending in -*tion*, *t* is the final letter of the base element and -*ion* is the suffix, but this pattern is often taught as -*tion*.

(pronounced /chən/ after a base element ending in -st)

combustion	digestion	ingestion
congestion	exhaustion	question

-ish   (origin, nature, or resembling; Anglo-Saxon; adjective)

amateurish	darkish	lavish	softish
babyish	devilish	longish	Spanish
biggish	dullish	loutish	strongish
bluish	foolish	reddish	stylish
bookish	fortyish	selfish	Swedish
boyish	freakish	sheepish	sweetish
British	frumpish	skittish	thickish
clownish	garish	sluggish	thinnish
dampish	girlish	smallish	youngish

-ism   (doctrine, system, manner, condition, act, or characteristic; noun)

absenteeism	egotism	industrialism	pessimism
altruism	exorcism	Judaism	pluralism
atheism	fatalism	materialism	positivism
baptism	feudalism	mechanism	radicalism
Buddhism	heroism	modernism	realism
capitalism	Hinduism	moralism	ritualism
Catholicism	humanism	optimism	terrorism
classicism	hypnotism	organism	ventriloquism
criticism	idealism	pacifism	verbalism
egoism	impressionism	patriotism	

-ist   (one who; noun [person])

abolitionist	bassoonist	colonist	druggist
accompanist	bicyclist	communist	egoist
alarmist	biologist	conformist	egotist
allergist	canoeist	copyist	essayist
archivist	cartoonist	cosmologist	extortionist
artist	cellist	cyclist	extremist
astrologist	chemist	dentist	federalist
Baptist	clarinetist	dramatist	florist

flutist
futurist
geologist
guitarist
harpist
herbalist
hobbyist
humorist
hypnotist
impressionist
jurist

linguist
lobbyist
loyalist
machinist
manicurist
modernist
moralist
motorist
oculist
opportunist
optimist

parachutist
pessimist
pharmacist
physicist
physiologist
pianist
positivist
psychologist
purist
reformist
reservist

revolutionist
scientist
socialist
taxidermist
terrorist
theorist
tourist
violinist

The suffix -ize is related to -ism and -ist and can be added to many of the same base elements to make nouns (e.g., socialism, socialist, socialize; terrorism, terrorist, terrorize).

-ite (*nature of, quality of, or mineral product;* **noun**)

alexandrite
amazonite
azurite
barite
calcite
chlorite
dolomite

dynamite
favorite
fluorite
graphite
hematite
Israelite
malachite

marcasite
meteorite
Muscovite
parasite
satellite
stalactite
stalagmite

sulfite
tanzanite
trilobite
Wisconsinite

-ium (*chemical element, or group;* **noun**)

ammonium
aquarium
atrium
auditorium
biennium
cadmium
calcium

crematorium
delirium
emporium
equilibrium
helium
honorarium
iridium

lithium
medium
millennium
planetarium
podium
premium
radium

sanatorium
sodium
solarium
stadium
tedium
titanium
uranium

The related plural noun suffix -ia can be added to some of the same base elements (e.g., atria, honoraria, podia, media).

-ive *(causing or making;* **adjective)**

abrasive	depressive	expensive	positive
active	descriptive	explosive	primitive
assertive	destructive	extensive	progressive
attentive	diffusive	furtive	provocative
cohesive	dissuasive	imperative	punitive
collective	divisive	impressive	receptive
comprehensive	effective	instinctive	recessive
congestive	effusive	intrusive	relative
consecutive	elaborative	massive	revulsive
constructive	elective	medicative	sensitive
cooperative	elusive	native	speculative
corrosive	eruptive	negative	stimulative
creative	evasive	offensive	submissive
cursive	excessive	oppressive	superlative
decisive	exhaustive	passive	
defensive	expansive	perceptive	

-ize *(make;* **verb)**

actualize	humanize	melodize	realize
apologize	hypnotize	memorize	scrutinize
colonize	idolize	minimize	sensitize
criticize	iodize	mobilize	socialize
dramatize	italicize	organize	standardize
economize	legalize	ostracize	tantalize
familiarize	liquidize	polarize	verbalize
fertilize	localize	politicize	vitalize
formalize	materialize	popularize	

The related suffixes *-ism* and *-ist* can be added to many of the same base elements to make nouns (e.g., *formalize, formalism, formalist; realize, realism, realist*).

-less *(without;* **Anglo-Saxon; adjective; primarily used with Anglo-Saxon base words)**

ageless	careless	endless	formless
blameless	cheerless	faceless	groundless
breathless	childless	faithless	hatless
breezeless	cloudless	faultless	heedless

helpless	moneyless	sailless	timeless
homeless	nameless	senseless	tireless
hopeless	noiseless	shameless	tuneless
joyless	painless	shiftless	voiceless
leafless	penniless	sleepless	voteless
lifeless	pointless	sleeveless	wingless
loveless	priceless	smokeless	wordless
matchless	restless	soundless	

-ling   (very small; diminutive; Anglo-Saxon; noun)

cageling	fledgling	kindling	underling
changeling	foundling	sapling	wiseling
darling	gosling	seedling	yearling
duckling	kidling	starling	youngling

-logy (-ology)   (science or study of; noun)

anthology	ecology	morphology	psychology
archaeology	ethnology	musicology	radiology
astrology	etiology	mythology	sociology
audiology	flaciology	neurology	technology
biology	geology	ophthalmology	terminology
cardiology	hydrology	ornithology	theology
chronology	immunology	paleontology	volcanology
cosmology	lexicology	pathology	zoology
criminology	meteorology	pharmacology	
dermatology	mineralogy	phonology	

The related forms -ologist (-ology + -ist), which denotes *one who deals with a specific topic* (e.g., dermatologist, cosmologist, criminologist, audiologist), and -logue can be added to many of the same base elements that -ology is added to.

Note that -logy is often considered a Greek combining form. See Appendix G for a more extensive list of -logy words.

-ly   (like or manner of; adverb)

absently	broadly	deadly	fearlessly
badly	candidly	delightedly	fervently
blindly	carefully	evasively	foolishly
briskly	cleanly	faintly	forcedly

forcefully	likely	prettily	smartly
friendly	lonely	primely	smilingly
gladly	longingly	proudly	sorely
goodly	loudly	quickly	stiffly
grandly	madly	rarely	swiftly
heatedly	maidenly	roundly	validly
hoarsely	morbidly	rudely	vividly
homely	namely	ruggedly	wisely
hurriedly	nicely	sadly	
jointedly	peacefully	sanely	
kingly	pleasantly	shakily	

-ment   (*act of, state of, or result of an action;* **noun**)

achievement	confinement	entertainment	payment
advertisement	derailment	excitement	postponement
agreement	detachment	government	punishment
amazement	disappointment	impeachment	refinement
amendment	employment	implement	replacement
announcement	encampment	infringement	resentment
argument	enchantment	instrument	retirement
arrangement	endorsement	integument	segment
basement	enforcement	management	sentiment
commandment	engagement	movement	settlement
commitment	enjoyment	nourishment	shipment
compliment	enlistment	ornament	statement
concealment	entanglement	pavement	testament

-most   (*most or nearest to;* **Anglo-Saxon; adjective [superlative]**)

bottommost	hindmost	middlemost	topmost
endmost	inmost	northernmost	undermost
farthermost	innermost	outermost	upmost
furthermost	lowermost	southernmost	uppermost

-ness   (*state of;* **Anglo-Saxon; noun; primarily used with Anglo-Saxon base words**)

alertness	busyness	flatness	happiness
ambitiousness	cautiousness	fleetness	hollowness
badness	exactness	furiousness	lightness
bigness	expertness	gladness	loudness
bluntness	fitness	greatness	madness

neatness	rightness	smartness	vastness
newness	roundness	softness	wellness
politeness	sadness	strictness	wetness
prettiness	shortness	sweetness	witness
promptness	shyness	swiftness	
quaintness	sleeplessness	tightness	
quietness	slowness	uproariousness	

-or   (one who; that which; noun; primarily used with Latin roots)

abdicator	confessor	fumigator	precursor
accelerator	contractor	generator	predecessor
actor	contributor	governor	predictor
adductor	creator	imitator	professor
advisor	creditor	impostor	projector
aggressor	curator	incinerator	prosecutor
agitator	defector	incisor	prospector
alternator	demonstrator	incubator	protector
ambassador	denominator	indicator	protractor
ancestor	depressor	instigator	radiator
arbitrator	detractor	instructor	reflector
auditor	dictator	interlocutor	refrigerator
aviator	director	inventor	respirator
bachelor	divisor	investigator	rotator
benefactor	donator	juror	senator
bettor	editor	legislator	solicitor
calculator	educator	lessor	spectator
capacitor	elevator	liberator	speculator
chancellor	erector	matador	supervisor
co-conspirator	escalator	mediator	survivor
collector	executor	moderator	tractor
communicator	extensor	narrator	transistor
competitor	exterminator	navigator	translator
compositor	fixator	numerator	ventilator
conductor	flexor	oppressor	visor

-ory   (relating to, quality, or place where; noun)

allegory	directory	inventory	rectory
category	dormitory	laboratory	refectory
conservatory	factory	lavatory	reformatory
crematory	history	memory	territory

-ory   (*of, pertaining to, or characterized by;* **adjective**)

accessory	cursory	manipulatory	satisfactory
advisory	declaratory	predatory	sensory
ambulatory	defamatory	proclamatory	signatory
auditory	exclamatory	promissory	speculatory
benedictory	exclusory	purgatory	supervisory
compulsory	inflammatory	reformatory	valedictory
contradictory	mandatory	salutatory	

-ous   (*full of or having;* **adjective; primarily used with Latin roots**)

adventurous	fabulous	monstrous	simultaneous
anonymous	famous	mountainous	slanderous
calamitous	felicitous	murderous	solicitous
calciferous	fibrous	nervous	spontaneous
cavernous	frivolous	odorous	stupendous
coniferous	generous	poisonous	synonymous
conspicuous	gluttonous	pompous	thunderous
credulous	hazardous	populous	tremendous
cruciferous	horrendous	ravenous	unanimous
dangerous	humorous	ridiculous	vigorous
deciduous	igneous	rigorous	villainous
desirous	jealous	ruinous	viscous
dextrous	joyous	scandalous	vociferous
enormous	meticulous	scrupulous	
extraneous	miraculous	serous	

Variants of -ous

-cious

atrocious	judicious	pernicious	specious
audacious	loquacious	precocious	suspicious
auspicious	luscious	pugnacious	tenacious
delicious	malicious	sagacious	vicious
ferocious	officious	salacious	vivacious

-ious

amphibious	dubious	hilarious	notorious
anxious	fastidious	laborious	obvious
curious	furious	litigious	precarious
delirious	glorious	melodious	previous
devious	gregarious	mysterious	rebellious

| religious | studious | uproarious | vicarious |
| serious | tedious | various | victorious |

-tious

ambitious	facetious	nutritious	scrumptious
conscientious	fictitious	pretentious	superstitious
contentious	flirtatious	propitious	vexatious
expeditious	infectious	repetitious	

In these words ending in -tious, t is the final letter of the base element and -ious is the suffix, but this pattern is often taught as -tious.

-s (noun [plural])

(pronounced /s/ with a base element ending in an unvoiced consonant)

| buckets | giraffes | traps |
| cats | graphs | trucks |

(pronounced /z/ with a base element ending in a vowel or a voiced consonant)

cars	halls	mountains	rings
cogs	knaves	news	trees
films	monkeys	reeds	

Variant of -s

-es (noun [plural]; used with base words ending in s, x, ch, sh, and z)

| boxes | gases | lunches |
| bushes | hutches | waltzes |

Many hundreds of other words contain plural suffixes.

-ship   (office, state, dignity, skill, quality, or profession; noun)

authorship	companionship	horsemanship	relationship
captainship	courtship	kinship	scholarship
censorship	dictatorship	leadership	seamanship
chairmanship	ensignship	lordship	sponsorship
championship	fellowship	membership	township
chaplainship	friendship	ownership	workmanship
citizenship	guardianship	partnership	
clerkship	hardship	readership	

-some *(characterized by a specified quality, condition, or action; Anglo-Saxon; adjective; primarily used with Anglo-Saxon base words)*

adventuresome	foursome	loathsome	twosome
awesome	frolicsome	lonesome	venturesome
bothersome	fulsome	meddlesome	wholesome
burdensome	gladsome	threesome	winsome
cumbersome	handsome	tiresome	
fearsome	irksome	toothsome	
flavorsome	lissome	troublesome	

-ster *(one who is associated with, participates in, makes, or does; noun)*

gangster	jokester	roadster	youngster
hipster	mobster	songster	
huckster	prankster	Teamster	

-tude *(condition, state, or quality of; noun)*

altitude	finitude	latitude	quietude
amplitude	fortitude	longitude	rectitude
aptitude	gratitude	magnitude	servitude
certitude	habitude	multitude	solitude
decrepitude	ineptitude	platitude	vicissitude
desuetude	infinitude	plentitude	
exactitude	lassitude	promptitude	

-ty, -ity *(state or quality of; noun)*

absurdity	felicity	negativity	sagacity
acidity	ferocity	ninety	scarcity
anxiety	finality	novelty	severity
automaticity	frailty	oddity	simplicity
calamity	frugality	paucity	solidarity
capacity	heredity	personality	solidity
captivity	humidity	perspicacity	specificity
commodity	integrity	plurality	stupidity
cruelty	legality	profanity	tenacity
domesticity	liberty	propriety	totality
eccentricity	liquidity	publicity	validity
elasticity	locality	quality	veracity
electricity	mentality	quantity	vivacity
entirety	multiplicity	reality	whimsicality
facility	nationality	rigidity	

-ure   (state of, process, function, or office; noun)

censure	erasure	measure	seizure
closure	failure	pleasure	tenure
configure	figure	pressure	
disfigure	leisure	procedure	
enclosure	manure	secure	

Variant of -ure

-ture

adventure	furniture	moisture	stricture
architecture	future	nature	structure
armature	gesture	overture	temperature
capture	indenture	pasture	texture
creature	juncture	picture	tincture
culture	lecture	portraiture	torture
curvature	legislature	posture	venture
expenditure	literature	puncture	vestiture
feature	mature	rupture	vulture
fixture	miniature	signature	
fracture	mixture	stature	

 In these words ending in *-ture*, *t* is the final letter of the base element and *-ure* is the suffix, but this pattern is often taught as *-ture*.

-ward   (expressing direction; Anglo-Saxon; adjective)

awkward	heavenward	onward	upward
backward	homeward	outward	wayward
earthward	inward	rearward	westward
eastward	leeward	seaward	windward
forward	northward	southward	

-y   (inclined to; adjective; primarily used with Anglo-Saxon base words)

blotchy	creaky	eighty	flirty
brainy	creepy	fishy	floppy
brawny	dreary	flabby	foggy
bushy	dumpy	flaky	funny
cloudy	earthy	flashy	gawky

greedy	lucky	shaky	soggy
groggy	mighty	shifty	splotchy
gushy	milky	shiny	spooky
hairy	muddy	showy	stocky
heady	muggy	skimpy	tacky
healthy	musky	skinny	touchy
itchy	rainy	sleepy	tricky
jerky	scraggy	slimy	weedy
jumpy	scrappy	smoky	whiny
lengthy	scruffy	snappy	windy
loony	seedy	sneaky	wordy

REFERENCES

The American heritage dictionary (2nd ed.). (1982). Boston: Houghton Mifflin.
The American heritage dictionary (4th ed.). (2000). Boston: Houghton Mifflin.
Random House unabridged dictionary (2nd ed.). (1993). New York: Random House.

Latin Roots

Words of Latin origin come to English from the Latin language spoken in ancient Rome and in Latium, a country in ancient Italy. The Latin roots in English words carry specific meanings. The root syllables usually receive the stress in the word and therefore contain either a short or a long vowel sound. Most Latin roots are bound morphemes. They are affixed; that is, one adds prefixes and/or suffixes to them. Most roots form the basis of hundreds of associated words with the addition of numerous prefixes and suffixes.

The roots in this appendix are given in alphabetical order, with rarer variants in parentheses. The meaning of each root family is also listed in parentheses. The teacher should introduce the most common word roots used in common words first. See Chapter 7 for a logical order of presentation. See Chapter 8 for a sequence of presentation of some less common Latin roots. The lists in this appendix are not complete but contain the most frequently found words containing the targeted roots.

When presenting a new root, the teacher can show the root on an index card and have students write the root on paper. The teacher can ask students to generate words containing the root on the board or on paper. The teacher can observe whether students pick up the meaning of the root from the words generated.

After presenting the roots, the teacher should have word lists ready for students to read. In addition, words can be dictated for spelling. The class can discuss the meanings of the words as they relate to specific roots. See Chapters 7 and 8 for additional activities involving Latin roots.

anni, annu, enni (*year*)

annals	bicentennial	interannual	sesquicentennial
anniversary	biennial	millennial	superannuate
annual	biennium	millennium	tercentenary
annualize	centenary	plurannual	tercentennial
annuitant	centennial	quadrennial	triennial
annuity	decennial	quadrennium	
biannual	decennium	quinquennial	
bicentenary	exannual	semiannual	

aud (*to hear or listen*)

audibility	audiogram	audiovisual	auditory
audible	audiologist	audiphone	audivision
audience	audiology	audit	inaudible
audio	audiometer	audition	subaudible
audioanalgesia	audiophiliac	auditor	
audiofrequency	audiospectogram	auditorium	

cad, cas, cid (*to fall or befall*)

accident	casual	decadent	occident
accidental	casualty	decay	Occident
cadaver	coincide	deciduous	occidental
cadaverous	coincidence	incidence	recidivism
cadence	coincident	incident	recidivist
cadenza	coincidental	incidental	
cascade	decadence	occasion	

cap, ceit, ceive, cep, cept, cip (*to take, catch, seize, hold, or receive*)

accept	capsule	conceptual	exception
acceptable	caption	deceit	exceptional
acceptance	captious	deceitful	forceps
anticipate	captivate	deceitfulness	incapable
anticipation	captive	deceive	inconceivable
anticipatory	captivity	deception	intercept
capability	captor	emancipate	interception
capable	capture	emancipation	interceptor
capacious	conceit	emancipator	municipal
capacitor	conceive	encapsulate	municipality
capacity	concept	encapsulation	participant
capstan	conception	except	participate

participation
perceive
percept
perceptible
perception

perceptive
principal
principle
receipt
receivable

receive
receptacle
reception
recipe
recipient

susceptibility
susceptible
unacceptable

capit, capt (chie, cip) *(head or chief)*

achieve
achievement
achiever
capital
capitalism
capitalist
capitalize
capitate
capitation
Capitol
capitular
capitulate
capitulation

caprice
capricious
captain
captaincy
chapter
chief
chieftain
decapitate
decapitation
handkerchief
kerchief
mischief
mischievous

occiput
overachiever
per capita
precipice
precipitate
precipitation
precipitous
recapitulate
recapitulation
underachiever
undercapitalization

cause, cuse, cus *(to cause; motive)*

accusation
accusative
accuse
accuser

because
causal
causality
causation

cause
causeless
excusable
excuse

inexcusable

cede, ceed, cess *(to go, yield, or surrender)*

abscess
accede
access
accessible
accession
accessory
ancestor
antecedent
cease
cessation
concede
concession

decease
decedent
exceed
excess
excessive
inaccessible
incessant
intercede
intercession
necessary
precede
precedent

precess
precession
predecessor
procedure
proceed
process
procession
recede
recess
recession
recessive
retrocede

secede
secession
secessionist
success
successful
succession
successive
supersede
unprecedented

cern *(to separate)*   **cert** *(to decide)*

ascertain	certificate	concern
certain	certification	discern
certainty	certify	discernment

cise *(to cut)*

circumcise	decision	incision	precise
circumcision	decisive	incisive	precision
concise	excise	incisor	scissors
concision	excision	indecision	
decide	incise	indecisive	

 The root *cise* and the suffix *-cide*, meaning *to kill*, come from the same Latin root, *caedere*.

claim, clam *(to declare, call out, or cry out)*

acclaim	clamor	disclaim	misclaim
acclamation	clamorous	disclaimer	proclaim
claim	conclamant	exclaim	proclamation
claimant	counterclaim	exclamation	proclamatory
clamant	declaim	exclamatory	reclaim
clamatorial	declamation	irreclaimable	reclaimable

claus, clois, clos, clud, clus *(to shut or close)*

clause	conclusion	foreclose	occlusion
claustrophobia	conclusive	foreclosure	occlusive
claustrophobic	disclose	include	preclude
cloisonné	disclosure	inclusion	preclusion
cloistral	enclose	inclusive	recluse
cloister	enclosure	inclusiveness	reclusive
close	exclude	malocclusion	seclude
closet	exclusion	occlude	seclusion
conclude	exclusive	occlusal	

cogn *(to know)*

cognition	cognizance	metacognitive	recognition
cognitive	cognizant	precognition	recognizable
cognizable	metacognition	precognitive	recognize

The root *cogn* is related to the Greek combining forms *gno* and *gnosi,* also meaning to *know.*

cred (*to believe*)

accredit	credible	credulity	incredible
accreditation	credit	credulous	incredulity
credence	creditable	creed	incredulous
credential	creditor	discredit	
credibility	credo	discreditable	

cur, curs (cours) (*to run or go*)

concourse	current	discursive	recourse
concur	curricular	excursion	recur
concurrent	curriculum	incur	recurrence
corridor	cursive	incursion	recurrent
courier	cursor	occur	succor
course	cursory	occurrence	
currency	discourse	precursor	

dent (*tooth*)

dental	dentilation	dentition	indent
dentation	dentin	dentofacial	indentation
denticulate	dentine	dentoid	indenture
dentiform	dentiphone	dentolingual	interdental
dentifrice	dentist	dentulous	labiodental
dentigerous	dentistry	denture	trident

dic, dict (*to say or tell*)

abdicant	dedicate	edict	predicament
abdicate	dedication	indicate	predicate
abdication	Dictaphone	indication	predication
addict	dictate	indicative	predict
addiction	dictation	indicator	prediction
addictive	dictator	indict	valedictorian
benediction	dictatorial	indictable	verdict
benedictory	dictatorship	indictment	vindicate
contradict	diction	interdict	vindication
contradiction	dictionary	interdiction	vindictive
contradictory	dictum	malediction	

duc, duce, duct   (*to lead*)

abduce	deduct	induce	reducible
abduct	deductible	inductance	reduction
abduction	deduction	inductee	reproduce
abductor	deductive	induction	reproduction
adduction	ducal	inductive	seduce
adductor	duchess	introduce	seduction
aqueduct	duchy	introduction	traduce
conducive	duct	postproduction	transduce
conduct	ductile	producer	transduction
conductor	ductility	product	viaduct
conduit	educate	production	
deduce	education	reduce	

fac, fact, fect, fic   (*to make or do*)

affair	defector	facility	infection
affect	deficient	facsimile	infectious
affection	deficit	fact	insignificant
affectionate	deification	faction	intensification
artifact	difficult	factious	justification
artifice	difficulty	factitious	magnification
artificer	disaffected	factor	magnificent
artificial	disinfect	factory	maleficence
beautification	disinfectant	factotum	maleficent
benefactor	disinfection	facultative	manufacture
beneficence	dissatisfaction	faculty	manufacturer
beneficent	diversification	falsification	modification
beneficial	edification	fiction	notification
beneficiary	edifice	fictional	office
certificate	effect	fictionalize	officer
certification	effective	fictitious	official
classification	effectual	fortification	officiant
coefficient	efficacious	gentrification	officiate
confection	efficacy	glorification	officious
confectionary	efficiency	gratification	pacification
confectioner	efficient	identification	perfect
confectionery	electrification	imperfect	personification
defect	facile	imperfection	proficiency
defection	facilitate	ineffective	proficient
defective	facilitation	infect	profit

profiteer	rarefaction	significant	suffice
purification	rubefacient	signification	sufficient
putrefaction	sacrifice	simplification	unification
qualification	satisfaction	specification	unsatisfactory
quantification	satisfactory	stupefaction	

The Latin suffixes *-fy* and *-ify* are related to the roots *fac, fact, fect,* and *fic.*

feal, feder, fid, fide   (*trust or faith*)

affiance	confidence	federacy	fiduciary
affidavit	confident	federal	infidel
bona fide	confidential	federalism	infidelity
confederacy	confidentiality	federalist	perfidious
confederate	diffidence	federation	perfidy
confidant	diffident	fidelity	Semper Fidelis
confide	fealty	fiducial	

fer   (*to bear or yield*)

afferent	difference	insufferable	referendum
aquifer	different	interfere	referent
circumference	differential	interference	referential
confer	efferent	odoriferous	referral
conferee	ferriferous	offer	suffer
conference	ferry	prefer	sufferance
conifer	fertile	preferable	teleconference
coniferous	fertilization	preference	transfer
crucifer	fertilize	preferential	transferable
defer	fertilizer	proffer	transference
deference	floriferous	refer	transferrin
deferential	infer	referee	vociferant
differ	inference	reference	vociferous

fin, finis   (*end*)

ad infinitum	definitive	financial	finite
affinity	final	financier	finitude
confine	finale	finial	indefinite
confinement	finalist	finis	infinite
define	finalize	finish	infinitesimal
definite	finance	finisher	infinity

paraffin   refinement   undefinable
refine   refinery

fix   (*to fix*)

affix   fixate   fixity   suffix
affixation   fixation   fixture   transfix
affixture   fixative   infix   transfixion
fix   fixator   prefix

flect, flex   (*to bend or curve*)

anteflexion   flexible   inflect   reflector
circumflex   flexile   inflection   reflectoscope
circumflexion   flexion   inflexible   reflex
deflect   flexor   nonreflective   reflexive
deflection   flexuous   reflect   retroflex
flex   genuflect   reflection
flexibility   genuflection   reflective

flu, fluc, fluv, flux   (*flow*)

affluence   fluctuant   fluidimeter   influence
affluent   fluctuate   fluidity   influx
afflux   fluctuation   fluidize   mellifluous
circumfluent   flue   flume   reflux
confluence   fluency   flush   superfluity
confluent   fluent   fluvial   superfluous
effluence   fluid   fluviograph
effluent   fluidic   fluviology

form   (*to shape*)

conform   format   informant   performer
conformist   formation   information   reform
conformity   formless   informative   reformation
deform   formlessness   informer   reformer
deformity   formula   misinform   transform
disinformation   formulaic   misinformation   transformation
form   formulary   nonconformist   transformer
formal   formulate   nonconformity   uniform
formality   inform   perform   uniformity
formalize   informal   performance

gen, genus (*race, kind, or species; birth*)

agenesis	genealogy	genocide	monogenesis
congenial	generable	genre	nitrogen
congeniality	general	gentile	photogenic
congenital	generate	gentility	primogeniture
degenerate	generation	genuine	progenitor
degeneration	generative	genus	progeny
degenerative	generator	heterogeneous	regenerate
disingenuous	generic	homogeneous	regeneration
eugenics	generosity	homogenize	telegenic
gendarme	generous	hydrogen	transgenic
gender	genesis	indigenous	
gene	genetics	ingenuous	

grad, gred, gress (*step, degree; to walk*)

aggradation	degree	gradual	regress
aggression	digress	graduate	regression
aggressive	digression	graduation	retrograde
aggressor	downgrade	gressorial	retrogress
biodegradable	egress	ingredient	transgress
centigrade	gradate	ingress	transgression
congress	gradation	postgraduate	upgrade
congressional	grade	progress	
degradation	gradient	progression	
degrade	gradiometer	progressive	

grat, gre (*thanks; pleasing*)

agree	disagreeable	gratification	gratulant
agreeable	disagreement	gratify	gratulatory
agreement	disgrace	gratis	ingrate
congratulate	disgraceful	gratitude	ingratiate
congratulation	grace	gratuitant	ingratitude
congratulatory	graceless	gratuitous	
disagree	grateful	gratuity	

greg (*crowd, group, flock, or herd; to assemble*)

aggregate	congregation	desegregation	segregate
aggregation	congregational	egregious	segregation
congregate	desegregate	gregarious	segregationist

jac, jec, ject   (*to throw or lie*)

abject	eject	object	projective
abjectness	ejection	objection	projector
adjacent	inject	objective	reject
adjectival	injection	objectivity	rejection
adjective	interject	project	subject
conjecture	interjection	projectile	subjective
deject	introject	projection	subjectivity
dejection	introjection	projectionist	trajectory

jud, judi, judic   (*judge*)

adjudge	judge	judicature	prejudge
adjudicate	judgment	judicial	prejudice
adjudicative	judicator	judiciary	prejudicial
injudicious	judicatory	judicious	unprejudicial

jur, jus   (*law or right*)

abjuration	conjure	juror	justification
abjure	conjurer	jury	justify
adjure	jurisdiction	juryman	readjust
adjust	jurisprudence	just	readjustment
adjustive	jurist	justice	
adjustment	juristic	justifiable	

lect, leg, lig   (*to choose, pick, read, or speak*)

acrolect	electable	intelligible	neglectful
basilect	elector	lectern	negligent
collect	electorate	lecture	prelect
collection	elegant	legend	sacrilege
collective	idiolect	legendary	sacrilegious
delegate	illegibility	legibility	select
delegation	illegible	legible	selection
dialect	intellect	legion	selective
diligence	intellectual	Legionnaire's	
diligent	intelligence	mesolect	
elect	intelligent	neglect	

The roots *lect*, *leg*, and *lig* are related to the Greek combining form *logos*, meaning *speech or word*.

leg (*law*)

illegal	legal	legalize	legislature
illegality	legalese	legislate	legitimate
illegitimate	legalism	legislative	privilege
legacy	legalistic	legislator	

lit, liter, litera (*letters*)

alliterate	illiterate	literalism	obliterate
alliteration	litany	literary	obliteration
alliterative	literacy	literate	transliterate
illiteracy	literal	literatim	transliteration

loc, loqu (*to speak, talk, or say*)

ambiloquent	elocution	loquacious	soliloquist
circumlocute	eloquence	loquacity	soliloquy
circumlocution	eloquent	magniloquence	somniloquent
colloquial	grandiloquence	magniloquent	somniloquy
colloquialism	grandiloquent	obloquious	uneloquent
colloquy	interlocution	obloquy	ventriloquist
elocute	interlocutor	omniloquent	ventriloquy

magna, magni (*great*)

magnanimity	magnification	magnify	magnum
magnanimous	magnificence	magniloquence	
magnascope	magnificent	magniloquent	
magnate	magnifico	magnitude	

matr, matri (*mother*)

alma mater	matricide	matrimonial	matronymic
maternal	matriculant	matrimony	
maternity	matriculate	matrix	
matriarch	matrilineal	matron	

mit, miss (*to send*)

admission	compromise	emit	mission
admit	dismiss	inadmissible	missionary
commission	dismissal	intermission	omission
commit	emissary	intermittent	omit
committee	emission	intromission	permissible

permission	promise	subcommittee	transmit
permissive	remiss	submission	transmitter
permit	remit	submit	
premise	remittance	transmission	

mob, mot, mov (*to move*)

automobile	immovable	motivation	move
commotion	locomotion	motivational	movement
countermove	mob	motive	movie
demobilization	mobile	motor	promote
demote	mobility	motorbike	promoter
demotion	mobilization	motorboat	promotion
emote	mobilize	motorcade	remote
emotion	mobster	motorcycle	removal
emotional	motion	motordrome	remove
immobile	motionless	motorist	
immobilization	motivate	movable	

patr, pater (*father*)

compatriot	paternity	patriot	patroon
depatriate	patriarch	patriotic	patrophile
expatriate	patriarchy	patriotism	philopatric
expatriation	patrician	patron	repatriate
paterfamilias	patricide	patronage	repatriation
paternal	patrilineal	patronize	unpatriotic
paternalism	patrimony	patronymic	

ped (*foot*)

aliped	expeditious	pedal	pedomotive
biped	expeditiousness	pedestal	peduncle
carpopedal	impede	pedestrian	pinniped
centipede	impediment	pedicure	quadruped
depeditate	millipede	pediment	uniped
expedite	multiped	pedogram	velocipede
expedition	octoped	pedometer	

The Latin root *ped* is different from the Greek combining forms *ped*, meaning *child*, and *ped*, meaning *soil*.

pel, puls (*to drive or push*)

compel	expulsion	propeller	repellent
compulsion	impel	propulsion	repulse
compulsive	impulse	pulsate	repulsion
compulsory	impulsive	pulsation	repulsive
dispel	propel	pulse	
expel	propellant	repel	

pend, pens (*to hang or weigh*)

appendage	dispensary	interdependence	penthouse
appendectomy	dispensation	interdependent	perpendicular
appendix	dispense	pendant	suspend
compensate	dispenser	pending	suspenders
depend	expend	pendulate	suspense
dependability	expense	pendule	suspenseful
dependable	expensive	pendulous	suspension
dependence	impending	pendulum	
dependent	independence	pension	
dispensable	independent	pensive	

port (*to carry*)

airport	exporter	portage	reportage
apportable	import	portal	reporter
carport	important	portamento	support
comportment	importer	porter	supportive
deport	insupportable	portfolio	teleportation
deportation	opportune	porthole	transport
deportee	opportunity	portmanteau	transportable
deportment	passport	purport	transportation
export	port	rapport	transporter
exportation	portable	report	unimportant

pos, pon, pound (*to put, place, or set*)

component	compositor	deposit	exponent
compose	composure	deposition	exponential
composer	compound	disposal	expose
composite	counterproposal	dispose	exposition
composition	depose	disposition	exposure

expound	opposition	postpone	purpose
impose	ponder	postural	purposeful
imposition	ponderous	posture	purposeless
impostor	pose	preposition	superimpose
impound	posit	prepositional	suppose
interpose	position	proponent	supposition
interposition	positive	proposal	transpose
opponent	positor	propose	transposition
oppose	post	proposition	
opposite	poster	propound	

put   (*to think*)

computable	deputize	disputatious	reputable
computation	deputy	dispute	reputation
compute	disputable	imputation	repute
computer	disputants	impute	
depute	disputation	putative	

rect, recti   (*straight or right*)

correct	erect	rectangular	regimental
correctable	erector	rectifiable	region
correction	incorrect	rectify	regional
corrective	indirect	rectilinear	regionalism
corrigible	indirectness	rectitude	regular
direct	irregular	rector	regularity
direction	irregularity	rectory	regulate
directive	reckon	redirect	regulation
directness	reckoning	regal	
director	rectangle	regiment	

rupt   (*to break or burst*)

abrupt	corruptible	eruption	irrupt
abruption	disrupt	incorrupt	irruption
bankrupt	disruption	incorruptible	rupture
bankruptcy	disruptive	interrupt	
corrupt	erupt	interruption	

scrib, script   (*to write*)

ascribe	conscription	indescribable	manuscript
ascription	describe	inscribe	nondescript
circumscribe	description	inscription	postscript
conscript	descriptive	interscribe	prescribe

prescription	scribble	scrivener	transcriber
proscribe	scribblemania	subscribe	transcript
proscription	scribe	subscriber	transcription
rescript	scribophobia	subscription	
scribable	script	superscription	
scribacious	Scripture	transcribe	

Verbs usually use *scribe,* as in *prescribe;* nouns usually use *script,* as in *prescription.*

sec, sect   (to cut)

dissect	intersection	sectile	segment
dissection	resect	section	segmental
insect	resection	sectional	transect
intersect	secant	sector	

spec, spect, spic   (to see, watch, or observe)

aspect	prospect	spectrogram
auspicious	prospector	spectroheliograph
circumspect	respect	spectrohelioscope
conspicuous	respectful	spectrology
despicable	respective	spectrometry
despise	retrospective	spectrophobia
disrespect	special	spectrophone
disrespectful	specialist	spectroscope
expect	species	spectrum
expectation	specify	speculate
inconspicuous	specimen	speculation
inspect	specious	speculator
inspection	spectacle	speculum
inspector	spectacular	suspect
introspection	spectator	suspicion
introspective	specter	suspicious
perspective	spectral	

spir, spire   (to breathe)

aspiration	disspirited	perspiration	spirit
aspire	expiration	perspire	spiritual
co-conspirator	expire	respiration	spiritualism
conspiracy	inspiration	respirator	transpire
conspire	inspire	respire	uninspiring

sta, sist, stat, stit (*to stand*)

assist	ecstatic	reconstitute	statistic
assistant	establish	reconstitution	status
assistive	establishment	resist	subsist
circumstance	estate	resistant	subsistence
circumstantial	insist	restitution	subsistent
consist	insistence	stamina	substance
consistency	insistent	stance	substandard
consistent	instance	stanch	substantial
constancy	instant	stanchion	substantiate
constant	instantaneous	stand	substantive
constitute	instantiate	standard	substitute
constitution	insubstantiate	standardization	superstition
constitutional	interstice	standardize	superstitious
desist	irresistible	stanza	transistor
destitute	obstacle	static	understand
destitution	obstinate	station	understandability
distance	persist	stationary	understandable
distant	persistence	stationer	
ecstasy	persistent	stationery	

stru, struct (stry) (*to build*)

construct	industrious	instrument	reconstructionist
constructive	industry	instrumental	restructure
construe	infrastructure	instrumentalist	structural
destruction	instruct	obstruct	structure
destructive	instruction	obstruction	superstructure
indestructible	instructive	obstructionist	
industrial	instructor	reconstruction	

tact, tag, tang, tig, ting (*to touch*)

contact	intangibility	tactical	tangential
contagion	intangible	tactician	tangibility
contiguous	tact	tactile	tangible
contingency	tactful	tactless	
contingent	tactfulness	tactlessness	
intact	tactic	tangent	

ten, tain, tin, tinu   (*to hold*)

abstain	continuous	maintainer	sustenance
abstainer	detain	maintenance	sustentation
abstinence	detainee	obtain	tenable
attain	detainment	obtainable	tenacious
attainment	detention	pertain	tenacity
contain	discontent	pertinence	tenant
container	discontentedness	pertinent	tenement
containment	discontinuation	retain	tenet
content	discontinue	retainer	tenure
contentment	entertain	retention	unattainable
continual	entertainer	retentive	untenable
continuation	entertainment	sustain	
continue	maintain	sustainer	

tend, tens, tent   (*to stretch or strain*)

antenna	extend	intensity	pretension
attempt	extension	intensive	pretentious
attend	extensive	intent	pretentiousness
attendance	extensor	intention	superintendent
attention	hyperextend	intentional	tendinitis
attentive	hyperextension	lieutenant	tendon
attentiveness	hypertension	ostensible	tenotomy
contend	hypotension	ostentation	tense
contender	inattention	ostentatious	tension
contention	inattentive	ostentatiousness	tent
contentious	inattentiveness	portend	tenuous
contentiousness	intend	portentous	unintentional
distend	intense	pretend	
distention	intensify	pretense	

tract   (*to draw or pull*)

abstract	contract	detractor	extraction
abstraction	contractor	distract	intractable
attract	contractual	distractible	protract
attraction	detract	distraction	protractor
attractive	detraction	extract	retract

retraction	tract	tractile	tractor
subtract	tractable	traction	
subtraction	tractibility	tractive	

ven, veni, vent (to come)

advent	contravene	inconvenient	preventive
adventitious	convene	intervene	revenue
adventitiousness	convenient	intervention	souvenir
adventure	convent	invent	unconventional
adventurer	convention	invention	uneventful
adventuresome	covenant	inventor	unpreventable
adventuress	event	inventory	venture
adventurous	eventful	misadventure	venturesome
adventurousness	eventual	prevent	
avenue	eventuality	preventable	
circumvent	inconvenience	prevention	

ver, veri (true or genuine)

veracious	verify	veritable
veracity	verisimilitude	verity
verdict	verism	very

vers, vert (to turn)

adversarial	conversant	inverse	varsity
adversary	conversation	inversion	versatile
adverse	converse	invert	versatility
advertise	convert	obverse	verse
advertisement	convertible	reverse	version
advertiser	diverse	reversible	versus
averse	diversification	reversion	vertebra
aversion	diversify	revert	vertebrate
aversive	diversion	subversion	vertex
avert	divert	subversive	vertical
controversial	extroversion	subvert	vertiginous
controversy	extrovert	universal	vertigo
converge	introversion	universe	vortex
convergent	introvert	university	

vid, vis   (*to see*)

advise	individual	supervision	visionary
adviser	indivisible	supervisor	visit
advisor	invisible	supervisory	visitation
divide	nonvisual	televise	visitor
division	provide	television	visor
divisor	providence	video	vista
envision	provider	visa	visual
evidence	provision	visage	visualization
evident	revise	visibility	visualize
improvisation	revision	visible	
improvise	supervise	vision	

The Middle English term *vewe*, which became *view*, came from Latin *videre*, meaning *to see*.

interview	review	viewfinder
preview	view	

vit, vita, viv, vivi   (*to live*)

antivivisectionist	survive	vivace	vividness
revitalize	vital	vivacious	viviparous
revival	vitality	vivacity	vivisection
revive	vitamin	vivarium	
survival	vitaminology	vivid	

voc, vok, voke   (*to call*)

advocacy	evocative	provoke	vocalic
advocate	evoke	revocable	vocalization
avocation	invocation	revocation	vocalize
convocation	invoke	revoke	vocation
equivocal	irrevocable	vocabulary	vocational
equivocate	provocation	vocabulist	vociferant
equivocation	provocative	vocal	vociferous

REFERENCES

The American heritage dictionary (2nd ed.). (1982). Boston: Houghton Mifflin.
The American heritage dictionary (4th ed.). (2000). Boston: Houghton Mifflin.
Random House unabridged dictionary (2nd ed.). (1993). New York: Random House.

Greek
Combining Forms

The word parts in this appendix come to us from the Greek language and usually appear in specialized words used in science and mathematics. Greek word parts are usually compounded—that is, two word parts are combined as in *photograph* and *psychology*—and are thus called *combining forms* in many dictionaries. Suffixes are often added as in *photographic* and *psychologist*. Some specific letter–sound correspondences are typically found in Greek words. Most common are *ph* as in *phonograph*; *ch* as in chemistry; and /ĭ/ or /ī/ as in *synonym* and *hydrogen*, respectively. Less common orthographic patterns include *ps* as in *psychiatry*, *mn* as in *mnemonics*, *pn* as in *pneumonia*, *rh* as in *rhinoceros*, and *pt* as in *pterodactyl*.

Students may not know the meanings of many of the words and are encouraged to predict the meanings based on the combining forms and to follow-up by looking in a dictionary. Although the following combining forms are listed in alphabetical order, teach the most common first. See Chapter 7 for a logical sequence of presentation. See Chapter 8 for a sequence of presentation of some less common Greek combining forms. These lists are not complete but include the most frequently found words containing the targeted combining forms.

andr, anthr (*man*)

andragogy	androgynous	androphobia
andranatomy	android	anthropoid
androcentric	andrology	anthropologist
androcracy	andromorphic	anthropology

anthropomorphic   philander   philanthropist
anthropomorphism   philanderer   philanthropy
anthroponym   philanthropic   polyandry

arch (chief or ruler)

anarchy	archimorphic	autarchy	monarchy
archangel	architect	biarch	myriarch
archbishop	architectonic	ecclesiarch	oligarchy
archconservative	architectural	endarchy	panarchy
archdeacon	architecture	hierarchy	patriarch
archduke	archthief	matriarch	patriarchy
archenemy	archvillain	matriarchy	pentarchy
archetype	autarch	monarch	polyarchy

archae, arche, archi (primitive or ancient)

archaeoastronomer	Archaeozoic	archetype
archaeological	archaic	archilithic
archaeologist	archaism	archimorphic
archaeology	archecentric	archives
archaeopteryx	archegenesis	archivist

ast, astro (star)

archaeoastronomer	astrological	astrophobia
asterisk	astrologue	astrophotograph
asteroid	astrology	astrophysics
asterozoa	astrometeorologist	Astros
astrobiology	astrometeorology	astrosphere
astrobotanist	astrometry	astrotheology
astrochemistry	astronaut	bioastronautics
astrograph	astronomer	disaster
astrokinetic	astronomical	disastrous
astrolabe	astronomy	radioastronomy
astrologer	Astrophil	

auto (self; usually used as a prefix)

autarchy	autochthon	autocratic	autoimmune
autism	autocide	autodermic	autoinfection
autoantibody	autoclave	autogenesis	Automat
autobiographical	autocracy	autograph	automatic
autobiography	autocrat	autohypnosis	automation

automaton	autonomy	autoscope	semiautomatic
automobile	autonym	autosuggestion	
automotive	autophobia	autotelic	
autonomous	autopsy	autotherapy	

biblio (*book*)

bible	bibliography	bibliophobia
biblical	biblioklept	bibliopole
biblioclast	bibliolatry	bibliosoph
bibliofilm	bibliology	bibliotheca
bibliogenesis	bibliomania	bibliotherapy
bibliographer	bibliophile	bibliotics
bibliographic	bibliophobe	photobibliography

bio (*life*)

abiosis	bioecology	biomaterial	biosphere
aerobiology	bioengineering	biome	biotechnics
amphibious	bioethics	biomechanics	biotechnology
antibiotics	biofeedback	biomedicine	bioterrorism
astrobiology	biogeographic	biometeorology	chronobiology
autobiographical	biogeographical	biometer	ecobiology
autobiography	biogeography	biometrics	hydrobiology
bioactive	biogeosphere	biomicroscope	macrobiotic
bioastronautics	biographer	biomotor	microbiology
biochemistry	biographic	bionavigation	parabiosis
biocompatible	biographical	bionic	photobiotic
biocracy	biography	biopesticide	phyllobiology
biocrat	biological	biophile	psychobiography
biodegradable	biologist	biophysics	symbiosis
biodiversity	biology	biopsy	zoobiotic
biodynamic	biomagnetism	bioregion	
bioecologist	biomarker	bioscope	

chrom (*color*)

achromachia	chromatogram	chromogenic
achromatic	chromatology	chromophobic
achromoderma	chromatolysis	chromoscope
chromatic	chrome	chromosomal
chromatid	chromium	chromosome
chromatin	chromogenesis	chromosphere

ferrochrome
heliochrome
heliochromoscope
hemochrome
hyperchromatic

hyperchromia
hypochromic
monochromatic
monochrome
orthochromatic

parachromatism
photochrome
polychromatic
polychrome

chron, chrono (*time*)

achroniasm
anachronistic
chronal
chronic
chronicle
chronicler
chronobarometer
chronobiology
chronognosis
chronogram
chronograph
chronographic

chronologer
chronological
chronologist
chronologize
chronology
chronometer
chronometric
chronometry
chronophobia
chronophotograph
chronoscope
chronotherapy

chronothermal
desynchronize
diachronic
diachronous
geochronic
geosynchronous
monochronic
parachronism
psychochronometry
synchronicity
synchronize
synchronous

cracy, crat (*rule, strength, or power;* **often used as a suffix**)

androcracy
aristocracy
aristocrat
aristocratic
autocracy
autocrat

autocratic
biocrat
bureaucracy
bureaucrat
bureaucratic
democracy

democrat
democratic
mediocracy
mobocracy
pancratic
plutocracy

plutocrat
plutocratic
technocracy
technocrat
technocratic
theocrat

cycl, cyclo (*wheel or circle; circular*)

bicycle
bicyclist
cyclamen
cycle
cyclic
cyclical
cycling
cyclist
cyclograph

cyclomania
cyclometer
cyclometry
cyclone
cyclonology
cyclopedia
cyclopedist
cyclophobia
Cyclops

cyclorama
cyclosporine
cyclotron
encyclopedia
encyclopedic
epicycle
geocyclic
kilocycle
megacycle

monocycle
motorcycle
pericycle
recycle
tricycle
unicycle

dem, demo (*people*)

antidemocratic	democratism	demophile	endemic
demagogue	demographer	demophobe	pandemic
democracy	demographics	demophobia	philodemic
democrat	demographist	demotic	polydemic
democratic	demography	demotics	

derm (*skin*)

achromoderma	dermatoglyphics	dermatotherapy	intradermal
adermia	dermatoid	dermis	megaderm
autodermic	dermatologist	ectoderm	pachyderm
blastoderm	dermatology	epidermis	pneumoderma
dermabrasion	dermatome	hyperdermic	taxidermist
dermal	dermatoplasty	hypodermic	taxidermy
dermatitis	dermatosis	hypodermis	

drome, dromos (*course or running*)

acrodrome	dromomania	hippodrome	prodrome
aerodrome	dromometer	hydrodrome	syndrome
airdrome	dromophobia	motordrome	
dromedary	dromos	palindrome	
dromograph	dromotropic	paradromic	

dyn, dynamo (*power, strength, or force*)

aerodynamics	dynamo	dynastic	hemodynamics
biodynamic	dynamoelectric	dynasty	hydrodynamic
dynagraph	dynamogenesis	dynatron	megadynamics
dynameter	dynamometer	dyne	monodynamic
dynamic	dynamometry	dynode	photodynamic
dynamism	dynamoscope	electrodynamic	thermodynamics
dynamite	dynamotor	geodynamics	toxicodynamic

eco (*house or home*)

bioecologist	ecogeography	ecomania	economy
bioecology	ecological	econometrics	ecophobia
ecoactivist	ecologist	economical	ecophysics
ecobiology	ecology	economics	ecophysiology
ecogeographic	ecomanagement	economist	ecospecies

ecosphere	ecotone	macroeconomics
ecosystem	ecotourism	microecology
ecoterrorism	ecotype	microeconomics

ecto   (outside, external, or beyond)

appendectomy	ectoderm	ectomorphic	ectoplasm
ectoblast	ectogenous	ectoparasite	ectosuggestion
ectocardia	ectoglobular	ectopia	ectoterm
ectocommensal	ectomorph	ectopic	ectothermic

ectomy   (cut out; often used as a suffix)

appendectomy	cystectomy	mastectomy	splenectomy
bursectomy	hysterectomy	pneumatectomy	tonsillectomy
cardiectomy	lumpectomy	pneumectomy	

geo   (earth)

biogeographical	geodesic	geologist	geophysics
biogeography	geodynamics	geology	geopolitical
biogeosphere	geoglyphic	geometric	geopolitics
ecogeographic	geognosy	geometry	geosphere
ecogeography	geographer	geomorphic	geosynchronous
geocentric	geographic	geophagia	geotechnics
geochemistry	geography	geophilous	geothermal
geochronic	geohydrology	geophone	
geocyclic	geological	geophysical	

gno, gnosi   (to know)

agnosia	diagnosis	ignorant	prognosticator
agnostic	diagnostician	prognosis	telegnosis
agnostician	geognosy	prognosticable	
chronognosis	ignorance	prognosticate	

 The Greek combining forms *gno* and *gnosi* are related to the Latin root *cogn*, also meaning *to know*.

gon   (angle)

diagonal	hexagonal	octagonal	polygon
goniometer	isogon	orthogonal	tetragon
heptagon	nonagon	pentagon	tetragonal
heptagonal	nonagonal	pentagonal	trigonometric
hexagon	octagon	perigon	trigonometry

gram, graph (*written or drawn*)

anagram
astrograph
astrophotograph
autobiographical
autobiography
autograph
bibliographer
bibliographic
bibliography
biogeographic
biogeographical
biogeography
biographer
biographic
biographical
biography
calligrapher
calligraphic
calligraphy
choreographer
choreographic
choreography
chronogram
chronograph
chronographic
chronophotograph
cinematographer
cinematographic
cinematography
cyclograph
demographer
demographics
demographist
demography
dromograph
dynagraph
dysgraphia
ecogeographic
ecogeography

electrocardiogram
electroencephalogram
epigram
epigraph
ethnography
geographer
geographic
geography
graph
grapheme
graphic
graphite
graphology
graphomania
graphometer
graphomotor
graphophonemic
heliograph
hologram
holograph
holographic
homograph
homographic
hydrograph
hydrographer
ideogram
isogram
kinematograph
lexicographer
lexicography
lexigraphy
limnograph
lithograph
lithographer
lithographic
lithography
lithostratigraphy
logogram
logograph

logographer
logographic
macrograph
macrophotography
megagram
microlithography
mimeograph
mimeographic
monogram
monograph
morphography
myelogram
oceanographer
oceanographic
oceanography
orthographic
orthography
pangram
paragraph
parallelogram
pathography
pantograph
petrograph
petrographic
phonocardiograph
phonogram
phonograph
photobibliography
photogram
photogrammetry
photograph
photographer
photographic
photography
photoheliograph
physiograph
physiographic
pictogram
pictograph

pneumatogram
pneumograph
polygraph
polygraphy
psychobiography
psychograph
radiograph
radiographic
seismograph

sonogram
spectrogram
spectroheliograph
stenographer
stenographic
stenography
stereogram
stereographic
stereography

tangram
telegram
telegraph
telegraphic
telephotography
thermograph
zoography

helio   (*sun*)

aphelion
heliocentric
heliochrome
heliochromoscope
heliofugal
heliogram
heliograph
heliomania
heliometer

heliophilous
heliophobia
heliophobic
heliophyte
Heliopolis
helioscope
heliosphere
heliostat
heliotherapy

heliotherm
heliothermometer
heliotrope
helium
perihelion
photoheliograph
spectroheliograph
spectrohelioscope

hema, hemo   (*blood*)

hematic
hematite
hematologist
hematology
hematoma
hemochrome
hemocyte

hemodynamics
hemogastric
hemoglobin
hemolysis
hemophilia
hemophobia
hemorrhage

hemorrhoids
hemospasia
hemostat
hemotose
hemotoxic
hemotropic
pseudohemophilia

hemi, demi, semi   (*half*; usually used as a prefix)

demigod
demigoddess
demimillionaire
demirelief
demisuit
demitasse
demitone
hemialgia
hemihedral

hemihedron
hemiplegia
hemisphere
hemispherical
semiannual
semiarid
semiattached
semiautomatic
semicentennial

semicircle
semicircular
semicivilized
semiclassical
semicolon
semicoma
semiconscious
semifinal
semifinalist

semiliterate
semimonthly
semiprecious
semipublic
semirigid
semiskilled
semitrailer

The combining forms *hemi, demi,* and *semi* can be added to many hundreds of other base elements.

hydr, hydra, hydro (*water*)

anhydride	hydraulic	hydroelectric	hydrophobia
anhydrous	hydrobiology	hydrofoil	hydrophone
dehydrate	hydrocarbon	hydrogen	hydroplane
dehydration	hydrocast	hydrogenated	hydroponic
geohydrology	hydrocephalus	hydrograph	hydroscope
hydrangea	hydrochloride	hydrographer	hydrosphere
hydrant	hydrodrome	hydrologist	hydrostat
hydrate	hydrodynamic	hydrology	hydrotherapy

hyper (*over, above, or excessive;* **usually used as a prefix**)

hyperacidity	hyperconscious	hyperlogia	hyperthermal
hyperactive	hypercritical	hypermetric	hyperthermia
hyperbola	hyperextension	hypersensitive	hyperthermic
hyperbole	hyperglycemia	hypersonic	hyperventilate
hyperbolic	hyperkinesia	hypertelic	hyperventilation
hyperbolize	hyperkinetic	hypertension	
hyperchromatic	hyperlexia	hypertensive	
hyperchromia	hyperlexic	hypertext	

hypn, hypno (*sleep*)

aphypnia	hypnoanalysis	hypnopathy	hypnotherapy
autohypnosis	hypnogenesis	hypnopedia	hypnotic
dyshypnia	hypnology	hypnophobia	hypnotism
hypnesthesia	hypnomania	hypnosis	hypnotize

hypo (*under;* **usually used as a prefix**)

acryhypothermy	hypocrisy	hypologia	hypothermia
hypoacidity	hypocrite	hypomania	hypothermic
hypoactive	hypocritical	hyposensitive	hypothesis
hypoallergenic	hypodermic	hyposomniac	hypothetical
hypochondria	hypodermis	hypotension	hypothyroidism
hypochromic	hypoglycemia	hypothermal	hypoventilation

kine, cine (*movement*)

akinesthetic	cinemascopic	cinerama	hyperkinetic
astrokinetic	cinematographic	dyskinesia	kinematics
cinema	cinematography	electrokinetics	kinematograph
cinemascope	cinephile	hyperkinesia	kinescope

kinesiology	kinesthesia	orthokinesis	telekinesia
kinesiometer	kinesthetic	photokinesis	telekinetic
kinesis	kinetic	photokinetic	

lex   (*word*)

alexia	hyperlexic	lexicography	lexigraphy
alexithymia	lexeme	lexicologist	lexis
dyslexia	lexical	lexicology	paralexia
dyslexic	lexicalize	lexicon	
hyperlexia	lexicographer	lexiconophonist	

lith, litho   (*stone*)

archilithic	lithologist	megalithic
cystolith	lithology	microlith
endolithic	lithometer	microlithography
lithic	lithophile	monolith
lithium	lithophyll	monolithic
lithogenesis	lithophyte	Neolithic
lithograph	lithosphere	Paleolithic
lithographer	lithostratigraphy	protolithic
lithographic	lithotomy	xenolith
lithography	megalith	zoolithic

log, logo, logue   (*speech or word*)

alogia	logical	logogram	logophasia
catalogue	logicaster	logograph	logorrhea
dialogue	logician	logographer	monologue
eclogue	logistical	logographic	syllogism
eulogy	logistics	logomachy	travelogue
hyperlogia	logocentric	logomania	
hypologia	logocentrism	logometric	
logic	logogogue	logopedics	

logy (ology)   (*science or study of*; **usually used as a suffix; derived from** *logos, logue:* **speech, word**)

aerobiology	astrology	bioecology
andrology	astrometeorology	biology
anthropology	astrotheology	biometeorology
archaeology	bacteriology	biotechnology
astrobiology	bibliology	cardiology

chromatology
chronobiology
chronology
climatology
criminology
cyclonology
demonology
dermatology
doxology
ecobiology
ecology
ecophysiology
ectobiology
endocrinology
epidemiology
ethnology
ethology
etiology
etymology
geohydrology
geology
gerontology
graphology
hematology

hydrobiology
hydrology
hypnology
ideology
kinesiology
lexicology
lithology
metrology
microbiology
microecology
micrology
mineralogy
morphology
musicology
neology
neurology
neuropathology
ophthalmology
paleontology
parapsychology
pathology
pathophysiology
pedology
pharmacology

philology
phobiology
phonology
photology
phrenology
phyllobiology
physiology
pneumatology
protozoology
psychology
psychopathology
Scientology
seismology
sophiology
spectrology
stereology
technology
teleology
theology
zoology
zoopathology
zoophysiology

macro (*large, long, or great;* **usually used as a prefix; opposite of** *micro*)

macrobiotic
macrocephaly
macrochemistry
macroclimate
macrocosm
macrocosmic
macrocyte
macrodont

macroeconomics
macrofossil
macrograph
macroinstruction
macromania
macrometer
macromolecule
macronucleus

macronutrient
macrophage
macrophotography
macrophysics
macrophyte
macroscopic

mania (*madness, frenzy, abnormal desire, or obsession*)

balletomania
bibliomania
cyclomania
dromomania

ecomania
egomania
graphomania
heliomania

hypnomania
hypomania
kleptomania
logomania

macromania
mania
maniac
maniacal

maniaphobia   phonomania   scribblemania   zoomania
megalomania   photomania   sophomania
micromania   pyromania   technomania
mythomania   schizomania   theomania

mega   (*large or great;* usually used as a prefix)

acromegaly   megafog   megameter   megaton
hepatomegaly   megagram   megaphone   Megatron
megabit   megahertz   megapod   megavolt
megabyte   megalith   megapode   megawatt
megacycle   megalithic   megascope   omega
megadactyl   megalomania   megascopic   splenomegaly
megaderm   megalophonous   megasecond
megadont   megalopolis   megatechnics
megadynamics   megalosaur   megatherm

meta   (*beside, after, later, or beyond;* usually used as a prefix)

meta-analysis   metacognitive   metamorphosis   metatarsal
metabolic   metaethics   metaphor   metazoa
metabolism   metalanguage   metaphrase   metazoan
metabolize   metalinguistics   metaphysical
metacarpal   metamorphic   metaphysics
metacognition   metamorphism   metaplasm

meter, metr   (*measure*)

altimeter   dromometer   hypermetric
anemometer   dynameter   interferometer
astrometry   dynamometer   interferometry
barometer   dynamometry   isometric
biometer   econometrics   kinesiometer
biometrics   geometric   lithometer
chronobarometer   geometry   logometric
chronometer   goniometer   macrometer
chronometric   graphometer   medimeter
chronometry   gravimeter   megameter
cyclometer   heliometer   meter
cyclometry   heliothermometer   metric
diameter   heptameter   metrical
dimeter   hexameter   metrication

metrology
metronome
micrometer
morphometric
odometer
parameter
parametric
pedometer
pentameter
perimeter
perimetric

photogrammetry
photometer
physiometry
pneumatometer
psychochronometry
psychometrician
psychometrics
quadrimeter
seismometer
sonometer
spectrometer

speedometer
spherometer
stereometry
symmetric
symmetry
telemetry
thermometer
trigonometric
trigonometry
trimeter
zoometry

micro   (*small or minute*; **usually used as a prefix; opposite of** *macro*)

biomicroscope
microacoustics
microanalysis
microbar
microbe
microbiology
microbrewery
microburst
microchemistry
microcircuit
microclimate
microcomputer
microcopy
microcosm

microculture
microdont
microdot
microecology
microeconomics
microenvironment
microfiber
microfilm
micrograph
microlith
microlithography
micrology
micromanage
micromania

micromechanics
micrometer
microorganism
microphone
microphysics
microplankton
microprocessor
microreader
microscope
microscopic
microsurgery
microwave
photomicroscope
stereomicroscope

mon, mono   (*one*)

monarch
monastery
monocellular
monochord
monochromatic
monochrome
monochronic
monocle
monocotyledon
monocracy

monocrat
monocular
monoculture
monocycle
monodactyl
monodrama
monodynamic
monogamy
monogenesis
monoglot

monogram
monograph
monogyny
monolith
monolithic
monologue
mononucleosis
monophobia
monophonic
monopoly

monosyllabic
monosyllable
monotheism
monotheistic
monotone
monotonous
monotony
monotreme
monounsaturated

morph   (form, shape, or structure)

allomorph	geomorphic	morphometric
andromorphic	metamorphic	morphophonemics
anthropomorphic	metamorphism	morphosis
anthropomorphism	metamorphosis	morphosyntax
archimorphic	morpheme	perimorph
ectomorph	morphemics	polymorphic
ectomorphic	morphic	polymorphous
endomorph	morphogenesis	protomorphic
endomorphic	morphography	theomorphism
exomorphic	morphology	zoomorphism

neo   (new or recent)

neoblastic	neoexpressionism	neology
neoclassical	neogenesis	neomodern
neoconservatism	neoimpressionism	neomodernism
neocortex	neoliberation	neonatal
neocosmic	Neolithic	neonate
neocritical	neologism	neophyte

nym, onym   (name or word)

acronym	autonym	homonymous	patronymic
allonym	characternym	matronymic	pseudonym
anonymity	eponym	metonym	synonym
anonymous	euonymus	metonymy	synonymous
anthroponym	heteronym	numeronym	synonymy
antonym	heteronymous	paronym	tautonym
antonymous	homonym	paronymous	toponym

ortho   (straight, correct, or upright)

orthocenter	orthoepy	orthokinesis	orthoscopic
orthochromatic	orthogenesis	orthomolecular	orthostatic
orthodontia	orthogenic	orthopedics	orthotics
orthodontics	orthogonal	orthopedist	orthotist
orthodontist	orthographic	orthopod	
orthodox	orthography	orthopsychiatry	

pan (*panto*) (*all*)

panacea	panegyric	panoply	pantheistic
panarchy	pangenesis	panoptic	pantheon
pancratic	pangram	panorama	pantograph
pandemic	panharmonic	pansophy	pantomime
pandemonium	panhuman	pantheism	

para (*beside, alongside, or position;* **usually used as a prefix**)

parabiosis	paradox	parallelism	paraphernalia
parable	paradoxical	parallelogram	paraphrase
parabola	paradromic	paralysis	paraprofessional
parabolic	paragon	paralytic	parapsychology
paracentral	paragraph	paralyze	parasensory
parachromatism	parajournalism	paramedic	parasite
parachronism	paralegal	parameter	parasympathetic
parachute	paralexia	parametric	parathyroid
paradental	parallax	paranoia	paratroopers
paradigm	parallel	paranormal	

path (*feeling, suffering, or disease*)

antipathy	pathogen	psychopathic
apathetic	pathogenesis	psychopathology
apathy	pathogenic	sociopath
empathize	pathography	somnipathy
empathy	pathological	sympathetic
homeopathy	pathologist	sympathomimetic
hypnopathy	pathology	sympathy
neuropathologist	pathophobia	telepathy
neuropathology	pathophysiology	telepathic
neuropathy	photopathy	theopathy
parasympathetic	protopathic	unsympathetic
pathetic	psychopath	zoopathology

ped (*child*)

hypnopedia	pedagogic	pedantic	pedocracy
orthopedics	pedagogue	pediatrician	pedodontics
orthopedist	pedagogy	pediatrics	pedodontist
pedagog	pedant	pediophobia	pedology

ped (*soil*)

pedalfer   pedocal   pedogenesis   pedology

The Greek combining forms *ped*, meaning *child*, and *ped*, meaning *soil*, are different from the Latin root *ped*, which means *foot*.

peri (*around or near;* **usually used as a prefix**)

pericardiac	perigon	periodic	periscope
pericardium	perihelion	periodical	periscopic
pericentric	perimeter	periodontal	peritoneum
pericranium	perimetric	peripatetic	
pericycle	perimorph	peripheral	
perigee	period	periphery	

phil, phila, phile, philo (*love or affinity for*)

Anglophile	Philadelphia	philogynist
audiophile	philander	philologist
bibliophile	philanderer	philology
biophile	philanthropic	philomath
cinephile	philanthropist	philomuse
demophile	philanthropy	philophobia
Francophile	philatelist	philosopher
gastrophile	philately	philosophize
geophilous	philharmonic	philosophy
hemophilia	philhippic	philotechnic
hemophiliac	philodemic	philotechnicist
lithophile	philodendron	pseudohemophilia
logophile	philodox	

phobia, phobic; phobe (*irrational fear or hatred; one who fears/hates*)

acousticophobia	astrophobia	cyclophobia	heliophobic
acrophobia	autophobia	demophobe	hemophobia
aerophobia	bibliophobe	demophobia	hydrophobia
agoraphobia	bibliophobia	dromophobia	hypnophobia
androphobia	chronophobia	ecophobia	monophobia
Anglophobe	claustrophobia	Francophobe	noctiphobia
aquaphobia	claustrophobic	heliophobia	ornithophobia

pathophobia	polyphobia	technophobe	zoophobia
philophobia	psychophobia	technophobia	
phobiology	pyrophobia	thermophobia	
photophobia	spectrophobia	xenophobia	

There are names for more than 500 phobias, most of which come from the field of medicine. See http://www.phobialist .com for a larger list of phobias, compiled by Fredd Culbertson.

phon, phono (*sound*)

allophone	hydrophone	phonograph
Anglophone	lexicophonist	phonology
antiphonal	megaphone	phonoscope
cacophony	microphone	phonostethoscope
chronophotograph	monophonic	phonotype
diplophonia	morphophonemics	spectrophone
euphonious	phoneme	stereophonic
euphony	phonemic	symphonic
Francophone	phonetic	symphony
geophone	phonetician	techniphone
gramophone	phonic	telephone
graphophonemic	phonics	vibraphone
heterophony	phonocardiograph	xylophone
homophone	phonogram	

photo (*light*)

aphototropic	photogram	photopathy
astrophotograph	photogrammetry	photophilia
chronophotograph	photograph	photophobia
macrophotography	photographer	photosensitive
photoallergy	photography	photosensitivity
photobiotic	photoheliograph	photosphere
photochrome	photojournalism	photosynthesis
photocopy	photokinesis	phototherapy
photodynamic	photokinetic	photothermic
photoelectric	photology	photothermy
photoengrave	photometer	phototropic
photoengraving	photomicroscope	telephoto
photogenic	photon	telephotography

phyll (*leaf or leaves*)

aphyllus	lithophyll	phylloid	sporophyll
chlorophyll	phyllo	phyllome	
gamophyll	phyllobiology	phyllopod	
heterophyllus	phyllode	phyllotaxy	

phys (*nature*)

astrophysics	physical	physiological
biophysics	physician	physiologist
ecophysics	physicist	physiology
geophysical	physicotherapeutics	physiometry
geophysics	physics	physiosophic
macrophysics	physiocrat	physiotherapy
metaphysical	physiogenesis	physiotype
metaphysics	physiognomy	physique
microphysics	physiograph	zoophysiology
pathophysiology	physiographic	

pneumo, pneumon (*breath or lung*)

bronchopneumonia	pneumectomy	pneumonectomy
pneumatic	pneumocardial	pneumonia
pneumatogram	pneumococus	pneumonitis
pneumatology	pneumocystis	pneumotherapy
pneumatometer	pneumoderma	postpneumonia
pneumatoscope	pneumogastric	
pneumatosis	pneumograph	

pod (*foot*)

megapod	podiatrist	podium
monopod	podiatry	tripod

pol, polis, polit (*city; method of government*)

acropolis	Heliopolis	police	politicking
Annapolis	Indianapolis	policy	politico
aquapolis	Interpol	politburo	politics
cosmopolitan	megalopolis	political	propolis
decapolis	metropolis	politician	Tripoli
geopolitical	metropolitan	politicize	
geopolitics	Minneapolis	politick	

poly (many; usually used as a prefix)

duopoly	polyclinic	polygyny	polypod
monopolize	polydactyl	polyhedron	polysyllabic
monopoly	polydemic	polymath	polytechnic
polyandry	polyester	polymorphic	polytendinitis
polyarchy	polyethnic	polymorphous	polytheism
polyarthritis	polygamy	polymyxin	polytheistic
polycentric	polyglot	polyneuritis	polyunsaturated
polychord	polygon	polynomial	
polychromatic	polygraph	polypharmacy	
polychrome	polygraphy	polyphony	

proto (earliest, original, or first in time; used as a prefix)

protocol	protolanguage	protoplasm	protozoan
protogalaxy	protolithic	protoplasmic	protozoic
protogyny	protomorphic	prototrophic	protozoology
protohistory	protopathic	prototype	
protohuman	protophyte	protozoa	

psych (mind or soul)

orthopsychiatry	psychochronometry	psychomotor
parapsychology	psychodrama	psychoneurosis
psyche	psychodynamics	psychopath
psychedelic	psychogenesis	psychopathic
psychiatric	psychogeriatrics	psychophobia
psychiatrist	psychograph	psychosis
psychiatry	psychohistory	psychosocial
psychic	psycholinguistics	psychotechnics
psychoacoustics	psychologist	psychotherapist
psychoallergy	psychologize	psychotherapy
psychoanalysis	psychology	psychotic
psychobabble	psychometrician	psychotraumatic
psychobiography	psychometrics	psychotropic

saur (lizard or serpent)

brontosaurus	megalosaur	saurischian	stegosaurus
dinosaur	paleosaurid	sauropod	teleosaurus
dinosaurian	pterosaur	saury	titanosaurus
ichthyosaur	saurian	secnosaurus	tyrannosaur
lepidosaur	sauries	sinosaurus	tyrannosaurus

scope   (to watch or see)

abdominoscope	helioscope	phonostethoscope
autoscope	horoscope	photomicroscope
baroscope	hydroscope	photoscope
biomicroscope	kaleidoscope	pneumatoscope
bioscope	kinescope	polariscope
bronchoscope	macroscopic	radioscope
chromoscope	megascope	seismoscope
chronoscope	megascopic	spectrohelioscope
cinemascope	microscope	spectroscope
cinemascopic	microscopic	stereoscope
dynamoscope	ophthalmoscope	stereoscopic
endoscope	orthoscopic	stethoscope
endoscopic	otoscope	telescope
gyroscope	periscope	telescopic
gyroscopic	periscopic	thermascope
heliochromoscope	phonoscope	

soph   (wisdom or cleverness)

bibliosoph	philosophy	sophistication	sophomoric
pansophic	physiosophic	sophisticator	theosophic
philosopher	sophic	sophistry	unsophisticated
philosophical	sophiology	Sophocles	
philosophism	sophism	sophomania	
philosophize	sophisticated	sophomore	

sphere   (circle)

astrosphere	geosphere	mesosphere	spherometer
atmosphere	heliosphere	petrosphere	spheroplast
biogeosphere	hemisphere	photosphere	stratosphere
biosphere	hemispherical	pyrosphere	thermosphere
chemosphere	hydrosphere	sphere	troposphere
chromosphere	ionosphere	spherical	
ecosphere	lithosphere	spheriform	
exosphere	magnetosphere	spheroid	

stereo   (solid, firm, or hard)

stereo	stereogram	stereography
stereochemistry	stereographic	stereological

stereology	stereoplasm	stereotype
stereomatrix	stereoscope	stereotypical
stereometry	stereoscopic	stereovision
stereomicroscope	stereotaxis	
stereophonic	stereotomy	

techn (*skill, art, or craft*)

biotechnics	philotechnicist	Technicolor	technology
biotechnology	polytechnic	technicon	technomania
electrotechnics	psychotechnics	techniphone	technophile
eutechnics	pyrotechnic	technique	technophobe
geotechnics	technical	technobabble	technophobia
megatechnics	technicality	technocracy	technostructure
neotechnic	technician	technocrat	zootechnical
philotechnic	technicist	technologist	zootechny

tele (*distant;* **usually used as a prefix**)

autotelic	telekinesia	teleportation
hypertelic	telekinetic	teleprinter
telecast	telemarketing	telescope
telecommunication	telemedicine	telescopic
telecommute	telemetry	teleshop
teleconference	teleology	teletherapy
telecourse	telepathic	telethon
telegenesis	telepathy	teletranscription
telegnosis	telephone	teletypist
telegram	telephoto	television
telegraph	telephotography	
telegraphic	teleport	

the, theo (*god*)

allotheism	pantheism	theocrat	theology
antitheism	pantheistic	theodicy	theomachy
astrotheology	pantheon	theogamy	theomania
atheism	philotheism	theogony	theomorphism
atheist	polytheism	theolatry	theopathy
atheological	polytheistic	theologian	theophany
monotheism	theocentric	theological	theophile
monotheistic	theocracy	theologize	

therm, thermo   (*heat or hot*)

acrohypothermy	megatherm	thermogram
chronothermal	philothermic	thermograph
endothermic	photothermic	thermolysis
euthermia	photothermy	thermometer
exothermic	thermal	thermomotor
geothermal	thermascope	thermonuclear
heliotherm	thermic	thermophilic
heliothermometer	thermistor	thermophobia
hyperthermal	thermoacoustic	thermoreceptor
hyperthermia	thermochemistry	thermoregulate
hyperthermic	thermocouple	Thermos
hypothermal	thermodynamics	thermosphere
hypothermia	thermoelectric	thermostat
hypothermic	thermoelectron	thermotherapy
isothermal	thermogenesis	thermotoxin

zo, zoo   (*animal*)

Archaeozoic	protozoan	zoolithic	zoophysiology
asterozoa	protozoic	zoological	zoophyte
azoic	protozoology	zoology	zooplankton
Cenozoic	Zodiac	zoomania	zooplasty
endozoic	zoobiotic	zoometry	zoospore
Mesozoic	zoochore	zoomorphism	zoosterol
metazoa	zoogenic	zoonosis	zootechnical
metazoan	zoogenous	zoonotic	zootechny
Paleozoic	zooglea	zoopathology	zootomy
Phanerozoic	zoography	zoophile	zootoxin
Proterozoic	zooid	zoophilic	
protozoa	zoolatry	zoophobia	

REFERENCES

The American heritage dictionary (2nd ed.). (1982). Boston: Houghton Mifflin.
The American heritage dictionary (4th ed.). (2000). Boston: Houghton Mifflin.
Random House unabridged dictionary (2nd ed.). (1993). New York: Random House.

Words Commonly Found in Textbooks

Students must learn to read and spell many words found in content area textbooks and lectures as well as learn the meaning of these words. The words in Appendix H are organized by subject area and grade level. The subject areas included are social studies (government, history, and psychology), science (biology, meteorology, physics, and chemistry), and mathematics. These lists are further subdivided according to topics that are often taught during the school year, such as the American Revolution, westward movement, state government, astronomy, physics, and so forth. Elementary grade lists are for third through sixth grades; secondary grade lists are for seventh through twelfth grades.

In addition to the spellings of the words listed, the meanings should be studied. Some terms have different meanings depending on the context. For example, *depression* has different meanings in psychology and geography, *conjunction* has different meanings in linguistics and astronomy, and *revolution* has different meanings in history and physics. In addition, students need to learn relationships among terms such as *legislative*, *judicial*, and *executive* when discussing government; *psychoanalyst*, *psychologist*, and *psychiatrist* when discussing psychology; and *recession* and *inflation* when discussing finance. Also note that many proper names of people and places appear in all content area texts and should be studied in addition to the words in this appendix.

The words in the lists may be used in many ways. Students may compare and contrast words such as *hurricane*, *earthquake*, and *tornado* or words such as *unicameral* and *bicameral*. Students may be asked to sort nouns, adjectives, and verbs within a group of words. Groups of students may draw webs of related words. See Chapters 7 and 8 for other possible activities using related and associated words.

WORDS FOUND IN SOCIAL STUDIES TEXTBOOKS

Teachers can make word lists for decoding and spelling practice using these topic lists and from vocabulary taken directly from student textbooks. In addition to the words listed for the elementary grades, these words are found in many social studies textbooks.

Elementary Grades

Early Explorers

cape	explorer	passage	trade
discovery	navigation	route	trader
exchange	navigator	scurvy	
exploration	ocean	spice	

Early America

barter	governor	Mayflower	pilgrimage
celebration	hardship	Compact	thanksgiving
charter	Indian	Native American	treaty
exchange		Pilgrim	winter

Revolutionary War

assembly	freedom	monarchy	redcoat
boycott	independence	musket	representation
colonist	indentured	oppression	revolution
colony	loyalist	proclamation	servant
constitution	Minutemen	rebel	taxation
declaration	monarch	rebellion	Yankee

Civil War and Reconstruction

abolition	escape	scalawag
abolitionist	freedmen	secede
assassination	freedom	secession
autonomy	Gilded Age	siege
battle	hiding	slavery
carpetbagger	independence	Underground Railroad
charge	massacre	Union
Confederacy	reconstruction	
Confederate	revolt	

Westward Movement

covered wagon	hardship	Pacific	trail
expansion	homesteading	pioneer	westward
frontier	movement	territory	

Weather and Geography

anthropology	hemisphere	ocean	relief map
community	hurricane	peninsula	rural
contour map	interdependence	physical	satellite
desert	irrigation	plateau	savannah
elevation	lake	political map	suburban
equator	latitude	pond	summit
equatorial	longitude	population	tide
foothill	manufacturing	prairie	tornado
geography	meridian	precipitation	transportation
glacier	meteorology	province	
globe	mountain	rain forest	
gulf	neighborhood	refinery	

Government and Citizenship

argumentative	emigrate	immigration	presidential
bicentennial	emigration	judicial	proletariat
caricature	emigré	legislative	re-elect
centennial	government	oppressor	senator
democracy	governor	perpetuate	sequential
dictatorship	hierarchy	politician	
electoral	immigrant	president	

Secondary Grades

Teachers can make word lists for decoding and spelling practice using these topic lists and from vocabulary taken directly from social studies textbooks. The following words are found in many secondary grade social studies textbooks.

Ancient Cultures

acropolis	city-state	cuneiform	god
amphitheater	civilization	decode	goddess
ancient	coliseum	delta	hieroglyph
aqueduct	constellation	gladiator	immortal

irrigation	offering	Rosetta stone	tunic
mortal	papyrus	ruin	valley
mummification	polytheism	sacrifice	viaduct
myth	pyramid	senator	ziggurat
mythology	republic	stadium	zodiac

Middle Ages and Renaissance

archbishop	crusade	loyalty	schism
armor	crusader	Magna Carta	scribe
beheaded	enlightenment	manuscript	scrivener
bishop	fealty	medieval	serf
cathedral	feudal	monarch	serfdom
chain mail	fief	monarchy	simony
chivalry	illumination	monastery	subjugation
conquer	inquisition	pike	sword
conqueror	invasion	plate mail	vassal
Constantinople	jousting	pope	
convent	knighthood	Renaissance	

Pre–World War I

antitrust	muckraker	tenement
bribery	muckraking	transcontinental
corporation	railroad	trustbusting
corruption	refinery	yellow journalism
doctrine	sabotage	
monopoly	stockyards	

World Wars I and II

aircraft	Axis	fascism
aircraft carrier	biplane	fascist
Allied	blackout	gunner
Allies	bomber	Holocaust
anti-aircraft	campaign	homeland
anti-Semitism	communism	invade
Archduke	concentration camp	invasion
armistice	debarkation	isolationism
assassin	devastation	isolationist
assassination	dictatorship	liberation
atomic	fallout	Marxism

mustard gas
Nazism
nuclear
parachute
peacetime

socialism
totalitarian
totalitarianism
treaty
trench

triplane
warfare
Zionism

Cold War

agent
airlift
anti-American
ballistic
Berlin Wall
blackball
collectivization
commission
communism

communist
counterintelligence
crisis
detente
escalation
intelligence
intercontinental
investigation
Iron Curtain

McCarthyism
missile
nuclear
spy plane
surveillance
testify
testimony
treaty
warhead

Government and Citizenship

alien
ambassador
amendment
appeal
apportionment
assembly
ballot
bicameral
Bill of Rights
bureaucracy
campaign
campaign promise
capital
Capitol
caucus
checks and balances
citizen
citizenship
civil rights
Congress
congressional

constituent
Constitution
constitutionalist
debate
delegate
democracy
Democrat
demonstration
denaturalization
desegregation
desegregationist
diplomacy
diplomatic
discrimination
disobedience
dissolution
economic
embassy
entrepreneur
executive
extradition

federalism
federalist
feminism
feminist
filibuster
gerrymandering
inalienable
judge
judicial
jurisdiction
jury
justice
law
legal
legislation
legislative
legislator
lobbyist
multiculturalism
naturalization
naturalize

nomination
party
passport
petition
plank
platform
precinct
press
protest
racism
racist
referendum
religion

repeal
representation
representative
Republican
running mate
segregation
segregationist
Senate
senator
signature
sovereignty
speech
suffrage

suffragist
support
supremacist
supremacy
Supreme Court
television
unicameral
urbanization
voter registration
voting
Whig

Psychology

adolescence
afferent
agoraphobia
amygdala
antidepressant
anxiety
aphasia
axon
behaviorism
catatonic
central
cerebellum
cerebral
cerebrum
circadian
cognitive
conditioning
consciousness
cortex
cyclothymia
deindividualism
dendrite
dizygotic
dysthymia

echoic
eclecticism
efferent
electroconvulsive
electroencephalogram
electromyogram
electrooculogram
etiology
extrinsic
extroversion
frontal
functionalism
hallucination
heterosexuality
heuristic
hippocampus
homeostasis
homophobia
homosexuality
hyperphagia
hypochondria
hypothalamus
interdisciplinary
intrinsic

introspection
introversion
limbic
lobe
localization
microelectrode
monozygotic
nervous
neurotransmitter
occipital
oculomotor
olfactory
operant
overregularization
parasympathetic
parietal
perception
peripheral
phenomena
physiology
pituitary
prefrontal
pseudodialogue
pseudoinsomnia

pseudomemory
psychoanalysis
psychoanalyst
psychobiography
psychophysics
psychosocial
psychotherapy
psychotropic
schema

schizophrenia
seizure
self-actualization
sensorimotor
sexuality
sociobiology
somatosensory
spinal
structuralism

synapse
synaptic
technocrat
tomography
transformation
trichromatic

WORDS FOUND IN MATH TEXTBOOKS

Elementary Grades

Arithmetic and Place Value

addend
addition
borrowing
calculation
calculator
carrying
decimal
denominator
digit
dividend

division
divisor
even
fraction
hundreds
hundredths
multiplication
multiplier
numerator
odd

ones
operator
percentage
place
quotient
reciprocal
regrouping
remainder
sign
subtraction

symbol
tens
tenths
thousands
thousandths
value
zero

Geometry and Shapes

acute
adjacent
angle
area
axis
circumference
congruent
cube
diagonal
diagonally
diameter
dimension

geometry
graph
hemisphere
heptagon
heptagonal
hexagon
hexagonal
horizontal
intersection
isosceles
linear
nonagon

nonagonal
obtuse
octagon
octagonal
opposite
parallelogram
pentagon
pentagonal
pentomino
perimeter
perpendicular
polygon

prism
protractor
pyramid
radius
rectangle
rectangular
reflection
rhombus
rotation
scalene
sphere
square

surface area	trapezoid	triangular	vertical
symmetry	triangle	vertex	volume

Units of Measure

millimeter	yard	centiliter	decigram
centimeter	mile	kiloliter	centigram
decimeter	cubic centimeter	ounce	kilogram
kilometer	milliliter	pound	
inch	liter	milligram	
foot	deciliter	gram	

Sampling, Statistics, and Problem Solving

algebra	extension	median
algorithm	formula	minimum
application	frequency	permutation
argument	greater than	prediction
average	greater than or equal to	probability
computation	identity	solution
cumulative	inequality	statistics
deduce	less than	strategy
deduction	less than or equal to	surveyed
diagram	likelihood	transaction
distribution	manipulative	validate
equation	mathematical	word problem
equivalent	mathematician	
estimate	maximum	

Secondary Grades

Algebra, Logic, and Sets

abscissa	coefficient	disjunction
absolute value	commutative	distributive
algebra	conjunction	exponent
associative	contrapositive	exponential
asymptote	constant	factorial
asymptotic	converse	factoring
base 10	coordinates	formula
binary	cube	identity
binomial	cube root	imaginary

integer	positive	set
intersection	power	slope
inverse	quadrant	square
irrational	quadratic	square root
multiplicative	rational	trinomial
negative	real	union
order of operations	rise	variable
ordinate	run	Venn diagram
polynomial	scientific notation	whole

Geometry and Trigonometry

arc	degree	leg	scalene
arccosecant	dodecahedron	line	secant
arccosine	eccentric	origin	segment
arccotangent	eccentricity	parabola	sine
arcsecant	ellipse	parabolic	square
arcsine	elliptical	parallel	supplementary
arctangent	equidistant	parallelogram	symmetric
asymmetric	equilateral	perpendicular	symmetry
asymmetry	exterior angle	pi	tangent
chord	foci	plane	tessellate
collinear	focus	point	tessellation
complementary	geometric	postulate	theorem
concentric	geometry	prism	transverse
concentricity	grad	proof	trigonometric
cone	icosahedron	pyramid	trigonometry
coplanar	interior angle	quadrilateral	vertex
cosecant	isoceles	radian	vertices
cosine	hyperbola	right angle	
cotangent	hyperbolic	right triangle	
cube	hypotenuse	rhombus	

Analysis and Calculus

cardioid	*e*	matrices	series
calculus	integrate	matrix	summation
delta	integration	maxima	
differential	logarithm	minima	
discrete	logarithmic	multivariable	

Statistics

bell curve	median	ratio
central tendency	mode	sample
confidence interval	outlier	sampling
distribution	percent	skew
error	percentile	standard deviation
histogram	population	subsample
mean	quartile	variance

WORDS FOUND IN SCIENCE TEXTBOOKS

Elementary Grades

Paleontology and Prehistory

ammonite	Jurassic	skeleton
archaeopteryx	mammoth	stegosaurus
brontosaurus	Mesozoic	Tertiary
Cenozoic	Paleozoic	Triassic
Cretaceous	Precambrian	triceratops
dinosaurs	pteranodon	trilobite
diplodocus	pterodactyl	tyrannosaurus rex
extinction	Quaternary	
glaciers	saber-toothed	

Geology, Meteorology, and Astronomy

asteroids	cumulus	metamorphic	satellite
astronomy	earthquake	meteor	sediment
atmosphere	environment	meteorite	sedimentary
cirrocumulus	fault	meteorology	shuttle
cirrus	friction	moon	spacecraft
climate	granite	nimbus	telescope
comet	gravity	orbit	tide
constellation	igneous	planet	tornado
core	lava	polar	volcano
crust	magma	precipitation	weightless
cumulonimbus	mantle	rocket	weightlessness

Animals and Plants

adapt	adaptation	amphibian	amphibious

biology	deciduous	mammal	reptile
chlorophyll	development	microorganism	warm-blooded
cold-blooded	ecosystem	nutrition	zoology
community	fibrous	pesticide	
coniferous	habitat	photosynthesis	

Experiments

adventure	equipment	interpretation	prediction
artificial	estimate	investigate	production
assumption	experience	measurement	requirement
calculation	experiment	microscope	sequence
classification	facsimile	neutral	spontaneous
communicate	hypotheses	numerical	virtual
complicated	hypothesis	observation	
conclusion	instrument	parallel	

Chemistry

aluminum	element	oxygen
catalyst	hydrogen	petroleum
chemical	nitrogen	solution

Applied Physical Science

Celsius	megaphone	photograph	translucent
construction	molecular	prism	transparent
cylinder	opaque	spectrum	ultraviolet
Fahrenheit	percussion	temperature	vibration
infrared	periscope	thermometer	

Electricity and Magnetism

attraction	electricity	galvanometer	positive
battery	electromagnet	magnet	short-circuit
bulb	electronic	negative	transistor
circuit	filament	pole	

Technology

binary	invention	photocopy	technology
computer	microwave	refrigerator	telegraph
digital	patent	silicon	telephone

Secondary Grades

Scientific Method

analysis	data	literature	scientific
bias	discussion	observation	scientific method
blind	double-blind	reliability	scientist
conclusion	empirical	replicate	validity
control	hypothesis	results	variable

Biology

adenosine triphosphate	dominant	microorganism
aerobic	double helix	mitochondria
amino acid	duodenum	mitosis
amoeba	dynamic equilibrium	molecule
anaerobic	enzyme	monozygotic
anaphase	esophagus	mutation
artery	evolution	natural selection
asexual	evolve	nomenclature
bile	genes	nuclear membrane
biome	genetic	nucleus
bolus	genome	ontogeny
botany	genotype	organ
capillary	genus	organelle
carbon dioxide	glucose	organic
carbon-based	glycogen	oxidative
cell	Golgi apparatus	phosphorylation
centriole	guanine	oxygen
chain	haploid	pancreas
chemosynthesis	heterozygotic	paramecium
chromatid	homozygotic	peristalsis
chromatin	insulin	phenotype
cytoplasm	interphase	phylogeny
cytosine	islet	prophase
deoxyribonucleic acid	Krebs cycle	protein
digestion	lactic acid	protozoa
diploid	large intestine	recessive
dissection	meiosis	reproduction
division	messenger RNA	respiration
dizygotic	metaphase	reticular

ribonucleic acid (RNA)
ribosome
sexual
small intestine
species

sphincter
spindle pole
stoma
stomach
taxonomy

telophase
thymine
transfer RNA
vein
zygote

Chemistry

absorption
acid
acidic
activation energy
adhere
adhesion
adhesive
adsorption
alkali
alkaline
alloy
anhydride
anhydrous
anion
aqueous
atom
atomic mass
atomic weight
Avogadro's number
base
basic
beaker
boil
bond
buffer
Bunsen burner
calorie
catalyst
catalyze
cation
caustic
centrifuge

chain
cohere
cohesion
cohesive
colloid
compound
concentrate
concentration
condensation
condense
covalence
covalency
covalent
crystal
crystalline
decay
dewpoint
dilute
dilution
dissolve
ductile
ductility
electrolysis
electrolyte
element
emulsifier
emulsion
endothermic
evaporate
evaporation
exothermic
flask

fluoresce
fluorescent
formula
freeze
gas
gaseous
group
half-life
heavy metal
humidity
hydrolysis
hydrolyze
hydrophilic
hydrophobic
inert
inorganic
ion
ionic
ionization
isomer
isomeric
isotope
lanthanide
liquid
luminance
luminescence
luminous
malleability
malleable
mass number
meniscus
molar

molarity
mole
molecular
molecular weight
molecule
noble gas
notation
orbital
oxidation
oxidize
ozone
period
periodic table
pH
phosphate
pipette

polymer
polymeric
precipitate
radiation
radioactivity
reaction
relative humidity
ring
shell
solid
solution
solvent
specific gravity
spin
state
stoichiometry

sublevel
subshell
substrate
surface tension
suspension
symbol
titrate
titration
univalent
valence
valency
vapor
viscosity
viscous

Physics[1]

absolute zero
acceleration
amperage
ampere
amplitude
angle
angstrom
angular momentum
applied
atmosphere
atmospheric
atom
atomic
axle
candela
capacitance
capacitor
centrifugal
centripetal

charge
coefficient
concave
conduction
conductor
conservation
constant
converge
convergent
convex
coulomb
current
cycle
differential
diffract
diffraction
dipole
dislocation
distance

diverge
divergent
dynamic
dyne
electromagnetic
electron
electrostatic
emission
energy
equilibrium
equipartition
exponential
farad
ferroelectricity
field
fission
fluctuation
fluid
fluid dynamics

[1]*Source:* Feynman, R.P., Leighton, R.B., & Sands, M. (1970). *The Feynman lectures on physics* (Vols. I–III). Reading, MA: Addison-Wesley.

force	molecule	relativity
frequency	momentum	resistance
friction	muon	resonance
fulcrum	neutrino	resultant
fusion	neutron	screw
gravitation	newton	semiconductor
gravity	nonlinear	simple machine
harmonic	nuclear	slope
henry	nuclei	solenoid
hertz	nucleus	spectrum
horsepower	opacity	spring scale
hydrostatic	opaque	static
ideal	optics	superconductivity
illumination	oscillation	superconductor
image	oxygen	superposition
inclined plane	parabola	symmetry
inductance	parabolic	synchrotron
inertia	parity	tesla
infrared	particle	theorem
ionic	pendulum	theoretical
irreversibility	period	theory
irrotational	periodic	thermal
joule	periodicity	thermodynamics
kelvin	polarization	translucence
kinetic	polarize	translucent
kinetic energy	potential energy	transparence
law	power	transparent
lens	pressure	ultraviolet
lever	principle	vector
lift	projectile	velocity
lumen	projectile motion	virtual image
magnet	proton	volt
magnetic	pulley	voltage
magnetism	quantum	watt
magnitude	quark	wave
mass	rate	wavelength
mechanical advantage	real image	weber
mechanics	reflection	wedge
model	refraction	wheel
molecular	relativistic	work

Astronomy

altitude	elliptical	magnetosphere	recalibration
aphelion	elongation	magnification	retrograde
arcminute	epoch	magnify	revolution
arcsecond	equinox	magnitude	rotation
ascension	estival	matter	sidereal
asteroid	event horizon	meridian	solar
astigmatism	exosphere	mesosphere	solstice
astrology	galactic	meteor	spectral
aurora	galaxy	nebula	spectrum
autumnal	giant	obliquity	sphere
azimuth	gibbous	observatory	stratosphere
binary	globular	occultation	supernova
binoculars	gravitational	opposition	telescope
black hole	gravity	optical	telescopic
celestial	hibernal	orbit	terminal velocity
comet	infrared	parallax	thermosphere
cosmic	interstellar	penumbra	troposphere
constellation	ionosphere	perihelion	ultraviolet
declination	latitude	planetarium	umbra
dwarf	light-year	planet	universe
eclipse	longitude	precession	vernal
ecliptic	luminosity	radiation	zenith
ellipse	lunar	recalibrate	zodiac

Geology

acid rain	bay	ebb	isobath
aftershock	bedrock	epicenter	isotherm
alluvial fan	bog	erosion	isthmus
alpine	canyon	estuary	karst
anticline	cape	fjord	kettle
aquiclude	clay	gneiss	lagoon
aquifer	conservation	granite	limestone
archipelago	contour line	groundwater	marsh
artesian	deforestation	gypsum	metal
atoll	delta	hydrology	mica
basalt	doldrums	inlet	mineral
batholith	dune	isobar	moraine

neap	Richter scale	silicate	syncline
oxbow	riverbed	silt	tectonic
peat	runoff	sinkhole	terrace
permeable	sandbar	slate	tide pool
petrified	sandstone	slump	topsoil
phosphorescence	scarp	stalactite	tsunami
pollution	sediment	stalagmite	water cycle
preservation	sedimentation	strait	watershed
reef	shale	swamp	wetland

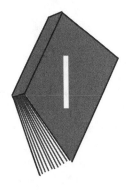

Glossary

The key terms used in this book are defined in this glossary. The definitions given are those that pertain to the study of language, reading, decoding, and spelling.

affix A bound morpheme attached to the beginning or end of a base or root that creates a new word with a meaning or function that is different than the base or root. *See also* prefix; suffix.

allomorph A variant form of a morpheme, such as the English plural, which is represented by *-s* in *cats*, *-es* in *horses*, and *-en* in *oxen*.

alphabetic code Letter–sound relationships in an alphabetic writing system, the understanding of which is crucial to decoding and spelling in that system.

alphabetic principle The representation of a phoneme by a graphic symbol, such as a letter or letters.

analytic phonics An instructional approach in which students learn whole words and deduce the component parts, such as phonemes.

assimilated prefix *See* chameleon prefix.

auditory discrimination The ability to discriminate between similar-sounding phonemes, such as /p/ and /b/, /t/ and /d/, and /f/ and /v/.

automaticity The immediate recognition of words while decoding.

base word A word, such as *spell*, to which prefixes and suffixes may be added to form related words, such *misspell* and *misspelling*.

blend *See* consonant blend.

blending The ability to say a word by fusing a sequence of sounds or syllables.

bound morpheme A prefix, suffix, or root that cannot stand alone, such as *re-*, *struct*, and *-ure* in *restructure*.

breve   The diacritical marking (˘) appearing over a vowel grapheme that denotes a short, or lax, pronunciation of the vowel.

chameleon prefix   A prefix in which the final letter of the prefix changes due to assimilation with the first letter of the base element (e.g., *con-* becomes a chameleon prefix in *collect, correct,* and *combine*). *Also called* assimilated prefix.

closed syllable   A syllable containing a short vowel sound and ending with one or more consonants, as in *hot* and *plant.*

combining form   In this book, word parts of Greek origin that can be combined with other combining forms or morphemes to form new words, such as *psych* and *ology,* which can be combined to make *psychology.*

compound word   A word that is composed of two or more smaller words and whose meaning is related to the constituent words, such as *bookcase, lamppost,* and *schoolhouse.*

consonant   1) A speech sound that is constricted or obstructed by the teeth, lips, roof of the mouth, and/or tongue during articulation; 2) a grapheme corresponding to a consonant sound.

consonant blend   Two or three adjacent consonants before or after a vowel sound in a syllable, such as /spl/ in *split* and /nt/ in *font. Also called* consonant cluster.

consonant digraph   Two adjacent consonants that represent one speech sound, such as *sh* in *ship* and *ch* in *church.*

consonant-*le* syllable   A syllable ending in a consonant followed by -*le,* such as -*ble* in *table* or -*zle* in *puzzle.*

decoding   The act of translating written words into vocal or subvocal speech. Decoding draws on certain linguistic skills and knowledge.

decoding–spelling continuum   A recommended sequence for integrated decoding and spelling instruction across grade levels.

deductive phonics   *See* analytic phonics.

derivational affix   A prefix or suffix added to a base or root that forms another word that is often a different part of speech from the base or root, such as *re-* in *return,* -*ful* in *hopeful.*

digraph   Two adjacent letters in a syllable that represent one speech sound, such as *th* for /th/ (as in *thin*) or *ai* for /ā/ (as in *rain*).

diphthong   1) A vowel in a syllable that produces two subtle sounds by gliding from one vowel sound to another, such as /oi/ in *boil* or /ô/ in *fawn*; 2) a grapheme corresponding to a diphthong sound. (*Note:* Some linguists disagree about how many diphthongs exist in English. Venezky, 1999, attributed this dispute to regional differences in vowel pronunciations. In this book, diphthongs are not distinguished from vowel digraphs.)

double-deficit hypothesis   The hypothesis that a child who has difficulty with both phonological processing and with naming speed will have more difficulty with reading than a child with only one of those problems.

dyslexia   A specific learning disability that is neurological in origin. It is characterized by difficulties with accurate and/or fluent word recognition and by poor spelling and decoding abilities. These difficulties typically result from a deficit in the phonological component of language that is often unexpected in relation to other cognitive abilities and in the provision of effective classroom instruction. Secondary consequences may include problems in reading comprehension and reduced reading experience that can impede growth of vocabulary and background knowledge (Hennessey, 2003; Hennessey is IDA president and quoted the newly approved definition in the IDA newsletter *Perspectives*). *Also called* specific language disability; specific reading disability.

etymology   The study of the history and origins of words by tracing their earliest use and changes in form and meaning.

fluency   The speed of decoding that is gained as one masters the alphabetic code.

free morpheme   A base word or root that can stand alone as a whole word, such as *spell, script,* or *graph.*

grapheme   A written or printed letter or letters that represent a phoneme, such as *m* for /m/ and *oy* for /oi/.

high-frequency word   *See* sight word.

homograph   One of two or more words that have the same spelling but that sound different and differ in meaning, such as *polish* (to rub to make shiny or a substance used while doing so) and *Polish* (the nationality).

homonym   One of two or more words that have the same sound and often the same spelling but that differ in meaning, such as *die* (stop living), *die* (a device for cutting/stamping objects), and *dye* (color); *pail* and *pale;* or *bear* and *bare. Also called* homophone.

homophone   *See* homonym.

inductive phonics   *See* synthetic phonics.

inflectional suffix   "In English, a suffix that expresses plurality or possession when added to a noun [*-s* in *cats*], tense when added to a verb [*-ed* in *walked*], and comparison when added to an adjective [*-er* in *bigger*]" (Harris & Hodges, 1995, p. 116).

irregular word   A word that does not follow typical letter–sound correspondences, usually in the vowel sound(s), such as *there* and *cough.*

lax vowel sounds   *See* short vowel sounds.

long vowel sounds   The vowel sounds that are also letter names, such as /ā/ as in *pale,* /ē/ as in *demon,* /ī/ as in *pilot,* /ō/ as in *hobo,* and /o͞o/ as in *Cupid.* Some long vowel sounds are represented by vowel digraphs, such as *ai* as in *rain* and *ee* as in *feed.* Long vowel sounds have a longer duration relative to short vowel sounds. *Also called* tense vowel sounds.

macron   The diacritical marking symbol (¯) appearing over a vowel grapheme that denotes a long, or tense, pronunciation of the vowel.

manuscript writing   A form of handwriting in which letters are separate from each other, unlike cursive writing. *Also called* printing.

metacognition   The act of reflecting on and monitoring cognitive activity.

metalanguage   The language used to talk about spoken and written language concepts.

metalinguistic awareness   Ability to think about and reflect on the nature and function of language.

morpheme   The smallest meaningful linguistic unit in a word.

morphology   "Study of the structure and forms of words, including derivation, inflection, and compounding" (Harris & Hodges, 1995, p. 158).

morphophonemic relations   The relationships between changing phonemic forms and constant written spellings, such as in *know* and *knowledge*.

multisensory instruction   Instruction using the simultaneous linking of visual, auditory, and kinesthetic-tactile modalities to enhance memory and learning.

open syllable   A syllable ending in a vowel sound, making the vowel sound long, as in <u>me</u>, <u>ho</u>bo, and <u>va</u> *cation*. Open syllables may or may not have an initial consonant (e.g., the first syllable in the word *open* is an open syllable with no initial consonant).

orthography   The writing (spelling) system of a language.

phoneme   The smallest unit of sound that conveys a distinction in meaning, such as /p/ of *pat* and /m/ of *mat*.

phonemic awareness   An awareness of the sounds that make up spoken words *and* an ability to manipulate sounds in words.

phonetics   1) The nature and articulation of speech sounds and their representation by written symbols; 2) the systematic classification of speech sounds in a language.

phonics   A teaching method that stresses letter–sound relationships in reading and spelling.

phonological awareness   An awareness of various levels of the speech sound system, such as syllables, accent patterns, rhyme, and phonemes.

phonology   1) The science of speech sounds; 2) the sound system of a language.

portmanteau word   A word formed by merging the sounds and meanings of two separate words, such as *brunch* (*breakfast* and *lunch*) and *smog* (*smoke* and *fog*). See the section in Chapter 8 called "Word Wisdom: Portmanteau Words" for more information.

prefix   A morpheme attached to the beginning of a base word or root, such as *dis-* in *disclaim*, that creates a new word with changed meaning or function.

printing   *See* manuscript writing.

rapid automatized naming (RAN)   The rapid naming of colors, numbers, letters, and objects. RAN appears to be an important factor in later reading acquisition.

***r*-controlled vowel**   A vowel that immediately precedes and whose sound is modified by /r/ in the same syllable, as in *car, for, her, bird, curl, tear, berry,* and *marry*.

regular word   A word that follows typical letter–sound correspondences in consonant and vowel sounds, such as *last* and *stump*.

root   The main part of a word to which affixes are added to derive new words. For example, *struct* is the root of *destructive*. Roots are often, but not always, bound morphemes.

schwa   The neutral vowel in unaccented or unstressed syllables in English words, such as the sound that corresponds to the grapheme *a-* in *asleep*. (The diacritical marking is /ə/.)

segmenting   Separating a word into syllables or phonemes.

short vowel sounds   The sounds of /ă/ in *map*, /ĕ/ in *bed*, /ĭ/ in *sip* or *gym*, /ŏ/ in *cot*, and /ŭ/ in *but*. Short vowel sounds have a relatively short duration. *Also called* lax vowel sounds.

sight word   1) A word that students know by sight without having to analyze it to pronounce it. Sight words may have regular (e.g., *jump, stop*) or irregular (e.g., *where, only*) spelling. *Also called* high-frequency word.

sound deletion   The act of removing a specific sound from a syllable or word; doing so is more difficult when the sound is being deleted from a consonant blend.

specific language disability   *See* dyslexia.

specific reading disability   *See* dyslexia.

spelling pattern   The letter or letter combinations representing specific phonemes. *See also* grapheme.

spelling rules   The principles guiding spelling, such as when to use *ck* instead of *c* or *k* to represent the /k/ sound.

suffix   A morpheme added to the end of a base or root that creates a new word with changed meaning or grammatical function, such as *-or* added to the verb *instruct* to make the noun *instructor*.

syllabication   The process of dividing words into syllables.

syllable   A unit of sequential speech sounds containing a vowel and consonants (if any) preceding or following that vowel, such as /ĭ/, /bĭ/, /ĭb/, and /bĭb/.

synthetic phonics   An instructional approach in which students learn letter–sound correspondences and blend parts to make whole words. *Also called* inductive phonics.

tense vowel sounds   *See* long vowel sounds.

VCE syllable   *See* vowel-consonant-*e* syllable.

voiced consonant   A consonant articulated with vibration of the vocal cords.

voiceless consonant   A consonant articulated with no vibration of the vocal cords. *Also called* unvoiced. (*Note:* /th/ in *this* is voiced; /th/ in *thin* is voiceless.)

vowel   1) A speech sound that is created by the free flow of breath through the vocal tract; 2) a grapheme corresponding to a vowel sound.

vowel digraph syllable   A syllable containing a vowel digraph, such as *meal* or *rain*. *Also called* vowel team syllable.

vowel-consonant-*e* (VCE) syllable   A syllable ending in a vowel, a consonant, and *e*, in that order, such as *made* or *cute*.

unvoiced consonant   *See* voiceless consonant.

word identification   The pronunciation of unfamiliar words with such methods as the use of context clues, phonics, or structural analysis.

word recognition   The swift identification of a previously learned word and its meaning.

word sorting   A word-study activity in which students group words according to categories such as spelling patterns, sounds, origin language, and/or meaning.

BIBLIOGRAPHY

This glossary was compiled using the following resources:

The American heritage dictionary (4th ed.). (2000). Boston: Houghton Mifflin.
Badian, N. (1997). Dyslexia and the double deficit hypothesis. *Annals of Dyslexia, 47,* 69-87.
Harris, T.L., & Hodges, R.E. (1995). *The literacy dictionary: The vocabulary of reading and writing.* Newark, DE: International Reading Association.
Hennessey, N. (2003, Winter). President's letter. *Perspectives, 2.*
Moats, L.C. (1995). *Spelling: Development, disability, and instruction.* Timonium, MD: York Press.
Moats, L.C. (2000). *Speech to print: Language essentials for teachers.* Baltimore: Paul H. Brookes Publishing Co.
Venezky, R.L. (1999). *The American way of spelling: The structure and origins of American English orthography.* New York: Guilford Press.

Index

Page numbers followed by *f* indicate figures; numbers followed by *t* indicate tables.